RISING CHINA'S
Soft Power in Southeast Asia

The **ISEAS – Yusof Ishak Institute** (formerly Institute of Southeast Asian Studies) is an autonomous organization established in 1968. It is a regional centre dedicated to the study of socio-political, security, and economic trends and developments in Southeast Asia and its wider geostrategic and economic environment. The Institute's research programmes are grouped under Regional Economic Studies (RES), Regional Strategic and Political Studies (RSPS), and Regional Social and Cultural Studies (RSCS). The Institute is also home to the ASEAN Studies Centre (ASC), the Singapore APEC Study Centre and the Temasek History Research Centre (THRC).

ISEAS Publishing, an established academic press, has issued more than 2,000 books and journals. It is the largest scholarly publisher of research about Southeast Asia from within the region. ISEAS Publishing works with many other academic and trade publishers and distributors to disseminate important research and analyses from and about Southeast Asia to the rest of the world.

Edited by
Leo Suryadinata

RISING CHINA'S Soft Power in Southeast Asia

Impact on Education and Popular Culture

YUSOF ISHAK INSTITUTE

First published in Singapore in 2024 by
ISEAS Publishing
30 Heng Mui Keng Terrace
Singapore 119614
E-mail: publish@iseas.edu.sg
Website: http://bookshop.iseas.edu.sg

All rights reserved. No part of this publication may be reproduced, stored in a retrieval system, or transmitted in any form or by any means, electronic, mechanical, photocopying, recording or otherwise, without the prior permission of the ISEAS – Yusof Ishak Institute.

© 2024 ISEAS – Yusof Ishak Institute, Singapore

The responsibility for facts and opinions in this publication rests exclusively with the authors and their interpretations do not necessarily reflect the views or the policy of the publishers or their supporters.

This publication is made possible with the support of Konrad-Adenauer-Stiftung.

ISEAS Library Cataloguing-in-Publication Data

Name(s): Suryadinata, Leo, editor.
Title: Rising China's soft power in Southeast Asia: impact on education and popular culture / edited by Leo Suryadinata.
Description: Singapore : ISEAS-Yusof Ishak Institute, 2024. | All chapters started as papers presented at the online workshop "China's Soft Power in Education, Language and Art with Special Emphasis on Chinese Education" in October 2022 at ISEAS in Singapore. | Includes bibliographical references.
Identifiers: ISBN 9789815203035 (soft cover) | ISBN 9789815203042 (PDF) | ISBN 9789815203059 (epub)
Subjects: LCSH: China—Foreign relations—Southeast Asia. | Southeast Asia—Foreign relations—China. | Chinese—Education—Southeast Asia. | Chinese in popular culture—Southeast Asia.
Classification: LCC DS525.9 C5R59

Cover design by Lee Meng Hui
Index compiled by Raffaie Nahar
Typeset by Superskill Graphics Pte Ltd
Printed in Singapore by Markono Print Media Pte Ltd

Contents

The Contributors   vii

Introduction: An Overview of Rising Chinese Educational Soft Power and Cultural Influence in Southeast Asia   1
Leo Suryadinata

PART I: GENERAL OVERVIEW OF CHINA'S SOFT POWER

1. Chinese Overseas and China's Soft Power   15
   Tan Chee-Beng

2. Southeast Asian States and China's Educational Soft Power   28
   Leo Suryadinata

3. Expatriate or Native Chinese Language Teachers for Maritime Southeast Asia?   42
   Neo Peng Fu

PART II: CHINA'S SOFT POWER AND EDUCATION IN MAINLAND SOUTHEAST ASIA

4. Chinese Soft Power in Thailand: The Influence of Chinese Education   61
   Sivarin Lertpusit

5. Understanding China's Educational Soft Power from Recipients' Perspectives: A Case Study of the Yunnanese Chinese in Northern Thailand   76
   Aranya Siriphon

6. China's Soft Power in Laos, with Special Reference to Chinese Education and Chinese Language Teaching   98
   Lim Boon Hock

7. Chinese Education and Educating Chinese in a Post-Conflicted State: Mandarin Education Systems in Cambodia   121
   Shihlun Allen Chen

PART III: CHINA'S SOFT POWER AND EDUCATION IN MARITIME SOUTHEAST ASIA

8. China's Educational Soft Power: A View from Malaysia   139
   Ngeow Chow Bing and Fan Pik Shy

9. Seek Knowledge as Far as China: *Santris'* Educational Mobility to China and Its Meanings for China's Soft Power Projection in Indonesia   161
   Ardhitya Eduard Yeremia

10. Assessment of China's Soft Power among China-Educated Filipinos: Impact on the Philippines   180
    Jane Yugioksing

11. Chinese Language Education in Brunei Darussalam: An Instrument of China's Soft Power?   200
    Hannah Ming Yit Ho and Chang-Yau Hoon

PART IV: CHINA'S SOFT POWER AND POPULAR CULTURE

12. The Power of Fantasy: Southeast Asians' Obsession with Chinese *Xianxia* Dramas   217
    Gwendolyn Yap

13. Impact of Chinese Popular Culture on Young People in Vietnam   237
    Tran Thi Xoan

14. PRC Soft Power and Chinese Indonesian Arts: Reports from the Ends of the Spectrum   252
    Josh Stenberg

Index   269

The Contributors

Aranya Siriphon is Associate Professor at the Department of Sociology and Anthropology, Faculty of Social Sciences, Chiang Mai University. Her research interests are in recent Chinese migrants and mobility in the Mekong region, and transnational migration studies.

Ardhitya Eduard Yeremia is a faculty member of the Department of International Relations, Faculty of Social and Political Sciences, Universitas Indonesia. His research interests include China's foreign policy, China-Southeast Asia relations, and Indonesia-China people-to-people exchanges. His research has been published in the *International Journal of China Studies*, *Pacific Review*, *Asian Perspective* and 南洋问题研究.

Chang-Yau Hoon is Professor of Anthropology at the Institute of Asian Studies, University of Brunei Darussalam. He is also Visiting Senior Fellow at the ISEAS – Yusof Ishak Institute. He specializes in the Chinese diaspora, identity politics, multiculturalism, and religious and cultural diversity in contemporary Southeast Asia. His latest books include *Christianity and the Chinese in Indonesia: Ethnicity, Education and Enterprise* (Liverpool University Press, 2023); *Southeast Asia in China: Historical Entanglements and Contemporary Engagements* (authored with Y.K. Chan; Lexington Press, 2023); and *Stability, Growth and Sustainability: Catalysts for Socio-economic Development in Brunei Darussalam* (edited with A. Ananta and M. Hamdan; ISEAS – Yusof Ishak Institute, 2023).

Fan Pik Shy is a Senior Lecturer at the Institute of China Studies, University of Malaya. She received her PhD in Chinese Language and Applied Linguistics from Capital Normal University (Beijing, China). Her research interests are Chinese language, culture and literature, and education in China.

Gwendolyn Yap is a Research Officer with the Regional Social and Cultural Studies Programme at the ISEAS – Yusof Ishak Institute. Her research interests include popular culture, media, East Asian studies, Southeast Asian studies, literature and gender.

Hannah Ming Yit Ho is Assistant Professor at the Faculty of Arts and Social Sciences at Universiti Brunei Darussalam. She is also a National University of Singapore fellow (Southeast Asia) attached to its Asia Research Institute. Her publications include journal articles in *Kritika Kultura, Asiatic, Southeast Asian Review of English, Suvannabhumi* and *International Journal of Asia Pacific Studies*. Her current research topics comprise Chinese language education in Brunei Darussalam and Chinese Bruneian literature in English, for which she has been awarded research grants. She co-edited *Engaging Modern Brunei: Research on Language, Literature and Culture* (Springer 2021).

Jane Yugioksing is former Director of the Chinese Studies Department at Ateneo de Manila University. She is a recipient of the Chinese Government Scholarship and is a current PhD candidate in International Relations at Jinan University. She is a member of the International Society for the Study of Chinese Overseas and the Philippine Association for Chinese Studies. Her most recent published chapter is "A Perception-Based Study: Chinese Filipino's Response to China's COVID-19 Prevention Measures" in *Philippines-China Relations at 45 During the COVID-19 Pandemic: New Discoveries, Recent Developments, and Continuing Concerns* (2021). She is currently researching the mobility of Chinese Filipino students and the social identity of new Chinese migrants in the Philippines.

Josh Stenberg is a senior lecturer in Chinese studies at the University of Sydney. The author of *Minority Stages: Sino-Indonesian Performance and Public Display* (University of Hawai'i Press, 2019), his research interests include *xiqu* (Chinese opera) in modern and contemporary periods, the culture of Sino-Southeast Asian communities, and Chinese translation studies.

Leo Suryadinata is currently Visiting Senior Fellow at the ISEAS – Yusof Ishak Institute, Singapore. He was formerly Professor in the Department of Political Science at the National University of Singapore. He has published extensively on Southeast Asian politics, ethnic Chinese in Southeast Asia, and China-ASEAN relations. His latest book is *Rising China and New Chinese Migrants in Southeast Asia* (ISEAS – Yusof Ishak Institute, 2022).

Lim Boon Hock obtained his PhD in Area Studies from Kyoto University, Japan, under the Monbukagaku-sho, a prestigious Japanese government scholarship. He conducted field research in Lao PDR and Cambodia for a project entitled "Southeast Asian Personalities of Chinese Descent: A Biographical Dictionary". He was then the country editor-cum-writer in charge of these two countries. In 2019, he made a career switch to set up an NGO in Lao PDR to conduct basic English Language classes for the Laotian children. Currently, he is employed as a School Principal by Lao-Japan School, in Vientiane, Lao PDR.

Neo Peng Fu is a senior lecturer at the National Institute of Education (Singapore) and Director of the Confucius Institute at Nanyang Technological University. He is a historian by training who publishes mainly in two areas: Chinese classics and language-in-education policy (with special reference to Chinese language teaching and learning in Singapore). His detailed publication list can be accessed at https://www.nie.edu.sg/profile/neo-peng-fu

Ngeow Chow-Bing is Director of the Institute of China Studies at the University of Malaya. Dr Ngeow received his PhD in Public and International Affairs from Northeastern University. He is the editor of *Populism and Nationalism in the South China Sea Dispute* (co-edited with Peng Nian; Springer, 2022), *Researching China in Southeast Asia* (Routledge, 2019) and *Southeast Asia and China: Exercises in Mutual Socialization* (co-edited with Lowell Dittmer; World Scientific, 2017). In addition, Dr Ngeow has written more than forty articles in scholarly journals and book chapters. He has also published short pieces in *South China Morning Post*, *ThinkChina*, *East Asia Forum* and *Channel NewsAsia*.

Shihlun Allen Chen is currently Associate Professor at the Center for Southeast Asian Studies, School of International Studies, Sun Yat-Sen University. His research mainly focuses on the studies of Cambodia and Overseas Chinese, economic anthropology, identity theory, ethnic organizations, transnationalism, development theories, and Cross-straits issues.

Sivarin Lertpusit is an Assistant Professor at the College of Interdisciplinary Studies, Thammasat University, and a researcher in the socio-political field. She was formerly a visiting fellow at the ISEAS – Yusof Ishak Institute, Singapore. She finished her doctoral degree in International Studies (Southeast Asian Studies) at the Graduate School of Asia Pacific Studies, Waseda University, Tokyo. Her studies focus on the Greater Mekong Subregion and the influence of China. Her previous works are *The Chinese*

Transborder and Its Socioeconomic Impact to Boten People (Laos), *Chinese Student Mobility*, and *New Chinese Migrants in Chiang Mai and Chiang Rai*.

Tan Chee-Beng (PhD, Cornell University, 1979) taught at the University of Singapore, the University of Malaya, the Chinese University of Hong Kong (CUHK) and Sun Yat-sen University, Guangzhou. He is currently Adjunct Professor with CUHK. A cultural anthropologist, he has done research in Malaysia and China. His major publications include, as author, *The Baba of Melaka* (2021, new edition by SIRD), *Chinese Religion in Malaysia* (Brill, 2018), *Chinese Overseas: Comparative Cultural Issues* (Hong Kong University Press, 2004), and as editor, *Routledge Handbook of the Chinese Overseas* (Routledge, 2013).

Tran Thi Xoan holds her MA in ASEAN Studies focusing on Chinese popular culture in Vietnam from Pridi Banomyong International College, Thammasat University, Thailand. She works as a foreign lecturer at Language Institute and Global Affairs, Chiang Rai Rajabhat University. She continues working on ASEAN Studies and Cross-Cultural Competence Embedded in the Teaching Curriculum, and English Language Analysis.

INTRODUCTION
An Overview of Rising Chinese Educational Soft Power and Cultural Influence in Southeast Asia

Leo Suryadinata

The recent rise of China and its impacts on the ethnic Chinese and non-Chinese in Southeast Asia have been one of the foci of the Regional Social and Cultural Studies (RSCS) Programme at the ISEAS – Yusof Ishak Institute. In 2014, an international workshop was held at ISEAS on rising China, the arrival of *xin yimin* (new Chinese migrants) and the ethnic Chinese in Mainland Southeast Asia. In 2020, another workshop, focusing mainly on rising China and the *xin yimin* in Maritime Southeast Asia, was organized.

The papers of these two workshops were selected, revised and later published in a book under the title *Rising China and Chinese New Migrants in Southeast Asia* (2022). In October 2022, a third workshop on China's soft power in education, language and art with special emphasis on Chinese education was held. During the workshop, speakers did not present on Brunei Darussalam or China's popular arts in Southeast Asia—hence two more papers were added to this volume to provide a well-rounded survey. The revised papers have now been edited and transformed into a book, which you are holding now. It should be noted with thanks that these three workshops and the earlier publication of the two books were generously sponsored by Konrad Adenauer Stiftung (KAS).

Enquiry into China's Soft Power

It is widely recognized that China has risen economically. But with the rise of China as an economic power and regional military power, are China's soft power and cultural influences also growing equally? Undoubtedly, China has been trying to promote its language, culture and education beyond its boundaries since its recent rise. American soft power has been influential in Southeast Asia and remains so today. South Korean soft power has also been rising, surpassing both Hong Kong/Taiwan and Japan in its strength. Is China's soft power, especially the Chinese language and its cultural products, becoming similarly popular and influential in the Southeast Asian region? This book aims to examine the above questions with special reference to the Chinese language and Chinese education, surveying not only the Chinese communities but also non-Chinese communities in Southeast Asia as well. The book is divided into four parts.

Part I: General Overview of China's Soft Power

The first part is the general overview of China's soft power, education and Confucius Institutes (CIs, 孔子学院). Tan Chee Beng's chapter (Ch 1) begins with a general overview of China's soft power in relation to Chinese overseas. The Chinese overseas are a potentially important resource for expanding China's soft power influence. His paper discusses China's major institutions involving Chinese overseas including the Overseas Chinese Affairs Office, the China public associations, the China Council for Promotion of Peaceful Reunification, as well as similar associations established among Chinese overseas in Southeast Asian countries such as Malaysia, Indonesia and Thailand.

Tan maintains that CIs and Chinese mass media play important roles in China's soft power policy, impacting the Chinese overseas. He notes that China is not sensitive to the feelings of both the ethnic Chinese and non-Chinese population of other countries which may affect the relations between China and many Southeast Asian states. As the rivalry between the US and China intensifies, Tan observes in his paper that "it is essential for China to build a good image among ordinary citizens of the countries where it invests, not just the ethnic Chinese. This can be accomplished by establishing centres and organizations that provide services that benefit them. The present policy of providing scholarships for higher education in China, for example, can be expanded."

In Chapter 2, Leo Suryadinata focuses on the role of the state and China's educational soft power in Southeast Asia. Initially Chinese schools were established by local Chinese communities without the involvement of the Chinese state and colonial state. Later on, China and Southeast Asian states began to participate in shaping Chinese education in Southeast Asia to different degrees of success. Many Southeast Asian states succeeded in nationalizing Chinese schools into local schools, with the exception of those in Malaysia and Laos.

Rising China also began to introduce CIs to promote Chinese culture through language, and also offered scholarships to not only ethnic Chinese but also non-Chinese students. China also established university branches in some Southeast Asian countries (Laos and Malaysia). As such, Chinese educational soft power began to have an impact on Southeast Asians, not only among the ethnic Chinese communities but also among non-Chinese. The popularity of Mandarin has increased but is not comparable to the English language yet. As the Chinese language is an aspect of China's soft power, the growth of the Chinese language's popularity in Southeast Asia is often seen as an example of China's increasing soft power, albeit limited. Indeed, the US-China rivalry might impact the further growth of the Chinese language but it would not be able to stop the gradual spread of the Chinese language as it is essential when dealing with China.

Thereafter, Chapter 3 by Neo Peng Fu examines the role of CIs in dealing with the Chinese language outside China. It examines the current and future role of CIs in Maritime Southeast Asia, namely Indonesia, Malaysia and the Philippines. Through his paper, the question of expatriate teachers in meeting the needs of the local populace is addressed. Neo observes that CIs initially provided the necessary resources (teachers, textbooks and techniques of instruction) for helping various countries develop an infrastructure for teaching Mandarin. However, the continuous strong demand in Southeast Asia for mastering the Chinese language may result in the inability of CIs to meet these demands through expatriate teachers.

He therefore argues that CIs (or China) may have made "a right and wise move" on the issue, namely by helping the host countries to nurture their own crop of Chinese language teachers to make up for the lack of expatriate teachers from China. This reminds me of English teaching in Southeast Asia where countries used local rather than expatriate teachers. Only when countries are self-sufficient in teaching Chinese will Mandarin be able to compete with English.

Part II: China's Soft Power and Education in Mainland Southeast Asia

Chinese schools in Southeast Asia have a long history before the establishment of CIs. These Chinese schools were mainly catered to ethnic

Chinese children. With the rise of Thai nationalism, Chinese schools in Thailand were unwelcome and restricted. However, the situation gradually changed in the mid-1970s after Bangkok established diplomatic relations with Beijing and severed diplomatic ties with Taipei. Chapter 4 by Sivarin Lertpusit describes the educational cooperation between Thai and Chinese governments after the establishment of diplomatic ties, and evaluates the impact of Chinese education in Thailand, particularly among the China-educated Thais. Sivarin argues that Sino-Thai cooperation has expanded from government-to-government to the people-to-people level. Chinese-educated Thais are now key actors in promoting intercultural exchange between China and Thailand. Sivarin points out that China is renowned for its Science, Technology, Education and Mathematics (STEM) and e-commerce programmes in Thai vocational schools and universities. Moreover, the high educational reputation of the Chinese, employment opportunities and available scholarships attract a growing number of Thai students. Finally, Sivarin maintains that those Thai who were China-educated tend to promote China's image in Thailand. They deliver information and positive perspectives of China. Via Chinese education, Chinese soft power has had considerable achievement in Thailand.

However, Chapter 5 by Aranya Siriphon on Thailand conveys a rather different picture of Chinese education. Aranya conducted a case study on Chinese education in the Yunnanese Chinese community in northern Thailand. Unlike the Chinese who migrated and worked across Thailand, Yunnanese Chinese continue to reside in a specific area near the borders. Aranya addresses the responses of these ethnic Chinese towards educational soft power from China and Taiwan. While Beijing's educational policy appears to be more effective with "overseas Chinese" communities in Thailand, it was less successful with the Yunnanese Chinese due to their lingering loyalty to Taiwan. Prior to Bangkok's recognition of Beijing, Thailand had diplomatic ties with Taiwan. Therefore, the schools in northern Thailand are divided into pro-Taipei and pro-Beijing schools. In these Yunnanese Chinese communities, the number of students in pro-Taipei schools remains larger than that of pro-Beijing schools.

Nonetheless, due to the limitation of donations and educational support from Taiwan, pro-Beijing schools are increasing in number and may also become more dominant in the future with the growth of the economic, political and military power of mainland China. Yet, at the moment these two types of schools continue to coexist, reflecting slightly different cultural values. While the pro-Beijing schools are more secular in values, pro-Taipei schools are more Confucian. The comparison also shows the complexity of Chinese education in Thailand and the impact of Chinese educational soft power.

China's educational power can also be seen in Laos. This is a result of China's rapid economic development and the Belt and Road Initiative (BRI) in this landlocked country. Lim Boon Hock in Chapter 6 argues that the massive China's investment projects in Laos created strong demands for Laotians who are proficient in Mandarin. However, Laos has not had sufficient resources to sustain Chinese education and hence had to rely almost entirely on Beijing for not only teachers, but also curriculums and textbooks. Lim offers a case study of a major Chinese school, Liaodu (寮都) Public School, which suffers from these deficiencies. However, the standards of the Chinese language are still not up to expectations. To train more Chinese-speaking Laotians, China also established the Su Zhou University (苏州大学) branch in Laos where they are required to study for one year on the Laos campus and in China for the remaining years.

China's BRI has already created unprecedented and heightened interest in the learning of the Chinese language in local schools in Laos. There is a deeply rooted perception that acquiring a higher Chinese language proficiency promises upward social mobility opportunities, and hence, a brighter future, among young Laotians. The enthusiastic pursuit of Chinese education is often at the expense of Laotian identity. Not surprisingly, Lim argues that "the desirable outcomes of China's soft power in creating and sustaining a multifaceted 'win-win' relationship between China and Laos are yet to be seen."

Laos' neighbour, Cambodia, also has a close relationship with Beijing, with Beijing having massive investment projects in Cambodia. In Chapter 7 regarding Cambodian Chinese education, Shihlun Allen Chen examines the impact and influences of Chinese education since the early years of Cambodia, with a focus on the period after 1993. He argues that Cambodia has experienced three facets of Chinese education, namely ethnic Chinese education, foreign Chinese education and domestic Chinese education.

In the first facet, ethnic Chinese education sought foreign aid mainly from China and hence became China-oriented. However, this education, except for one secondary school, was limited to primary school levels. But after the rise of China and Beijing-Phnom Penh relations improved, Cambodian education entered the second facet, which was foreign education. This was characterized by the establishment of CIs in the country. CIs not only introduced the Chinese language at the primary level but also at the secondary level. Moreover, it offered Cambodian adults the opportunity to learn Mandarin. Even Chinese companies also offered

Mandarin courses for their employees. Chen finally argues that "[t]he final facet saw Cambodia building up their domestic Chinese education with the aid of Chinese universities. Chinese became part of the public school curriculum, alongside Khmer, English and French. However, even with the increase in scholarships to China, the number of students that head to China for higher learning remains low."

Chen did not explicitly discuss China's soft power and its impacts; however, it is obvious that China's educational soft power impacted Cambodians via Chinese education. Nonetheless, Chinese-educated Cambodian intellectuals remain small in number, just like the situation in many other Southeast Asian states.

Part III: China's Soft Power and Education in Maritime Southeast Asia

Malaysia, and at one time Singapore as well, had quite a complete Chinese educational system, ranging from primary school level to tertiary school level. However, the situation changed after Singapore gained independence in 1965. All Chinese schools in Singapore have been converted into national-type schools using English as the main language of instruction, Chinese is taught as a mother tongue (second language). Nanyang University merged with Singapore University in 1980 and formed the National University of Singapore (NUS). In Malaysia, primary and secondary Chinese schools remain. However, for Chinese tertiary education, Chinese Malaysians had to go to Taiwan, and later to Mainland China.

In recent years, more Malaysian Chinese are receiving education in Mainland China. In Chapter 8, Ngeow Chow Bing and Fan Pik Shy examine various groups of China-educated Malaysians, including both Chinese and non-Chinese. These China-educated are not only educated in China's tertiary education but also China's university branches in Malaysia. Courses were also conducted by CIs in Malaysia mainly for non-Chinese (i.e., the Malays). Many China-educated Malaysians later joined the organization known as *Liu Hua* (留华) in Malaysia which served as a platform "to connect its members, articulate and magnify their voices and interests, mobilize resources and liaise with other bodies and entities, including those from China".

Ngeow and Fan argued that from the perspective of China's soft power, all these categories of "China-educated Malaysians" generally (though not necessarily entirely) hold positive views about China. In their paper, they noted that "[t]hose who have been to China are, in general, impressed by its rapid economic and technological development, the orderliness of its cities, and the dynamism of its people and society. However, some express concerns about the growing political restrictions within China and feel uncomfortable about this trend." However, Ngeow and Fan maintained that for those Malaysians who received Chinese education through Xiamen University (厦门大学) Malaysia branch or courses via CIs, China is perceived positively but at a superficial level. This is attributed to their limited exposure to China.

Ngeow and Fan also note that the "China-educated Malaysians" remain a minority group despite increasing numbers among the broader population of Malaysians receiving foreign education. They also observe that "there are currently no prominent political leaders, top civil servants, or think-tank analysts in Malaysia with a China education background". Nonetheless, as China's universities continue to attract students from Malaysia, China-trained or -educated important Malaysian leaders may emerge in Malaysian society over time.

Over in Indonesia, Chinese education experienced ups and downs. Chinese education was confined mainly to ethnic Chinese in Indonesia. During the Suharto New Order period (1966–98), Chinese education was banned. Nevertheless, after the fall of Suharto, "Chinese schools" re-emerged, but these Chinese schools are no longer Chinese-medium schools, but are national schools-plus. Simply put, it is an Indonesian school with the Chinese language as an extra subject. However, the post-Suharto period also witnesses the rise of CIs in Indonesia and its outreach to non-Chinese. China also offered scholarships to non-Chinese students to study at China's universities. Ardhitya Eduard Yeremia in his chapter (Ch 9) discusses indigenous Indonesians, especially Muslim Indonesians, who started learning Mandarin and even furthered their studies in China.

During the Sukarno era (1957–65), indigenous Indonesians went to study in China, but the number was very small, and they did not have any impact on the indigenous population or society. However, the situation in the post-New Order period (post-May 1998) has been outstanding. Not only that there were ethnic Chinese but also *santri* (Muslim students or graduates of the *pesantren* [Islamic boarding schools]) who studied in China. After returning to Indonesia, many of them became activists who defended China. China's educational soft power has entered Indonesian society and even into the political scene.

Yeremia's chapter focuses on the increasing trend of *santri* Indonesians pursuing further education in China. Chinese culture has often been seen to be incompatible with Islam. The presence of these pro-Beijing

Indonesian indigenous Muslims has challenged the previous perception. However, Yeremia also noted that "China alone does not determine the overall outcome of its soft power projection in Indonesia. Power asymmetry between Indonesia and China does not imply that China always holds the dominant position in their interaction."

The chapter further demonstrates the limitations of the *santris'* activism in bridging the Indonesian Muslim community and China. For example, despite *Chaguan*—a social media programme run by China-educated *santris*—consistently highlighting the favourable aspects of China, it has not received overwhelmingly positive responses from its viewers. Yeremia finally assesses the limited impact of China-educated *santri* on Indonesia-China relations.

China's educational soft power in the Philippines is also limited. Like Thailand, the Philippines also had diplomatic relations with Taiwan before severing ties in order to establish official diplomatic ties with the People's Republic of China. Chinese education is now dominated by Beijing. CIs in the Philippines are welcoming an increasing number of Philippine Chinese and non-Chinese. There are also Filipinos who receive Chinese education in Mainland China. Jane Yugioksing in Chapter 10 discusses the China-educated Filipinos and their perceptions of the PRC. She conducted a small study based on in-depth interviews with twelve China-educated Philippine students. Due to various constraints, the study is small and hence the findings are not representative of the entire population of China-educated scholars in the Philippines.

Nevertheless, Yugioksing's research provides interesting preliminary findings and may offer some directions regarding China-educated Filipinos. For instance, "regardless of the duration of their studies, first-hand experience plays an important role in increasing appreciation and understanding of China, its people, and its society". The opportunities provided through China's scholarship have contributed to a more positive outlook on China among Filipino scholars. Despite controversial issues such as the West Philippine Sea (South China Sea) dispute, participants often expressed belief that China has never colonized any country and that bilateral talks remain the best approach.

Yugioksing also found that economic growth in China influenced many Filipino scholars to study the Mandarin language and pursue degrees in China. Additionally, despite China's different political system, these scholars were impressed by Chinese economic progress after experiencing China first-hand. Therefore, first-hand experience in China is effective in making Filipinos friendly with China. However, Yugioksing concluded that "due to the relatively small number of China-educated recipients, the impact of China's soft power is not widely felt in mainstream Philippine society".

Chapter 11 on Chinese education in Brunei Darussalam is jointly authored by Hannah Ming Yit Ho and Chang-Yau Hoon. Chinese education had a long history in Brunei but after Brunei attained independence, Chinese schools have been nationalized into trilingual schools and are no longer merely Chinese-medium schools. English, Malay and Chinese (Mandarin) are taught in these schools. Notably, Brunei is the only Southeast Asian state which does not have any CIs. Therefore, the development of the Chinese language in Brunei has become a domestic issue.

Ho and Hoon examine the popularity of Chinese language in Brunei and discover that there was no "Mandarin fever" among Bruneians. Nevertheless, Chinese and non-Chinese in Brunei continue to send their children to "Chinese schools" to study Chinese. The two authors interviewed parents of "Chinese school" students from five schools and enquired about their motivations for wanting their children to learn Chinese. They found that Bruneian parents are not specifically concerned with China's global power in terms of its economic status and soft power within Southeast Asia. On the contrary, academic rigour, institutional reputation and cultural diversity of these Chinese schools are cited as topmost reasons for pursuing a Chinese language education. In other words, the two authors argue that the Chinese-language issue has been depoliticized.

Part IV: China's Soft Power and Popular Culture

China's soft power is also reflected in popular culture such as *wuxia* (武侠) drama, *xianxia* (仙侠) drama, folktales, pop songs and popular performing arts such as *Potehi* (*bu dai xi* 布袋戏). The soft power of China had entered the Southeast Asian arena in the past but was never very forceful. However, rising China has given an opportunity for its popular culture to re-enter Southeast Asia in a more significant way. Chapter 12 on the *xianxia* drama written by Gwendolyn Yap, shows the most recent development of China's popular culture in many Southeast Asian countries.

Xianxia that combines Chinese mythology and culture with fantasy and action has been well-received by Southeast Asian audiences. According to Yap, there are two factors which made *xianxia* drama popular in this region: one is that *xianxia* has been able to become a hybrid cultural product constructed to appeal to regional audiences, and the other is the recent foray of Chinese streaming services into Southeast Asia. However, the popularity of *xianxia* is threatened by domestic restrictions in China such as the crackdown on online literature where *xianxia* came from. Nonetheless, the continued popularity of *xianxia* in Southeast Asia has led to further China-Southeast Asian collaborations in entertainment and other East Asian countries picking up on the trend. Nevertheless, Yap notes that while *xianxia* gains more attention in the region, how it will benefit China and Chinese policymakers remains unclear. However, she concludes that "from the continued growth of Chinese TV shows in the region and the increased demand for new *xianxia*s, it appears that China's rise in popular entertainment in the region will only continue".

Tran Thi Xoan's chapter (Ch 13) is about the impact of China's popular culture in Vietnam, especially among Vietnamese young people. The spread of this China's soft culture has been closely linked with the rise of China since the turn of the twenty-first-century. China's cultural products have been able to enter international markets and successfully compete with Western and some other Asian countries. Xoan provides an overview of Chinese popular culture products among Vietnamese youth in the last four to five years. She discovered that these products shared a significant proportion of the Vietnamese market for foreign products. Localization of these products made them more popular among Vietnamese youth and in turn, affected their positive perception of China.

Improved ties between Beijing and Hanoi offered opportunities for Vietnamese people to receive more Chinese popular cultural products such as *wuxia* novels, detective literature, TV programmes and movies. Chinese celebrities have also become familiar and closer to Vietnamese audiences. The volumes of these cultural products increased remarkably with Mandarin-language content. Moreover, the Chinese also knew to grasp the boom of consumers who devoted time and money to social media products, especially films and online literature. The online literature, which dealt with "unhealthy" romantic themes, was so popular among the Vietnamese youth that it alarmed the authorities. However, this popularity could not be stopped as these romantic novels are readily available online with numerous websites and fan pages dedicated to them.

The final chapter (Ch 14) in this book is on Chinese Indonesian arts by Josh Stenberg. This chapter is interesting as it covers two aspects of Chinese culture in Indonesia. On the one hand, an older Chinese pop culture has been integrated into a local cultural scene, and hence is no longer linked to the soft power of China; while the other, which is relatively more recent, is still linked to contemporary China, and hence related to China's soft power.

Josh Stenberg presents two case studies related to Chinese culture in Indonesia. One case is the *Potehi* which originated in Fujian, southern China. It gradually became a kind of *wayang* performance which was performed by the Indonesian Chinese in relation to their religious activities connected with the *klenteng* (Chinese temple). *Potehi* usually adopted Chinese historical fiction such as the legend of Sie Jin Kui and Fan Li Hua during the Tang Dynasty. This *Potehi* initially used Hokkien but gradually was replaced by Javanese and Indonesian. The *Potehi* today has become *Wayang Cina* (Chinese Wayang). As it has dissociated itself from the religious activities of its origin, it is now appreciated not only by Peranakan Chinese but also by the *pribumi* population.

The second case is *Yinhua Wenxue* (印华文学) or Indonesian Chinese literature written in Chinese (which differs from Peranakan Chinese literature written in Indonesian. This literature emerged only in the twentieth century but was not well developed. Initially, these authors were nationals of China and hence saw things from China's perspective. During the Suharto period, Chinese schools, organizations and media were banned, and *Yinhua* literature barely survived. After the fall of Suharto, the work of *Yinhua* authors was revived but became more complex. As many Indonesian Chinese nationalized into Indonesian citizens, the works also reflect their national identity. Younger writers preferred to express their ethnic and even Chinese cultural identity that is beyond national boundaries.

Josh Stenberg states that "[t]he two case studies presented serve as illustrations of separate ends of the spectrum of Chinese Indonesian activity: one in which an originally Chinese cultural product becomes absorbed into Indonesian culture, leaving only notional and folkloric traces, and another in which the bond between ethnic, cultural, linguistic, and political identity is deemed valid. These tendencies vary in intensity and proportion regionally and across social classes". Stenberg finally notes that "it is essential to keep both possibilities in mind when discussing not only Chinese soft power in the diaspora but also any aspect of contemporary Chinese Indonesian identity".

Conclusion

The book has addressed the issues of China's soft power in Southeast Asia during the rise of China. This soft power includes Chinese-language education and popular culture. With regard to Chinese education, before the rise of China, Chinese schools were catered to mainly/solely overseas Chinese children. Non-Chinese seldom received Chinese education. But the rise of China and the export of CIs changed the landscape as CIs are meant for the non-Chinese population as well. China's educational soft power penetrated into the larger non-Chinese community, making Chinese soft power more effective. Chinese popular culture has also infiltrated the non-Chinese population.

Various chapters in this book show that the rising China's soft power in Southeast Asia has grown quite significantly, particularly in terms of the Chinese language and Chinese popular culture. Nevertheless, its popularity still lags behind American soft power. The Chinese language is still not as popular as the English language. The same could also be said for Chinese popular culture. Chinese soft power has met many challenges, especially during intensifying US-China rivalry. The growth of China's soft power faces tremendous challenges in the Southeast Asian region. In my view, its further growth would depend on China's continuous economic power and cordial relations with the Southeast Asian countries.

Part I
GENERAL OVERVIEW OF CHINA'S SOFT POWER

1

CHINESE OVERSEAS AND CHINA'S SOFT POWER

Tan Chee-Beng

INTRODUCTION

The concept of soft power refers to the use of cultural and economic resources by a country to gain the support of overseas organizations and foreign governments or to get them to act in line with the interests of a country without the use of military power. This concept was proposed by Joseph S. Nye in 1990 (Nye 1990). He explains that "hard power is like brandishing carrots or sticks; soft power is more like a magnet" (Nye 2021, p. 6).

This paper describes China's soft power in relation to the Chinese overseas. It will show that the Chinese overseas constitute an important resource for China's soft power. Although there are similar patterns, the ways that China uses this resource may differ from region to region. The receptivity of, and impacts on, the Chinese overseas also differ from country to country. China's soft power policies are important for mobilizing international cooperation with China, gaining support for its promotion of national unification and rebuttal of Western anti-China rhetoric. Influential ethnic Chinese businesspeople and politicians in other countries play important roles in this and in enhancing cooperation that benefits both China and their country of residence.

The label "Chinese overseas" (海外华人 or *haiwai huaren*) is preferred by scholars who study people of Chinese origins living overseas. Strictly speaking, it refers to Chinese who have identified with their respective countries. However, its use, as in this paper, may include new immigrants who are mostly *huaqiao* (华侨 or overseas Chinese), meaning citizens of China residing overseas. As for the term "overseas Chinese", it is historically a term that refers to *huaqiao* or "Chinese sojourners". The term "Chinese diaspora" is best used to refer to new immigrants who are sojourners, who still see China as home, but many scholars also use it to include ethnic Chinese belonging to different nationalities.

Overseas Chinese Institutions

The Overseas Chinese Affairs Office of the State Council (OCAO, 国务院侨务办公室) is the state institution that deals with the Chinese overseas. Its forerunners were the Republican government's *Qiaowu Weiyuanhui* (侨务委员会) or Overseas Chinese Affairs Council (established in 1926) and the Chinese Communist Party's Yan'an Overseas Chinese Office (established in 1937). Taiwan still has its *Qiaowu Weiyuanhui*, but in 2006, its English name was changed from Overseas Chinese Affairs Council to Overseas Community Affairs Council (OCAC) to avoid confusion with the one in the People's Republic of China (PRC). In the PRC, the roles of the OCAO have changed over time. During the Maoist era, overseas Chinese played an important role in lessening the sufferings of the Chinese population in China in the face of the US economic blockade (Peterson 2012). Following China's opening and reforms initiated by Deng Xiaoping, Chinese overseas were encouraged to invest in China and to help in the development of emigrant regions (侨乡 or *qiaoxiang*). The latter process was broadly and well facilitated by *Qiaolian* or the Federation of Returned Overseas Chinese from the national to the county levels. In my contacts with *Qiaolian* leaders in Yongchun County and Quanzhou Municipality in Fujian, I was impressed with their knowledge of rich Chinese businesspeople and other well-known Chinese personalities in different Southeast Asian counties. These leaders conduct trips abroad to network with relevant Chinese associations and individuals. They connect visiting Chinese overseas groups and individuals with their respective ancestral villages and help arrange donations from rich Chinese from overseas to build schools, hospitals and roads.

In 2018, the OCAO was administratively placed under the United Front Work Department of the CPC Central Committee (中共中央统一战线工作部, 简称中央统战部), as was the **National Ethnic Affairs Commission (NEAC)** of the People's Republic of China (中华人民共和国国家民族事务委员会). This may be seen as a shift towards an emphasis on the grand unification of China internally (further integrating the minorities) and externally (the unification of Taiwan with the mainland). By the 2000s, China had become an economic power and no longer needed to rely on Chinese overseas for its development, and so placing OCAO under the United Front Work Department can be seen as paying greater attention to soft policy consideration, to further engaging overseas Chinese organizations and individuals to promote China's national interest, especially pursuing national unification with regard to Taiwan. Soon after the establishment of the People's Republic of China in 1949, China established friendship associations in some countries to promote bilateral cooperation and friendship. For example, the China-Vietnam Friendship Association (中国越南友好协会) was established in 1950. In Indonesia, the Indonesia-China Friendship Association (印尼中国友好协会) was established in the 1950s. There was also the Thai-Chinese Relationship Association (泰中关系协会). Influential local Chinese were actively involved in these associations.

In 1987, China established its China Public Relations Association (CPRA, 中国公共关系协会). One of its aims is to strengthen links with organizations and individuals worldwide in aid of China's international relations.[1] In fact, the CPRA relies a lot on Chinese overseas. In Malaysia, there is a Malaysia-China Public Relations Association (马中公共关系协会). On 30 September 2019, a number of its executive committee members issued a statement to the press denouncing groups in Malaysia which had demonstrated in support of the protests in Hong Kong against its government and China.[2]

In 1988, China established the China Council for the Promotion of Peaceful Reunification (中国和平统一促进会), seeking to promote a good relationship between Taiwan and the mainland as well as the unification of the island with the mainland. The council encourages the formation of Associations for Promotion of Peaceful Reunification of China (APPRC) overseas. The president of APPRC in a country is always an influential local Chinese leader. In Trinidad, for instance, the president of the Trinidad and Tobago Association for Promotion of Peaceful Reunification of China is also vice president of Central and South America Association for Promotion of Peaceful Reunification of China (中南美洲中国和平统一促进会), and president of the China Society (中华总会), Trinidad.[3] In August 2013, I interviewed the President of the Indian Ocean-China Society for the Promotion of Peaceful Reunification in Mauritius (印度洋中国和平统一促进会). He was quite influential as he was then also President of the Federation of Chinese Societies (Mauritius) (毛里求斯华人社团联合会, established in 1988), which aimed to unite the Chinese associations in Mauritius as well as to promote friendship with PRC.[4]

There are also APPRC associations in Southeast Asia, albeit with slightly different names. The Thailand-China Association for Promotion of Peaceful Reunification of China was established on 7 February 2001, just after the Philippine-China APPRC was formed on 2 January 2001.⁵ The one in Indonesia originally was called East Java-China Association for Promotion of Peaceful Reunification of China (印尼东爪哇中国和平统一促进会), although it has since been called Indonesian Chinese-China Association for Promotion of Peaceful Reunification of China (印尼华人中国和平统一促进会). On the day of its official formation on 19 March 2007, it condemned Chen Shui-bian's call for Taiwan's independence.⁶

There is a transnational association of the Chinese overseas from Vietnam, Kampuchea and Laos for the promotion of peaceful reunification of China. Called World Vietnam Kampuchea and Laos Chinese-China Association for Promotion of Peaceful Reunification of China (世界越棉寮华人中国和平统一促进会), it was established in 1983 in Guangzhou, and has been holding its general meetings and forums on a rotation basis in different countries, including Hong Kong and Macau.⁷ For example, it held a forum in Hong Kong on 4 July 2004,⁸ and it was active in criticizing the independence movement in Taiwan and the protests against mainland China in Hong Kong.

In Malaysia, the Malaysia One China Association for Promotion of Peaceful Reunification of China (马来西亚一中和平统一促进会) emphasizes *yizhong* (一中 or "one China"). It was initiated by the prominent Chinese Malaysian businessman Lim Geok Tong (林玉唐) and his business colleagues in 2004.⁹ On 8 October 2021, this association issued a statement to condemn AUKUS, the trilateral security pact between Australia, the United Kingdom and the United States. Indeed, overseas Chinese pro-China associations serve to speak up for China on major international issues. On 15 July 2021, for instance, various such pro-Beijing associations in Malaysia, including Malaysia's One China Association for Promotion of Peaceful Reunification of China, Malaysia-China Public Relations Association (马来西亚中国公共关系协会) and the Malaysia One Belt One Road Committee (马来西亚一带一路委员会) issued a joint statement which called upon the US and Western countries not to politicize COVID-19 and insult China.¹⁰

China's soft power approach has been rather reliant on directly establishing organizations that blatantly promote China's interests as well as on encouraging influential Chinese from overseas to establish pro-China associations. While such efforts gain the support of the Chinese overseas who are generally already pro-China against the Western unfriendly treatment of China, its impact on non-Chinese is unclear. In countries where there are many ethnic Chinese, such as in Malaysia, such efforts are useful for China, and it is easy to form pro-China associations. This is not just because there are influential Chinese businesspeople who are close to China for business or historical reasons, but also Chinese politicians and businesspeople who are interested in gaining prestige through such an association.

Confucius Institutes

An important institution of Chinese soft power is the Confucius Institute (CI) which promotes the study of Chinese language and civilization overseas whilst cementing good relations between China and the host countries. Its headquarters under the Ministry of Education in Beijing was known as the Office of Chinese Language Council International (*Hanban* or 汉办); in July 2020, it was renamed Center for Language Education and Cooperation or CLEC (教育部中外语言交流合作中心). Besides the CIs which are attached to universities in foreign countries, there are also Confucius Classrooms (孔子学堂) established in local schools. The first CI was established in Seoul in 2004. By December 2019, there were 550 such institutes in 162 countries.[11]

The institutes are welcomed by those who wish to study Chinese and are encouraged by the emergence of China as a global economic power. In countries where there is no good opportunity to learn Chinese, the local Chinese also welcome the services provided by CIs. In fact, a CI may be headed by a local Chinese academician.[12]

In ASEAN, as of 2021, there were thirty-three Confucius Institutes and thirty-five Confucius Classrooms.[13] Only Brunei and East Timor do not have any Confucius Institute, whilst Myanmar has only three Confucius Classrooms. Thailand has the most, sixteen in all. This shows the popularity of learning Chinese in that country.[14] There are eight Confucius Institutes in Indonesia, but they are called Pusat Bahasa Mandarin or Mandarin Language Centre, such as the one at Al Azhar University of Indonesia in Jakarta. This is most likely an adjustment in a country where any perception of intervention by China is sensitive.

Many universities outside China welcome Confucius Institutes as they are financed by China and there is a demand for studying Chinese. However, in Malaysia where the local Chinese already have a system of Chinese education, the introduction of Confucius Institutes (the first one established at the University of Malaya is called Kongzi Institute, adopting the Chinese name of Confucius) is not enthusiastically welcomed by the local Chinese. These Confucius Institutes serve mainly to teach Chinese as a foreign language to non-Chinese students, and this contradicts the local Chinese view of *Huayu* (华语 or Mandarin) as their mother tongue (Ngeow and Tan 2018, p. 106).

In most countries, Confucius Institutes are welcomed for providing opportunities for the study of the Chinese language and Chinese culture, and in some cases, Chinese medicine too. However, in the West, governments and China critics see Confucius Institutes as the Chinese Communist Party's attempt to carry out global propaganda. The anti-China attitude, no doubt, contributes to this but the management of the institutes under the Chinese Ministry of Education also adds to the suspicion that China has ulterior motives. Jennifer Hubbert points out that while the students in the US appreciated the learning of Chinese, they found the curriculum tedious, and they were sceptical of what they perceived as Chinese government propaganda (Hubbert 2019; Matthews 2021). The adoption of the new name, CLEC, and related administrative adjustments may be seen as an attempt to reduce the suspicious attitude towards Confucius Institutes.

China also pursues its soft policy by supporting local initiatives for the teaching of Chinese. An interesting example is the Asia International Friendship College (亚洲国际友好学院) in Medan, and its Indonesian name mentions specifically the study of foreign language (Sekolah Tinggi Bahasa Asing Persahabatan Internasional Asia). This college was initiated in December 2004 by the local Chinese leaders in Medan after the tsunami in Aceh to provide education for the disaster victims, Chinese and non-Chinese alike. To coordinate the various works of assistance and to collect donations, the Chinese in Medan formed a pan-Chinese association called the Association of Community of Social and Education of Indonesia North Sumatra Indonesian Chinese (印尼苏北华社慈善与教育联谊会), of which building an education facility was the main aim. One donation from the Malaysian-based newspaper *Sin Chew Daily* helped a lot towards establishing an educational centre. On 20 August 2008, Asia International Friendship College was officially established.[15] The college offers the study of Chinese, and the students are mostly ethnic Chinese.[16] It has the support of the School of International Culture of South China Normal University (华南师范大学) which provided teachers and helped to design the curriculum. The China Overseas Association (中国海外交流协会) in China as well as its branch in Guangdong also help in recruiting Chinese language teachers paid by the Chinese government.

Mass Media

In our globalized world today, people have access to international media and therefore, global media coverage is important to soft power projection.

China has the English GCTN and the Chinese *Zhongguo Guoji* (China International), which broadcast news and feature programmes in English and Chinese respectively for the global audience. GCTN English news reporting generally does not follow the rather fixed pattern of other Chinese broadcast programmes by first reporting about President Xi Jinping and other senior ministers before reporting other news. However, when there is an important party celebration or forum related to China's soft power, GCTN often devotes time mainly to reporting about China. The audiences of China International are Chinese speakers. Based on the author's long-term observation, it is more blatant in its support of China: programmes can be taken out last minute to report matters of national interest, and programmes (including TV dramas) showing patriotism can be repeated a few times.

China's civilization, rich fauna and flora, diverse foodways, martial arts, and intangible heritage no doubt are of interest to many people worldwide, Chinese and non-Chinese alike. Programmes on these are not only informative but also serve soft power objectives. In rebutting Western anti-China rhetoric, China's media could be made more effective by relying on more concise reporting and analyses that do not appear propagandistic. However, there is a tendency to emphasize propaganda to the extent of counter-productiveness even when the audience is a global one. CNN and BBC are effective in convincing at least their internal audience (such as in portraying China and Russia as evil) because they report it in a concise way that does not appear propagandistic, even though their reports are rather biased and may be full of distortions. For example, when reporting about the war between Russia and Ukraine, they report as if this is a purely Ukraine problem due to Russian aggression and shift the audience's attention away from the security threat that the US and the North Atlantic Treaty Organization (NATO) have imposed on Russia. Even when CNN reports about certain achievements of China, it always reminds its audience about some negative aspects of China, such as its authoritarianism or human rights violations. China can learn to appear not propagandistic while not having to follow CNN's and BBC's biased reporting. It can give a concise and balanced news analysis and still exposes the real intention of the US and its lies about China.

China's mass media have a significant impact on Chinese overseas, especially those who speak Mandarin. This is because the Chinese overseas share with the Chinese in China the common Chinese civilization. In particular, the common language (Mandarin) brings people together even though the Chinese overseas identify politically with their respective countries. Such civilizational identification (Tan 2001, p. 225) is, no doubt, significant in making the Chinese overseas an important resource in China's soft power policy. China's annual TV programme for Lunar New Year celebrations, for example, is of interest to many Chinese overseas and is planned to appeal to both China's citizens and the Chinese overseas.

Overseas, local Chinese mass media, especially Chinese newspapers like those in Malaysia, generally carry more news about China and Chinese culture than newspapers in other languages. Speeches of the Chinese ambassador are generally given more coverage, and this no doubt helps in furthering China's soft power. In the case of countries with a small Chinese population, the opening up of China allows the newspapers' management to hire editors from China, who run mostly news on mainland China (Tan 2016, p. 16). Ethnic Chinese users of Internet media like WhatsApp, WeChat, Facebook, Instagram and TikTok often receive and resend news and videos about China's infrastructure and socio-economic achievements, retorts of Western anti-China messages, Chinese civilization, food culture, Chinese arts and music, and China's natural beauty. While there are also negative messages found in mass media, all these reinforce the pride of the Chinese overseas about the Chinese civilization and influence their attitudes towards China positively, helping to oppose what is perceived as anti-China campaigns and strategies. Language and mass media thus play important roles in China's soft power.

A Softer Approach for Chinese and Non-Chinese

In his comment on China, Nye points out that "China should realize that most of a country's soft power comes from its civil society rather than from its government" and that "[p]ropaganda is not credible and thus often does not attract" (2021, p. 10). The US has Hollywood and various types of popular culture industries to help promote its soft power. To promote their good image, the United Kingdom has the British Council and Germany has the Goethe Institute in many countries. While the Malaysian locals know that these are centres provided by the governments of the United Kingdom and Germany, to them these are centres that provide services which they can participate in without feeling that they are targets of propaganda. Before the COVID-19 period, the British Council in Malaysia conducted seminars such as leadership training and career advancement for youths in different cities in Malaysia. These seminars, although they serve the United Kingdom's soft power objectives, are seen as useful to the locals rather than British propaganda. China can learn from their soft power approach instead of exhibiting patriotism in its outreach. A soft rather than a blatant approach is more effective for achieving soft power objectives. Such a blatant approach is different from Nye's "sharp power" which refers to inserting false information into the political processes of other countries (Nye 2021, p. 7), which can be better described as a subversive soft power.

An example of an institution from China that has a softer approach appreciated by both the local Chinese and non-Chinese is the China Cultural Center of Mauritius (毛里求斯中国文化中心), which offers instructions in Chinese language, Chinese martial arts and Chinese crafts. I was impressed with the local children, Chinese and non-Chinese, producing art of not only Chinese motifs but local motifs as well. Its Chinese language classes attracted both Chinese and non-Chinese. Even some older Chinese who were Hakka-speaking signed up as they wanted to learn to speak Mandarin.[17]

In fact, since the 1980s, China has established thirty China Cultural Centres worldwide, and these include ten in Asia (Japan, Korea, Mongolia, Thailand, Sri Lanka, Laos, Nepal, Pakistan, Singapore and Vietnam). The one (not to be confused with Singapore Chinese Cultural Centre) in Singapore was opened in 2015. The aim mentioned on its website "is to introduce Chinese culture and arts to Singapore and to enhance the understanding and friendship between the two peoples". The centre "offers a variety of cultural activities, including lectures and training programs, performances, exhibitions and consulting sessions".[18]

The cultural dimension of China's soft power is focused on the teaching of Chinese language and civilization. Given China's achievements in economy, science and technology, organizing seminars and training camps on these themes for people from different walks of life would be most welcome. This would enhance its soft power impact in the long run.

Conclusion

There is a lot more one can write about China's soft power policy, and one can do so more comprehensively by using the six categories (government, culture, education, global engagement, enterprise, and digital) that scholars have used to analyse different countries' soft power.[19] Nevertheless, the discussion above shows that China's soft power policy extensively involves the Chinese overseas. Over the years, the PRC has established a number of institutions that utilize the Chinese overseas as a resource for pursuing

China's soft policy interests. The Chinese language, Chinese education, as well as traditional Chinese medicine, Chinese arts and craftsmanship, music and dances, martial arts and culinary knowledge are all important cultural resources that play important roles in China's soft power, and they have influences on the Chinese overseas as well. The sharing of Mandarin and the Chinese writing script (in the case of those Chinese overseas who read and write Chinese) and Chinese civilization in general foster the cultural link with China as a land of Chinese civilization. This civilizational ethnicity (Tan 2001, p. 225) helps in contributing ethnic Chinese support to China against anti-China manoeuvres by the US and her Western and Asian allies like Britain and Japan.

However, the Chinese overseas are heterogeneous, and rather diverse from country to country, and their perception of China's soft power policy also differs. In island societies such as Mauritius, Trinidad and Tobago, and Tahiti, I observed that even the localized Chinese welcome China's economic and cultural inputs. Both the old and new immigrants rely on China's help to promote Chinese arts and cultural performances. Both Mauritius and Trinidad and Tobago governments (Tahiti is still under the French) are also friendly with China and support the local Chinese effort to involve China in local economic and urban development (such as the development of the Chinatown in Mauritius). In Southeast Asia (especially Malaysia and Singapore), the ethnic Chinese do not have to depend on China to promote their cultural activities although cultural troupes from China are always welcome. In both Mauritius and Southeast Asia, China's soft power strategies gain support from the ethnic Chinese leaders to liaise with the local governments, and this may include cooperation on major local economic projects.

The influential roles that ethnic Chinese business leaders and politicians play in Southeast Asia naturally make them an important resource for China's soft power strategy in the region. In return, China provides these ethnic Chinese leaders with status and socio-economic networks in China. Its ambassadors now and then show concern about ethnic Chinese interests by giving donations to Chinese schools and even imply giving protection (Ngeow and Tan 2018, pp. 108–10). Nevertheless, China needs to be sensitive to the feelings of both the ethnic Chinese and the non-Chinese populations. The local Chinese do not wish for China's activities to stir up the feelings of the non-Chinese majority against them. But while they may be proud of the achievements of China and welcome its support in cultural matters, they need to be careful about its "suffocating embrace" (Wang 1981, p. 278).

Indeed, with increasing US anti-China manoeuvres supported by its Western and some Asian allies, the local Chinese leaders who have been willing to support China for their business and personal interests need to attend to local Chinese interests in their relations with the majority local population and the government. It is necessary to help ensure that the local government is not caught in the conflict between the big powers, mainly between the US and China. The border wars between China and India in 1962 and China and Vietnam in 1979 show that any serious conflict between a local government and China is disastrous for the local Chinese. The local Chinese also cannot afford to ignore local corruption practices that benefit China as revelations of such practices may create not only anti-China but also anti-local Chinese feelings. In China's game of soft power involving China and the Chinese overseas, both sides need to be aware of such underlying tensions.

With its expansion of the Belt and Road Initiative, especially in Africa, Middle East Central Asia, South Asia and Southeast Asia, China needs to pay more attention to building its image in the countries of these regions. Other than the Confucius Institutes and providing scholarships, China has also established various kinds of institutions of cooperation and for image-building. These include the Forum on China-Africa Cooperation (FOCAC), China-African Union Strategic Dialogue (China-AU Strategic Dialogue), and Manila Forum for China-Philippines Relations (Manila Forum). The Chinese investment in building dams, ports, railways, and other kinds of infrastructure in many countries is impressive, but it has to cope with accusations of putting these countries in debt, involvement in corruption and co-optation of senior government and military officials. It is essential for China to build a good image among ordinary citizens of the countries where it invests, not just the ethnic Chinese. This can be accomplished through establishing centres and organizations that provide services that benefit the local people. The present policy of providing scholarships for higher education in China, for example, can be expanded.

Notes

1. See www.cpra.org.cn
2. See https://www.sinchew.com.my/20190930/斥大马撑港马中公共关系协会
3. I interviewed Mr Yung Gen Siu (萧容庆) at his restaurant, Port-of-Spain, Trinidad, on 19 May 2012.
4. Interview with Mr Tang Yun Sing (邓旭升) at his home in Port Louis, Mauritius on 29 August 2013.
5. See http://www.pcpprc.com/portal.php?mod=list&catid=2

6. See https://xueshu.baidu.com/usercenter/paper/show?paperid=cc3f3457421e62f03e0694b730041ed7&site=xues; see also the 21 March 2007 report in China Qiaowang (www.chinaqw.com.cn).
7. See http://www.zhongguotongcuhui.org.cn/hwtchzs/201210/t20121031_3258366.html
8. See www.chinanews.com
9. See https://news.sohu.com/2004/06/03/96/news220369655.shtml
10. See http://yn.people.com.cn/n2/2021/0716/c372459-34822938.html
11. See https://baike.baidu.com/item/%E5%AD%94%E5%AD%90%E5%AD%A6%E9%99%A2/812632
12. For instance, the one in Tahiti was located on the campus of the University of French Polynesia, and it was headed by an ethnic Chinese professor from the university at the time of my visit in September 2015.
13. See http://union.china.com.cn/zfgl/2021-12/16/content_41824559.html, 16 December 2021.
14. See "Confucius Institutes around the World", 2021, https://www.digmandarin.com/confucius-institutes-around-the-world.html
15. The information on Asia International Friendship College was derived from both interviews and the epigraphic record at the college, visited on 28 August 2017.
16. At the time of my visit on 28 August 2017 together with a colleague from Sun Yat-sen University, the President is a Batak, assisted by three ethnic Chinese.
17. I visited the China Cultural Center of Mauritius on 29 August 2013.
18. See China Cultural Center 中国文化中心, chinaculture.org
19. See https://softpower30.com/what-is-soft-power/

References

Hubbert, Jennifer. 2019. *China in the World: An Anthropology of Confucius Institutes, Soft Power, and Globalization*. Honolulu: University of Hawai'i Press.

Mathews, Gordon. 2021. "Book Review of *China in the World: An Anthropology of Confucius Institutes, Soft Power, and Globalization* by Jennifer Hubbert". *Asian Anthropology* 20, no. 4: 290–92.

Nye, Joseph S. 1990. *Bound to Lead: The Changing Nature of American Power*. New York: Basic Books.

Nye, Joseph S. 2021. "Soft Power: The Evolution of a Concept". *Journal of Political Power* 14, no.1: 196–208.

Ngeow, Chow-Bing, and Tan Chee-Beng. 2018. "Cultural Ties and States' Interests: Malaysian Chinese and China's Rise". In *China's Rise and the Chinese Overseas*, edited by Bernard P. Wong and Tan Chee-Beng, pp. 96–116. London and New York: Routledge.

Peterson, Glen. 2012. *Overseas Chinese in the People's Republic of China*. London and New York: Routledge.

Tan, Chee-Beng. 2001. "Chinese in Southeast Asia and Identities in a Changing Global Context". In *Chinese Populations in Contemporary Southeast Asian Societies:*

Identities, Interdependence and International Influence, edited by M. Jocelyn Armstrong, R. Warwick Armstrong, and Kent Mulliner, pp. 210–36. Richmond, UK: Curzon.

Tan, Chee-Beng. 2016. "Voluntary Associations of the Chinese Overseas: Mauritius, Trinidad and Comparison with the Asia Pacific". *Asian Culture* 40: 1–24.

Wang, Gungwu. 1981. "China and the Region in Relation to Chinese Minorities". In *Community and Nation: Essays on Southeast Asia and the Chinese*, edited by Wang Gung Wu, pp. 274–85. Singapore: Heinemann Educational Books (Asia) Ltd.

2

SOUTHEAST ASIAN STATES AND CHINA'S EDUCATIONAL SOFT POWER

Leo Suryadinata

INTRODUCTION

Chinese education in Southeast Asia emerged during the colonial period. Initiated by the local Chinese community, the Chinese schools were not controlled by the colonial or local government. However, when the colonial states felt that "undesired" elements were arising within these schools they began to intervene.

After Southeast Asian countries obtained independence, Southeast Asia states too did not immediately intervene in Chinese education. Only when they started the nation-building process, did the states then begin to pay closer attention to Chinese education, especially since China as a foreign power was perceived to be influencing local Chinese education. The measures introduced by Southeast Asian states differ from country to country, resulting in the emergence of several types of schools reflecting the local conditions of the different Southeast Asian states. Nevertheless, with the recent rise of China as an economic and technological power, the Southeast Asian states have started to modify their attitude and policy towards Chinese language and Chinese education.

This chapter attempts to examine the measures taken by Southeast Asian states towards dealing with China's soft power through Chinese education during the modern and contemporary periods, especially during the twenty-first century. Chinese migration to Southeast Asia has a long history, but massive migration took place from the nineteenth to early twentieth century (modern period), and again from the end of the twentieth to the early twenty-first century (contemporary period). When

Chinese people migrated during these periods, they also brought their language and culture with them. Unsurprisingly, Chinese language and Chinese education can also be found in Southeast Asia.

During the modern period, Southeast Asian countries (except for Thailand), were ruled by Western colonial powers, only achieving independence after the Second World War. Understandably, ethnic Chinese in Southeast Asia were mainly China-oriented rather than locally oriented. The contemporary period, however, brought about a different political situation. China has risen as a major power, if not a global superpower, and all countries in Southeast Asia have been independent for several decades. As ethnic Chinese identity grew, China also became stronger and now seeks to export its soft power. This in turn has largely affected Chinese language education in Southeast Asia.

Before proceeding further, it is necessary to identify the different characteristics of Chinese migrants in the aforementioned periods. Firstly, there exists a difference in migration destination. During the modern period, partially due to transportation difficulties, Southeast Asia was a major destination for Chinese migrants. In the contemporary period, however, new migrants identify developed countries (such as the United States, Canada, Japan, Australia and New Zealand) as their main destination, with only about 20 per cent of these migrants migrating to Southeast Asia.

The second characteristic is the place of origin of the Chinese migrants. In the modern period, the absolute majority of migrants came from southern provinces, while in the contemporary period, new migrants came from all over China. The third characteristic is the background of new migrants. In the modern period, the majority of migrants were poor with little to no education. Meanwhile, new migrants of the contemporary period are wealthier and better educated, with some possessing large capital and high skills. This also leads to the fourth characteristic, where migrants in the modern era are less mobile and tend to remain in Southeast Asia, while new migrants in the contemporary period are more mobile and transitional. These characteristics have greatly affected the trajectory of Chinese language and education in the region of Southeast Asia.

THE MODERN PERIOD (NINETEENTH TO EARLY TWENTIETH CENTURY)

During the modern period, Chinese migrants in Southeast Asia would organize themselves by clan and province. This led to the emergence of clan and provincial associations, known in Chinese as *Zongxiang Huiguan*

(宗乡会馆). They were sometimes also called dialect group (speech group) associations. These *Huiguan* were created to help new migrants survive in the new and foreign land by establishing temples, funeral associations and Chinese schools. This was particularly relevant in the twentieth century when modern Chinese education began to flourish. The Chinese modern language form, *Baihuawen* (白话文), was used in Chinese schools, instead of the classical form *Wenyanwen* (文言文).

In colonial Southeast Asia, except for Siam/Thailand which was not colonized, race became the foundation of society. The Westerners (Europeans) were at the top of the hierarchy, with the Chinese in the middle, and the so-called natives at the bottom. The colonial powers followed a divide-and-rule policy, using the racial hierarchy to maintain colonial rule and ensure that the Chinese would not join the locals to rebel against colonial masters. To maintain the racial divide, colonial masters established different schools for different races. Only later, when there was a need to train administrators to help colonial governments, did they allow a small number of Chinese individuals to enter Western schools. A handful of Chinese and indigenous elites were able to receive tertiary education in the country of their colonial masters. Later, mainly in the twentieth century, a few Western medical and technological colleges were also built in the colonies to respond to local demand.

The majority of the Chinese in Southeast Asia went to Chinese primary schools and later on Chinese secondary schools which were built in a later period. Those who graduated from secondary schools went to China for tertiary education, though it was not easy for them to get into Chinese universities. As a result, Tan Kah Kee (1874–1961), a wealthy businessman and philanthropist specially built Chip Bee schools, and later Xia Men (Amoy) University for overseas Chinese students to receive higher education.[1] Despite all this, the majority of Chinese in Southeast Asia remained without higher education.

In the mid-1950s, there was a significant development in Singapore and Malaya (currently known as Malaysia)—the establishment of the first and only Chinese-medium university in Southeast Asia, known as Nanyang University (*Nanyang Daxue* or 南洋大学). The Chinese business community was led by Tan Lark Sye, leader of the Hokkien (*Fujian* or 福建) association. The establishment of Nanyang University (1955–80) marked the furthest development of Chinese education in Southeast Asia. During the twenty-five years of its existence, it produced about 12,000 graduates, many of whom served as schoolteachers in Chinese schools in Singapore/Malaysia and beyond.

There have also been many Chinese-medium schools in Southeast Asia, some of which have become quite well-known beyond the region. Though some schools have disappeared completely, the majority of them survived. These schools may have developed under different names, while others continue to use their localized names (see Table 2.1).

Since the 1948 closure of *Nanyang Zhongxue* (南洋中学), a Chinese secondary school, Thailand has not had any genuine Chinese schools (Zhou 1982, p. 281). All "Chinese schools" were in fact Thai schools that were allowed to teach Chinese as a foreign language. Many of these "Chinese schools" still exist but have been transformed into Thai-medium schools (Siriphon 2022).

After the establishment of the People's Republic of China (PRC) in 1949, these Chinese schools were divided into pro-Taipei and pro-Beijing schools. A school's political orientation was influenced by state relations. If the Southeast Asian state recognized Taiwan (e.g., Thailand and the Philippines), most of the schools would be oriented towards Taiwan instead of Beijing. However, if there were two types of orientations within one state (e.g., Indonesia), the pro-Beijing schools would eventually dominate the scene.

As time passed, the states in Southeast Asia began to pay more attention to Chinese-medium schools, particularly when the government stressed nation-building. As local nationalism in Southeast Asia grew, some countries (e.g., Indonesia) allowed only the children of foreigners to study in Chinese schools, before eventually closing all Chinese schools in 1966. Other states like Thailand and the Philippines restricted the operation of pure Chinese schools and only allowed the Chinese language to be taught in schools for limited hours. Yet others like Singapore transformed all Chinese schools into national schools, where Chinese is taught as a "mother tongue" (known as a second language).

The nationalization or localization of Chinese-medium schools took place in many Southeast Asian countries in the last century, coinciding with their nation-building processes. The result of this is the decline in the Chinese language standard in many of these Southeast Asian countries.

The Contemporary Period (Late Twentieth to Early Twenty-First Century)

If we examine the Chinese language and Chinese education in the contemporary scene, one can see that all of the Southeast Asian states, except for Malaysia and possibly Laos, have introduced a national education system

TABLE 2.1
Some Major Chinese High Schools in Southeast Asia

School	Location	Remarks
Pah Cheng Tsung Hsueh 巴城中学（巴中）	Jakarta, Indonesia	Pro-Beijing; closed down in 1966; and revived in 1990 mainly as a primary school
The Chinese High School 中华中学（华中）	Jakarta, Indonesia	Pro-Beijing; closed down in 1966
Pa Hoa School 八华学校	Jakarta, Indonesia	Neutral in orientation; closed down in 1966; Revived after 1998 as a trilingual school
The Chinese High School 华侨中学（华中）	Singapore	Transformed into a national-type school: Hwa Chong Institution
Chung Cheng Chung Hsueh 中正中学	Singapore	Transformed into a national-type school
Foon Yew High School 宽柔中学	Johor, Malaysia	Transformed into a national-type school
Confucian School 尊孔中学	Kuala Lumpur, Malaysia	Divided into a national-type school and a private independent school
Chung Ling High School 钟灵中学	Penang, Malaysia	Divided into a national-type school and a private independent school
Tiong Se Academy 中西学院	Manila, the Philippines	Transformed into a language school
Philippine Cultural College 菲律賓侨中学院	Manila, the Philippines	Transformed into a language school
Liaodu Gongxue 寮都公学	Vientiane, Laos	Transformed into a bilingual school
Duanhua Xuexiao 端华中学	Phnom Penh, Cambodia	Transformed into a bilingual school
Nanyang Zhongxue 南洋中学	Bangkok, Thailand	Closed in 1948; Since then, there are no more genuine Chinese schools in Thailand

in which either English or the national language has become the medium of instruction, and the Chinese language is taught as either the "mother tongue" or second language. While private schools run by ethnic Chinese are allowed (again except for Malaysia and possibly Laos) they are "tuition schools" that supplement national schools rather than full-fledged schools.

It is also worth noting that there are many national-type educational institutions in Southeast Asia run by ethnic Chinese, but their medium of instruction and curriculum are similar, if not identical, to the government schools. Some offer the study of the Chinese language as a foreign language while others do not. Moreover, some countries have even established universities based on national or international models.

Due to historical developments, some countries in Southeast Asia recognized Taiwan first while others recognized Beijing from the beginning. As mentioned earlier, the recognition of Taipei or Beijing also influenced the Chinese language education in the country concerned. In Thailand and the Philippines, the Chinese language was first influenced by Taipei. They used long-form *Fanti Zi* (繁体字) and teaching materials that came from Taiwan, but later shifted to short-form *Jianti Zi* (简体字) with teaching materials coming from Beijing. Although the influence from Beijing appears to be more dominant, language dualism continues to exist. There are still language schools and institutes in these countries that are linked to Taiwan.

There are many types of so-called "Chinese schools" in contemporary Southeast Asia, especially in the twenty-first century. Generally, they can be divided into five types of Chinese schools. The first type is the full-fledged Chinese-medium schools, such as those in Malaysia and Laos. In Malaysia, there are full-fledged, privately run, Chinese-medium schools known as *Duli Zhongxue* (独立中学) which means independent school. In these schools, apart from using Chinese as the medium of instruction, Malay and English are also taught. Their qualifications are not recognized by the Malaysian government. Apart from Malaysia, Laos also has full-fledged Chinese-medium schools, the largest of which is *Liaodu Gongxue* (寮都公学). Since this is a full-day school, the Chinese language is taught in the morning and Lao and English languages are taught in the afternoon.[2] This private school is considered to be a "good" school as its certificate is recognized by the Laos government.

The second type of school is a half-day Chinese school such as those in Cambodia. These schools are full-fledged Chinese schools attended mainly by Chinese students. They teach subjects such as Chinese, history, geography and mathematics, with Chinese as the medium of instruction.

One of the largest schools is *Tuanhoa (Duanhua) Xuexiao* (端华学校) in Phnom Penh which has 11,000 students.³ Nevertheless, the certificate issued by the school is not recognized by the Cambodian government. The third type of Chinese schools are mainly tuition schools such as those in Thailand and the Philippines. These Chinese schools are supplementary schools attended by Chinese children after regular school hours.

The fourth type of Chinese schools are national-type schools such as those in Indonesia and also in Malaysia. They are private Chinese schools that follow the national curriculum and teach Chinese as a foreign language. These schools in Indonesia are often called "National Plus" schools, or "*Sanyu Xuexiao*" (三语学校, meaning "trilingual school") as called by the Mandarin-speaking Chinese in Indonesia. But in Malaysia, these national-type schools have a unique characteristic. At the primary school level, Mandarin is still used under the national school system. The secondary schools, however, will need to conform to the national curriculum to acquire government subsidies. This is different from the private independent schools, *Duli Zhongxue*. The last type of school is the one in Singapore which teaches Chinese as a "mother tongue" (for Chinese children). Some of these secondary schools also offer advanced Chinese comparable to a first language standard. As the Singapore population consists of 75 per cent Chinese, naturally the majority of the school students are ethnic Chinese. They are not Chinese schools but Singapore national schools.

It is important to note that these "Chinese schools" now rely less on Beijing or Taipei for teaching materials. They have become concerned with the national contents of the textbooks. Singapore and Malaysia, for instance, have developed their Chinese language textbooks reflecting their own national identity. The contents lean towards creating individual identities in Southeast Asia rather than that of China. According to some reports, Singaporean and Malaysian Chinese textbooks have also been used by many private schools in other Southeast Asian countries, at least before the COVID-19 pandemic.

As ethnic Chinese in Southeast Asia became nationals of the country where they were born or now reside, they called their language *Huayu* (华语, meaning language of the Hua people) rather than *Hanyu* (汉语, meaning language of Han people) or *Guoyu* (国语, meaning National Language). *Huayu* is derived from *Hanyu*, but they are not the same. In Southeast Asia, *Huayu* has undergone localization. It is also interesting to note that the base of *Huayu* is Southeast Asia; thus, the language may deviate from the *Hanyu* of Mainland China. The former contains a lot of local words and displays a deeper national identity.

Confucius Institutes

Many Chinese schools were the product of local Chinese immigrants; but with China on the rise, the situation is changing. China has started to export its language, i.e., *Hanyu*, overseas. The organization responsible for the spread of the Han language is called the Office of Han Language, termed *Hanban* (汉办). *Hanban* is located in the Prime Minister's Office of China and has been tasked with establishing Confucius Institutes (*Kongzi Xueyuan*, 孔子学院) in Southeast Asia and beyond since 2005. These Confucius Institutes are usually established within foreign universities, with each Confucius Institute paired with a university in China.

Since 2005, *Hanban* has set up forty Confucius Institutes in Southeast Asia, of which the largest number is in Thailand with sixteen altogether; Indonesia has the second largest number with eight institutes. There are four established in the Philippines and the rest of the countries in Southeast Asia have only one or two. There is no Confucius Institute in Brunei Darussalam (Suryadinata 2017; Neo 2022).

These Confucius Institutes were established to teach the Chinese language to Southeast Asians, both ethnic Chinese and non-Chinese. At the same time, it aimed to expose them to Chinese culture. According to some reports, many Southeast Asian government officials have been taking Chinese language lessons from the Confucius Institutes. The students at Confucius Institutes are also given opportunities to further their studies in China.

In the West, many suspect Confucius Institutes to be spy organizations and Chinese Communist Party (CCP) propaganda; these issues have not been raised in Southeast Asia. Southeast Asian governments seem to feel that they are able to control the situation and benefit from the presence of such Institutes. Nevertheless, in Indonesia, major universities such as Universitas Indonesia (UI) and Universitas Gajah Mada (UGM) do not have Confucius Institutes, as many staff members are still very critical of China.

In some countries, like Indonesia, Confucianism is considered as a religion; thus, in many Indonesian universities, the Confucius Institutes are called "Mandarin Language Centres" (Pusat Bahasa Mandarin) instead. The purpose is not to confuse the language with the Confucian Religion. Nevertheless, when it is reported in the Chinese language, the Chinese name *Kongzi Xueyuan* (孔子学院, "Confucius Institute" in Chinese) is still used.

Confucius Institutes offer courses in *Hanyu* rather than *Huayu*, except in Singapore, where both *Hanyu* and *Huayu* are taught in the institute. The students are made fully aware that *Hanyu* is the language used in China, while the official language of Singapore is *Huayu*.

Additionally, Confucius Institutes offer scholarships for students to upgrade their *Hanyu* skills in China's universities. While each Confucius Institute only offers about twenty scholarships each year, the number of applicants has always exceeded the quota, indicating that many Southeast Asian students are interested in studying the Chinese language. In Indonesia, for instance, those who study the Chinese language are mainly non-Chinese, as few Chinese Indonesians want to become Chinese language teachers; they prefer to study other courses that are more practical and would generate better income.

Expansion of China's Tertiary Education and Chinese Students

In what can be seen as an attempt to spread and expand China's soft power, Beijing has established overseas university campuses in Southeast Asia. The first overseas China's university was established in Vientiane, Laos in October 2012. It is called Lao Soochow University, or Soochow University in Laos.[4] This university emphasizes international economics, finances and trade, and the major medium of instruction is Chinese (Mandarin). The Lao students are required to study one year on the Laos campus, but from the second year to the fourth year, they have to study at the Soochow University China campus. They have to be proficient in the Chinese language before they can graduate. According to one report, by 2017, 200 Lao students had passed undergraduate or postgraduate degrees from Soochow University, and they would get two degrees, one from Soochow University in China and the other from Laos. According to the same information, the "1+3" model (i.e., one year in Laos and three years in China) would gradually be changed to the "2+2" model in future. The graduates are meant to serve in China or Laos-China joint companies as they are mastering the Chinese language rather than English or other foreign language.

However, Xiamen University in Malaysia follows a different model, which requires the students to only study on the Malaysian campus with a different teaching medium. The Xiamen University in Malaysia was established in 2016. Unlike its counterpart in China, the university in Malaysia is an international university; all the courses, except for Chinese Studies and Traditional Chinese Medicine (TCM), are taught in English. The university offers engineering, economics, sciences and more. Half of its students are from China, but the other half are from Malaysia and beyond. When the university opened its doors, 180 students were accepted. In 2019, it had 120 graduates. Currently, there are 4,000 students enrolled in the university, and the university expects that student enrolment will reach 10,000 students in a decade.[5]

The establishment of the university campus has aided in spreading China's soft power. It should be noted that despite the strong anti-Communist sentiments of the youth of the United Malays National Organization (UMNO), a major political party in Malaysia, UMNO did not protest against the establishment of the Xiamen University in Malaysia mostly because it agreed with then UMNO leader and former Malaysian Prime Minister Najib Razak (Chang 2022). The arrangement of establishing the university was approved by Najib himself.

While no major Chinese university has established a branch in Thailand, the Open University of Fujian recently began a joint venture with the Thai Walailak University to set up an Overseas Chinese College in Bangkok,[6] suggesting that this college will strongly attract not just Chinese students but also Thai students.

Many Chinese students in mainland China have expressed interest in Western education or overseas education. Their first destinations were Western countries such as the United States, Canada, the United Kingdom and Australia. However, because of racism in the West, some students, especially those who do not have the opportunity to go to universities in China, decide to enter Southeast Asian universities instead. There are at least four popular countries in Southeast Asia for Chinese students: Singapore, Thailand, Malaysia and the Philippines.

Some of these Southeast Asian universities are known as "good" universities, and many students try to learn the English language or use their attendance at these universities as stepping stones to the West. In Malaysia alone, there are more than 10,000 mainland Chinese university students, with a large number of them studying in private Western universities. There are also over 10,000 mainland Chinese students in Thailand. In the Philippines, a few hundred Chinese students are currently enrolled in various universities and colleges.

Singapore houses perhaps the largest number of mainland Chinese students of all ages. It is common for mainland Chinese parents to send their young children to primary and secondary schools. Therefore, one may often come across *Peidu Mama* (陪读妈妈, translated literally as Study Mama) in Singapore.[7] Apart from young children, there is also a large number of Chinese university students in Singapore tertiary institutions, numbering between 13,000 and 15,000.[8]

Inversely, China itself has also become the country in which Southeast Asian students aspire to study. The Chinese government, various Chinese universities and foundations often offer scholarships to these students. In the past century, and especially during the Cold War, only overseas Chinese students were attracted to study in China. As China was a communist state, the implementation of anti-communist policies meant that many countries refused to allow students who studied in China to return to Southeast Asia. However, in the twenty-first century, as Chinese communist ideology was played down and China itself moved towards a "capitalist economy" (also deemed "Socialism with Chinese characteristics"), many Southeast Asian students began studying or even working and living in China.

Those who study in China are mainly tertiary students located at various universities all over the country. It is also worth noting that they study not only language and social sciences but also technology, sciences, economics and business administration. Many of these students are scholarship holders and private students. According to 2018 statistics, the largest number of Southeast Asian students in China came from Thailand, followed by those from Indonesia, Laos, Vietnam and Malaysia (see Table 2.2). Students from the other five Southeast Asian countries exist in low numbers; according to some reports, they range from several hundred (the Philippines) to a couple of thousand (Indonesia). Very few students came from Brunei Darussalam.

TABLE 2.2
Southeast Asian Students in China and Chinese Students in Southeast Asia

Country	Number of Southeast Asian Students in China	Number of Chinese Students in Southeast Asia
Thailand	28,608	10,000
Indonesia	15,050	A few hundred
Laos	14,645	N.A
Vietnam	11,299	N.A.
Malaysia	9,479	10,000
Singapore	N.A.	13,000–15,000

Source: 2018 China's statistics and others; various sources.

Conclusion

In the past, Chinese schools in Southeast Asia were all established by the local Chinese communities. The states, both China and the countries of Southeast Asia, were not involved in the establishment of these schools. As most of the Southeast Asian states were colonies, and there was no local "national identity" yet, the ethnic Chinese were mainly oriented towards China. During the Kuomintang's (KMT) rule in China, the KMT promoted "Chinese nationalism" among the Chinese overseas, particularly in Southeast Asia, and further enhanced Chinese orientation towards China.

However, after Southeast Asian countries attained independence and local nationalism began to grow, the majority of ethnic Chinese became local nationals/citizens. This also affected local Chinese schools and education. The Southeast Asian states began to intervene, and the Chinese school curriculum became localized. After 1949, the division between the Republic of China (ROC) and PRC educational systems impacted Chinese education in Southeast Asia; but gradually, the PRC language system became the dominant system.

Due to the "nationalization" of Chinese schools in Southeast Asia, the standards of the Chinese language among ethnic Chinese have gradually declined. Except for Malaysia and Laos, most of the "Chinese schools" have been transformed into local schools that offer the Chinese language only as a subject that is taught for several hours a week. Many of their teachers are not well qualified, and there is no conducive environment for ethnic Chinese children to learn the Chinese language. Anti-China and anti-ethnic Chinese attitudes in many countries in the region have also impacted Chinese language learning.

However, with the rise of China and its dramatic economic development, the Chinese language has become valuable again. A strong command of the Chinese language is often required to establish economic ties with the PRC or to find work in China's overseas companies. China's *Hanban* introduced Confucius Institutes in all Southeast Asian states but one. These institutes not only offer ethnic Chinese but also non-Chinese Southeast Asians the opportunity to study Chinese. The Chinese language has become rather popular among non-Chinese, although its popularity cannot be compared with that of the English language. As the Chinese language is an aspect of China's soft power, the limited growth of the Chinese language's popularity in Southeast Asia is often seen as an example of China's growing soft power.

Nevertheless, it does not mean that China's educational soft power is not without its challenges. In the China-US rivalry, some anti-China elements would use the ideological argument to stop the further development of Chinese education. Although China itself has de-emphasized the ideological contents in its overseas education, and many countries also see Chinese language and education as purely economic and technological tools, the politicization of China's educational institutions may present a problem in Southeast Asian states that are based on Western or religious ideology. This will be a challenge for the further development of China's overseas Chinese education in some Southeast Asian countries.

Notes

1. For a detailed study on Tan Kah Kee, see C.F. Yong, *Tan Kah Kee: The Making of Overseas Chinese Legend* (Singapore: Oxford University Press, 1989).
2. 老挝汉语教学现状概述.pdf (uai.ac.id), see also Lim Boon Hock's Chapter 6 in this volume.
3. See 柬埔寨华文教育的现状和发展趋势 (gqb.gov.cn) (accessed 17 September 2022).
4. "Soochow University in Laos Pioneers Chinese Education Abroad", China-ASEAN – China Report ASEAN (accessed 25 June 2023).
5. Ibid., p. 97.
6. See *Bangkok Post*, "The ASEAN-Bangkok Learning Center, College of Overseas Chinese, Walailak University Center is officially open!", 30 June 2022, https://www.bangkokpost.com/thailand/pr/2337213/the-asean-bangkok-learning-centre-college-of-overseas-chinese-walailak-university-centre-is-officially-open-
7. Primary or secondary students from China who come to study in Singapore were often accompanied by their mothers, hence the term *peidu mama*.
8. See *People's Daily*, "Singapore New Mecca for Chinese Students", 16 May 2002.

References

Neo, Peng Fu. 2022. "Confucius Institutes in Southeast Asia: An Overview". In *Rising China and New Chinese Migrants in Southeast Asia*, edited by Leo Suryadinata and Benjamin Loh, pp. 49–67. Singapore: ISEAS – Yusof Ishak Institute.

Chang, Peter T.C. 2022. "China's Soft Power and the Chinese Overseas: Case Study of Xiamen University and the Confucius Institute in Malaysia". In *Rising China and New Chinese Migrants in Southeast Asia*, edited by Leo Suryadinata and Benjamin Loh, pp. 91–106. Singapore: ISEAS – Yusof Ishak Institute.

Siriphon, Aranya. 2022. "Between Taipei and Beijing: Education Options among the Yunnanese Chinese of Northern Thailand". *ISEAS Perspective*, no. 2022/78, 4 August 2022.

Suryadinata, Leo. 2017. *The Rise of China and Chinese Overseas: Beijing's Policy Towards Southeast Asia and Beyond*. Singapore: ISEAS – Yusof Ishak Institute.

Zhou, Yi-e. 1982. *Dongnanya Huawen Jiaoyu* 东南亚华文教育 [Southeast Asia Chinese Education], p. 281. Guangzhou: *Jinan daxue chubanshe* 济南大学出版社 [Jinan University Press].

3

EXPATRIATE OR NATIVE CHINESE LANGUAGE TEACHERS FOR MARITIME SOUTHEAST ASIA?

Neo Peng Fu

INTRODUCTION

What is the current landscape of teaching and learning Chinese in the world? This paper begins with an observation of the global demands for Chinese government-sponsored teachers hosted by the Confucius Institutes (CI) in the past few years. It believes that the changes in the number of demands for these expatriate teachers by the various countries may serve as a gauge for reviewing the relevance of China's global CI project. By implication, it maps the rise or fall in the interest of learning the Chinese language by the world communities. Nevertheless, this paper attempts to show that reliance on the supply of teachers from China may not be the way to meet the growing demands for Chinese language instruction outside China. By focusing on the three states in maritime Southeast Asia, namely, Indonesia, Malaysia and the Philippines, this paper aims to address the question: could or should the regional countries continue to rely on expatriate teachers to meet their needs in teaching the Chinese language to the local populace?

CURRENT GLOBAL DEMANDS FOR TEACHERS HOSTED BY THE CONFUCIUS INSTITUTES

A CI is a language school that teaches Mandarin (the standard form of the modern Chinese language) and operates outside China.[1] The institute functions as a partnership between a Chinese university and a host university in the country in which it operates. In this partnership, the Chinese side is mainly responsible for providing teaching materials and instructors. The teachers who conduct language and culture classes at the CIs of the host countries are sent and sponsored by China. They are employed by the Chinese government in the form of contracts for service. The contract usually has a two-year term and provides a salary and overseas allowance. As such, they are essentially expatriate teachers based at the CIs hosted by various countries.

Every year, the central agency responsible for recruiting these teachers, firstly *Hanban* and subsequently the *Yuhe Zhongxin* (语合中心),[2] will send out notices to invite qualified and interested individuals to apply for these opened positions.[3] All applications (or registered of interest) are to be done through a centralized online platform (then: http://kzxyshizi.hanban.org, now: https://pmplatform.chinese.cn). Nevertheless, individual applications would have to be endorsed and recommended by the relevant provincial or local authorities where the applicants come from.[4] The whole process will commence in the spring season of the year, starting with the application and recommendation period from mid-March to early April. This is to ensure that there will be enough time to complete the selection and training (or more of a professional orientation course) of these teachers, before sending them overseas to assume their positions in autumn (between July and September).

The exact number of teachers to be recruited for the year is determined by the separate requests raised by the CIs around the world, so as to meet their teaching needs. These individual requests from the CIs will be collated and compiled (by *Hanban* and *Yuhe Zhongxin*) into a list, which not only indicates the distinct openings in the various CIs, but also the overall worldwide demands of these teachers, for the year.[5] The total number of openings recorded in these annual lists is therefore a good indication of the level or magnitude of demands for these Chinese language and culture teachers from around the world.[6] As such, this paper looks into the 2018, 2019 and 2022 lists of demands for expatriate teachers from China.[7] Firstly, to have a sketch of the recent international landscape of learning and teaching Chinese; and secondly, to analyse the varied developments as observed in different parts of the world.

The first CI in the world was established in Seoul, Republic of Korea (or South Korea) in 2004. By 2018, there were 548 CIs in 154 countries.[8] Based on a computation of the figures provided on the "Table of Overseas Teaching Positions Funded by the Government for 2018 at the Confucius Institutes" issued by *Hanban*, the total number of sponsored teachers requested for the year by the global CIs was 1,158. The numbers were

818 for 2019, dropping to 602 for 2022, according to the 2019 and 2022 "Table of Overseas Teaching Positions Funded by the Government at the Confucius Institutes" issued by *Hanban* and *Yuhe Zhongxin* respectively.

On the face of it, China's global CI project might appear to have suffered a great setback or lost its momentum, if one were to judge it from the continued decrease in demand for expatriate Chinese teachers from 2018 to 2022. Nevertheless, if we take a closer look at the numbers, we may find that the picture is not that simple. One key point to note is that the rate of decrease in demand for these sponsored teachers from China varies according to regional divisions. If we categorized the global CIs into six main groups according to their geographical identity, a more heterogeneous development could then be observed. Firstly, the decrease in demand for sponsored teachers from China is most drastic from the three countries in the North American region, from 352 in 2018 to 213 in 2019 and then merely 16 in 2022.[9]

Secondly, the decrease in demand for sponsored teachers from China has also been significant for the regions of Africa and Asia. The 43 countries in Africa which hosted CIs' operations had requested a total of 206 teachers in 2018, but the number was reduced to 98 in 2019 and 91 in 2022.[10] The 30 countries in Asia which hosted CIs' operations had requested a total of 249 teachers in 2018, but the number was reduced to 168 in 2019 and 113 in 2022.[11] Thirdly, there is no significant decrease or increase in demand for the sponsored teachers from China for the Central and South America, and Oceanic regions. The 22 countries in Central and South America which hosted CIs' operations had requested a total of 59 teachers in 2018. Although the number was reduced to 35 in 2019, it had bounced back to 61 in 2022.[12] Similarly, the four Oceanic countries which hosted CIs' operations had requested a total of 18 teachers in 2018, and although the number rose to 35 in 2019, it came down to 16 in 2022.[13]

On the contrary, there was a growth in demand for sponsored teachers from China in the region of Europe. The 39 European countries which hosted CIs' operations had collectively raised a request for 274 teachers in 2018. And the number was 269 in 2019 and 306 in 2022.[14] These developmental trends, as seen in the past few years, are summarized in Table 3.1.

Do these numbers support the perception that China's global CI project is no longer relevant? Perhaps we could start by understanding the reason that led to the drastic drop in demand for sponsored teachers from China in the North American region.

The answer is quite straightforward. The reason that led to the decrease is basically political in nature. The United States National Defense

TABLE 3.1
Developmental Trends of Expatriate Teachers According to Regions, 2018–22

Regions	Number of Teachers Requested in 2018	Number of Teachers Requested in 2019	Number of Teachers Requested in 2022
Asia	249	168	113
Africa	206	98	91
Europe	274	269	306
North America	352	213	16
Oceanic	18	35	16
Central and South America	59	35	61
Total	1,158	818	602

Authorization Act for Fiscal Year 2021 and the United States Innovation and Competition Act of 2021, enacted by the US Congress, had made it extremely difficult for the universities there to continue hosting a CI on their campuses. In 2017, there were 103 CIs in the US, but the number has fallen sharply to 18 by April 2022. Moreover, there was also a strong indication among these remaining CIs that they had plans to cease operations.[15]

It is worth noting that, the US, as a single country, used to be the largest requester for the teachers who were sent and supported by *Hanban*. Figures in the teachers' request lists indicate that in 2018, the CIs in the US had raised a total request for 323 teachers, which was 27.9 per cent of the grand global demand of 1,158 teachers for the year. In 2019, the CIs in the US made an overall demand of 202 of these expatriate teachers, which was also about a quarter of the total global demand of 818 teachers for that year. Nevertheless, in 2022 the request from the US had dropped to zero. It is clear that this drastic fall in demand, from more than a couple of hundred to nought in just a couple of years, was not a natural happening but a man-made suppression. This drastic fall does not reflect that the number of people interested in learning Chinese in the US has gone flat. The number of demands for these teachers by the CIs in Canada had also reduced from twelve in 2018 to nine in 2019, and subsequently three in 2022. But the number of demands for these expatriate Chinese teachers raised by the CIs in Mexico was seventeen in 2018, two in 2019, and thirteen in 2022. In other words, the numbers have been relatively stable in the other parts of the North American region.

The rather significant decrease as witnessed in Africa and Asia would be less easy to pinpoint. Nevertheless, two possible explanations could be proposed. The first likely reason could be that for some of the countries in these two regions, a stabilization or saturation in demand for Chinese language teachers has begun to take shape, after an explosive growth in the initial period when the global CI project jumpstarted its operation. This may partially explain why the number of demands made by the CIs of African countries appears to be stabilized at 98 for 2019 and 91 for 2022, after a height of 206 for 2018. Similarly, the number of demands made by the CIs of Asian countries appears to be stabilized at 168 for 2019 and 113 for 2022, after a height of 249 for 2018.

The second possible reason could be that certain African and Asian countries are now able to groom their own talents to complement the expatriate teachers in providing Chinese language instructions to the local populace. Simply put, some of the countries in the two regions could now rely on their own people, the natives who have had an opportunity to receive the requisite linguistic training in China (or elsewhere), and had become qualified instructors to fill up the teaching positions for Chinese classes, instead of continuing to depend on China to provide them with expatriate teachers.

One must realize that starting about two decades ago, the Chinese government was already actively giving out scholarships to students in Africa and Asia (and beyond) to pursue a tertiary education in China. This initiative, after being implemented for an uninterrupted and extended period, has resulted in producing a group of local teachers, called *bentu jiaoshi* (本土教师), qualified to conduct Chinese language and culture classes in their home countries. This could be the added factor contributing to the decrease (or stabilization) in demands as reflected in the annual request lists of 2018, 2019 and 2022. Perhaps it is meaningful to mention that, during the COVID-19 pandemic period, Hanban and its successor had tried to encourage CIs to source for *bentu jiaoshi* to keep their programmes running when the regular supply chain for expatriate teachers was disrupted. This point will be further elaborated in the next section with Southeast Asia as an example.

Requesting or Nurturing Chinese Language Teachers for Southeast Asia

Figures in the 2018, 2019, and 2022 "Table of Overseas Teaching Positions Funded by the Government at the Confucius Institutes" issued by *Hanban* and *Yuhe Zhongxin* appear to indicate that demands for expatriate teachers from China from Southeast Asia have remained stable between the pre- and post-pandemic periods. The eight Southeast Asian countries on these lists raised a total demand of seventy-eight teachers for the year 2018, fifty-five for 2019 and sixty-four for 2022.[16] A breakdown of the demands by the individual states is given in Table 3.2.

These figures seemingly indicate that for most of the Southeast Asian countries, their demands for expatriate Chinese language teachers have not been growing, or even weakened slightly, in the past few years. Does this mean that the number of Southeast Asians interested in learning or improving their mastery of the Chinese language has shrunk? Could it be that the scale and magnitude of the enterprise of teaching the Chinese language in Southeast Asia have diminished? This has not been the case, as it turns out.

Some Southeast Asian countries have witnessed exponential growth among their populace an interest in learning the Chinese language in the last decade. For example, in 2011, the Philippine government started to offer Chinese as an elective foreign language subject for public high school

TABLE 3.2
Request for Expatriate Chinese Teachers from
Southeast Asian Countries, 2018–22

Country	Number of Teachers Requested in 2018	Number of Teachers Requested in 2019	Number of Teachers Requested in 2022
Cambodia	12	4	9
Laos	3	3	0
Myanmar	4	0	0
Thailand	36	26	38
Vietnam	0	2	2
Indonesia	6	2	10
Malaysia	0	7	0
The Philippines	17	11	5
Total	78	55	64
Subtotal for Indo-China Southeast Asia	55	35	49
Subtotal for Maritime Southeast Asia	23	20	15

students in the country. By 2019, some 11,000 students in the nation studying at ninety-three public high schools had opted to study the subject.[17] It is obvious that with a student size of this magnitude, it would be unrealistic for the country to expect that it could rely on China (or any other nation) to supply it with a body of expatriate teachers significant enough to meet the explosive growth in demands for Chinese language instruction at home. A more sensible way to cope with the developing demands would be by grooming its own talents to become Chinese teachers. This is indeed what the Chinese and Philippine governments had accomplished through bilateral cooperation. In December 2019, the Philippine Ministry of Education signed an agreement with *Hanban* to run a master's degree programme at the Confucius Institute at the Angeles University Foundation, targeting to groom 300 graduates in five years. Trainees of the programme will attend classes in both the host university and its Chinese partner university, the Fujian Normal University. The aim is to deploy them to the Philippine high schools as qualified Chinese language teachers after their successful completion of training.[18]

A similar project for training local Chinese language teachers had already been put in place by the Malaysian government—much earlier than that of the Philippines'. In 2011, the Ministry of Education in Malaysia added Chinese (Bahasa Cina) as an elective subject in their National Primary School Curriculum (Kurikulum Standard Sekolah Rendah, or KSSR) by offering it as an optional language curriculum for the national primary schools, an education system that uses the Malay language as the medium of instruction. One must realize that this is a policy implemented with well-prepared groundwork. Three years before the implementation of this policy in 2008, the Malaysian government had already taken the initiative to kick-start a collaboration with the Beijing Foreign Studies University (BFSU) (also the Chinese partner university of the CI hosted at the University of Malaya, named Kong Zi Institute for the Teaching of Chinese Language) by commissioning the latter to offer a five-year Chinese Studies programme for a selected group of Malaysian students sent to study in China. These are a group of Malay or Indian, namely non-ethnic Chinese, Malaysians who have received their Malaysian Certificate of Education (SPM) and have been chosen to enrol on this programme through a scholarship scheme. After completing their study at BFSU, these scholarship recipients would then proceed to complete a Postgraduate Diploma in Education training at the Malaysian Institute of Teacher Education (ITE), before being posted to the national primary schools to become Chinese language teachers.[19] It is estimated that more than 500 trainees of this programme have completed their studies at BFSU to date.[20] There were 2,069,109 students studying at the 5,865 national primary schools in the nation in 2013, a system of elementary education catered mainly for the Malay (and Indian) communities in Malaysia.[21] One could thus safely infer that there must be a considerably high demand from the non-ethnic Chinese parents of the children enrolled in the national primary schools to allow their kids to have an opportunity to start learning Chinese at the onset of their school journey, that had prompted the Malaysian government to come up with the 2008 and 2011 initiatives.

Another factor which may have led to the decision to offer Chinese as a curricular subject in the national primary schools could be that more and more Malay and Indian parents in Malaysia have instead chosen to enrol their children in Chinese primary schools, an education system which uses Chinese as the medium of instruction and runs parallel with that of the National Primary Schools. The Malaysian Minister for Education, Dr Mohd Radzi Md Jidin, revealed that the percentage of Malay students enrolled in the nation's Chinese primary schools has been on the rise since the last decade. He mentioned that the percentage of ethnic Malay students among the total student population of the Chinese primary schools had increased from 9.5 per cent in 2010, to 15.33 per cent in 2020. Similarly, the percentage of ethnic Indian students among the total student population of the Chinese primary schools had also increased from 1.67 per cent in 2010, to 2.75 per cent in 2020.[22] There are more than 1,200 Chinese primary schools in Malaysia. The minister did not disclose the absolute figure of the total number of Malay and Indian students studying in these schools. However, according to statistics published by the United Chinese Schools Committees' Association of Malaysia (Dong Zong 董总),[23] the total number of non-ethnic Chinese students studying in the nation's Chinese primary schools was 81,011 in 2012.[24] The percentage of non-ethnic Chinese children among the total number of children enrolled in Chinese primary schools has been on a steady rise since the late 1980s. The figure was 3.05 per cent (or 17,309 students) in 1989, 5.52 per cent (32,203) in 1994, and 10.66 per cent (or 65,000) in 1999.[25] This indicates that the base of the Chinese language learners in Malaysia has expanded. More and more non-ethnic Chinese Malaysians, who would either choose not to learn the Chinese language or had been denied the opportunity to do so in the past, have now opted to learn the language. That is to say, compared with any historical period in the nation, the Chinese language is now more widely learned by all the ethnic communities of Malaysia.

Indonesia has also accomplished much, vis-à-vis its Malaysian and Filipino counterparts, in the aspect of grooming a corps of local Chinese language teachers. By June 2022, besides hosting eight Confucius Institutes, the country also has twenty-nine universities offering thirty-one Chinese language and culture-related majors. This clearly signifies that there is a substantial pool of Indonesians who opted to learn the Chinese language (and China-related subjects) at the tertiary level. But the key point to be noted here is that the teaching duty at these Chinese majors' departments, basically is being fulfilled by faculty members who are local Indonesians. The size of this corps of teachers of higher institutions currently stands at 232, of which, 187 or 81 per cent are female, and 45 or 19 per cent are male. The majority of them, 212 in total, hold a master's degree; and 17 a doctorate. A more remarkable point to be noted is that 158 of these local Indonesian teachers have received their training at a Chinese university (mainly in the mainland with some in Taiwan) and graduated with a master's degree.[26] That is to say, their training, qualifications, and credentials have enabled them to become competent native Indonesian teachers for Chinese language (and culture) instruction.

How did Indonesia manage to groom this sizeable group of Chinese language teachers of Indonesian descent? Beginning around 2005 and 2006, the Chinese government began to offer scholarships to young Indonesians to pursue a degree programme in China. But unlike the developments observed in Malaysia and the Philippines, the Indonesia case started as more of a private and non-government-led initiative. It means that these Chinese scholarships were awarded through personal recommendations by Indonesian citizens (most of whom were the older generation Indonesian Chinese language teachers), and by liaising with the Chinese embassy and consulates in Indonesia. The condition for these scholarships, offered respectively by *Hanban* and *Qiaoban* (侨办 or Overseas Chinese Affairs Office of the State Council) is that the recipients would need to return to Indonesia after their study, to take up teaching positions in the local tertiary institutions. The recommender would also serve as a guarantor to see that this obligation is fulfilled. Incidentally, many of these scholarship recipients had moved on to do a master's (also with scholarship support) after completing their undergraduate study, before returning to Indonesia.[27] This was the background which brought about the core group of native Indonesians capable of managing the Chinese language and culture courses currently being offered in the tertiary institutions of their own country. It appears that Indonesia is set to be able to rely on its very own Chinese language instructors to train its people to master the Chinese language.

Willy Berlian, Chairman of the Indonesian Federation of Chinese Education, was recently reported to have lamented that although Indonesia had incorporated Chinese language education into its formal school system and allowed its children to learn Chinese as a foreign language in their national curriculum, "fully integrating Chinese language education into the Indonesian education system remains difficult" because there are "no rules or standards being applied by (the) Chinese language institutions" in the nation.[28] It is not surprising at all to note that, Indonesia, being a multi-ethnic country with close to 300 million population living in thirty-eight provinces, such "problems" could and do exist. Nevertheless, developments in the Indonesian tertiary institutions allow us to see that there are indeed encouraging bright spots in the overall landscape of Chinese language education in the country, despite these challenges.

If this is the evolving landscape of teaching and learning of the Chinese language in Malaysia, Indonesia and the Philippines, how does it help to answer the research questions this paper meant to address: Is China's global CI project still relevant? Could or should the regional countries continue to rely on expatriate teachers to meet their needs in teaching the Chinese language to the local populace?

Conclusion

When China started to emerge as a global economic powerhouse more than two decades ago, it ensued a worldwide surge of interest in learning the Chinese language, especially among people whose countries had developed closer economic ties with China. But many, if not most, of these countries did not have the resources to run Chinese language courses for their public. The Confucius Institute is meant to deal with this situation. If the purpose of the CI is to provide necessary resources (teachers, textbooks and techniques of instruction) for helping the various nations develop an infrastructure for delivering Chinese language instructions at home, it would appear that the global CI project is still highly relevant. As can be seen by the developments in Southeast Asia, the demands in learning and upskilling the mastery of the Chinese language by the people in the region remain strong and steady.

But it has also come to a point where such ever-growing demands have grown so large to the extent that it has far exceeded the scope of CIs' existing model of supporting Chinese language instruction in the host countries. That is, the scale of the teaching needs in the host countries has greatly surpassed the amount of expatriate teachers CIs could realistically deploy.

It is simply impractical, and also not right, to expect that China should make the financial commitment to send an unlimited number of sponsored teachers to conduct Chinese classes overseas. As such, CIs (or China) may have made a right and wise move in light of this development, namely, by helping the host countries to nurture their own corps of Chinese language teachers to make up for the expatriate teachers from China.

Notes

1. For an updated review of the major scholarly works in English on Confucius Institutes or China's global CI project, see Emily T. Metzgar and Jing Su, "Friends from Afar? American media coverage of China's Confucius Institutes", in *Journalism Practice* 11, no. 8 (2016): 1000–25; and Zhou Xizhuang Michael, "Confucius Institute to the South Seas: A Case of Localization and Soft Power in Singapore", *China Review*, vol. 22, no. 1 (February 2022): 179–210. For a focused discussion of the CIs in Southeast Asia, see Neo Peng Fu, "Confucius Institute in Southeast Asia: An Overview" in *Rising China and New Chinese Migrants in Southeast Asia*, edited by Leo Suryadinata and Benjamin Loh, pp. 49–67 (Singapore: ISEAS – Yusof Ishak Institute, Singapore, 2022).

2. *Hanban* is the acronym for Hanyu Guoji Tuiguang Lingdao Xiaozu Banggongshi 汉语国际推广领导小组办公室, i.e., Office of Chinese Language Council International or Confucius Institute Headquarters. The organization, located in Beijing, was the central agency overseeing the operations of the global CIs from 2004 to July 2020. After which, the "operation of the brands of Confucius Institute and Confucius Classroom" has been "transferred" to the Chinese International Education Foundation, i.e., Zhongguo Guoji Zhongwen Jiaoyu Jijinhui 中国国际中文教育基金会. Nevertheless, the annual exercise of recruiting CI teachers conducted by *Hanban* is now taken over by a newly established agency called Center for Language Education and Cooperation of the Ministry of Education (of China), i.e., Jiaoyubu Zhongwai Yuyan Jiaoliuhezuo Zhongxin 教育部中外语言交流合作中心, abbreviated as *Yuhe Zhongxin*.

3. For example, the notice issued by *Hanban* for the 2018 recruitment exercise is titled "Guanyu zuzhi 2018 nian chunji kongzixueyuan zongbu/guojia hanban guoji gongpai chuguo jiaoshi tuijian xuanba gongzuo de han" (关于组织2018年春季孔子学院总部/国家汉办国际公派出国教师推荐选拔工作的函). According to which, applicants need to be full-fledged faculty of higher institutes of learning (*gaodeng yuanxiao*), or primary and high school teachers who have a minimum of two years' teaching credentials.

4. These authorities refer to the Education Department (*jiaoyu ting*) of the provinces, autonomous regions, and directly administered municipalities, as well as the relevant tertiary institutions of the Ministry (*bushu youguan gaodeng xuexiao*) in China.

5. These lists are called "Table of Overseas Teaching Positions Funded by the

Government for 2018 (or 2019 and 2022) at the Confucius Institutes". The names of these lists, in their Chinese original, are: "2018学年度国家公派出国教师岗位汇总表（孔子学院）", "2019学年度孔子学院总部国家公派出国汉语教师岗位需求表（孔子学院）", and "2022年中方合作院校申报资助外派教师岗位需求汇总表". As they would be broadly announced by the relevant schools and colleges in China through their respective websites, the lists are thus easily attainable via a keyword search on the World Wide Web. For example, for the 2018 list, see its announcement on the website of Zhejiang Sci-Tec University: https://www.zstu.edu.cn/info/1063/2287.htm; the 2019's by Sichuan International Studies University: http://wsc.sisu.edu.cn/info/1098/5067.htm; and the 2022's by Hunan Institute of Technology: https://www.hnit.edu.cn/gjjl/info/1058/1726.htm.

6. These teachers are categorized into two main groups: language teachers (*Hanyu jiaoshi* 汉语教师 or *Zhongwen jiaoshi* 中文教师) and culture teachers. The latter includes instructors for: martial arts (*wushu* 武术), Chinese medicine (*zhongyi* 中医), arts and crafts (*meishu* 美术), music and dance (*yinyue wudao* 音乐舞蹈), vocational trainings (*zhiye jiaoyu* 职业教育), and food culture (*shipin wenhua* 食品文化). But the former remains the dominant group, which constitutes 92.4, 97.4 and 96.3 per cent of all the teaching positions advertised for 2018, 2019 and 2022 respectively.
7. Recruitment exercises for 2020 and 2021 were disrupted because of the outbreak of the COVID-19 pandemics.
8. *Confucius Institute Annual Development Report 2018* (Beijing: Confucius Institute Headquarters, 2018), p. 8.
9. These three countries are Canada, Mexico and the US.
10. The forty-three African countries which hosted CIs' operations by 2022 are: Angola, Benin, Botswana, Burundi, Cabo Verde, Cameroon, Comoros, Côte d'Ivoire, Democratic Republic of the Congo, Djibouti, Egypt, Equatorial Guinea, Eritrea, Ethiopia, Gabon, Ghana, Guinea, Kenya, Lesotho, Liberia, Madagascar, Malawi, Mali, Mauritius, Morocco, Mozambique, Namibia, Nigeria, Republic of the Congo, Rwanda, São Tomé and Príncipe, Senegal, South Africa, Sierra Leone, Seychelles, Sudan, Tanzania, Togo, the Gambia, Tunisia, Uganda, Zambia and Zimbabwe.
11. The thirty Asian countries which hosted CIs' operations by 2022 are: Afghanistan, Armenia, Azerbaijan, Bahrain, Bangladesh, Cambodia, Georgia, India, Indonesia, Iran, Japan, Jordan, Kazakhstan, Kyrgyzstan, Laos, Lebanon, Malaysia, Mongolia, Myanmar, Nepal, Pakistan, the Philippines, South Korea, Sri Lanka, Tajikistan, Thailand, Türkiye, United Arab Emirates, Uzbekistan and Vietnam.
12. The twenty-two Central and South American countries which hosted CIs' operations by 2022 are: Antigua and Barbuda, Argentina, Barbados, Bolivia, Brazil, Chile, Colombia, Costa Rica, Cuba, Dominica, Ecuador, El Salvador, Grenada, Guyana, Jamaica, Peru, Panama, Suriname, the Bahamas, Trinidad and Tobago, Uruguay and Venezuela.
13. The four Oceanic countries which hosted CIs' operations by 2022 are: Australia, Fiji, New Zealand and Samoa.

14. The thirty-nine European countries which hosted CIs' operations by 2022 are: Albania, Austria, Belarus, Bosnia and Herzegovina, Bulgaria, Belgium, Croatia, Cyprus, Czechia, Denmark, Estonia, Finland, France, Germany, Greece, North Macedonia, Hungary, Iceland, Italy, Ireland, Latvia, Lithuania, Malta, Moldova, Montenegro, Netherlands, Norway, Poland, Portugal, Romania, Russia, Spain, Serbia, Slovakia, Slovenia, Sweden, Switzerland, Ukraine and the United Kingdom.
15. Congressional Research Service, "Confucius Institutes in the United States: Selected Issues" (updated 20 May 2022), see https://crsreports.congress.gov (accessed 30 August 2022).
16. The requests from Myanmar in the 2018 list were from two Confucius Classrooms but not CIs. The three Southeast Asian countries which are not on the lists issued by *Hanban* or *Yuhe Zhongxin* are Brunei, Singapore and Timor-Leste. Although Singapore hosted a Confucius Institute, namely, Confucius Institute of Nanyang Technological University, it has never requested any language teacher from China, because the CI there can rely on qualified local teachers to run its programmes. Brunei and Timor-Leste probably still do not have any CI in operation. But about fourteen years ago, H.E. Mme. Tong Xiaoling, the then Ambassador of the People's Republic of China to Brunei Darussalam, mentioned in an interview with the *Brunei Times*, the country's leading English newspaper, on 19 September 2009, that she "believes the establishment of a Confucius Institute in Brunei is possible in the future". See the website of the Chinese embassy in Brunei: http://bn.china-embassy.gov.cn/eng/sgxws/200909/t20090921_10117500.htm (accessed 23 May 2023).
17. See Hanban's website, http://www.hanban.org/article/2019-12/05/content_795096.htm and the Confucius Institute at Angeles University Foundation's (CI-AUF) website, http://confucius.auf.edu.ph/courses.php (accessed 26 November 2020)].
18. See *Hanban's* website, http://www.hanban.org/article/2019-12/05/content_795096.htm and CI-AUF's website, http://confucius.auf.edu.ph/courses.php (accessed 26 November 2020).
19. This group of Chinese language trainee teachers in Malaysia has been identified as non-native Chinese-speaking (NNCS) trainee teachers whose mastery and confidence of the Chinese language attracted scholars' attention. See, for example, Yap Teng Teng and Chee Siew Lan, "Language Proficiency, Self-efficacy and Challenges Facing Non-native Chinese-Speaking Trainee Teachers", in *Non-Native Chinese Speakers in Malaysia: Perspectives and Challenges*, edited by Yap Teng Teng, pp. 147–66 (Kuala Lumpur, Malaysia: Universiti Malaya Press, 2023).
20. The author wishes to thank Dr Yap Teng Teng, Senior Lecturer at the Department of Malaysian Languages and Applied Linguistics, University of Malaya, for providing this estimated figure, via e-mail correspondence in February 2023.
21. See the *60th Anniversary Souvenir Journal of the United Chinese Schools Committees' Association of Malaysia* (Dong Zong 60 nian huiqing tekan 董总60年会庆特刊), p. 1295, Table 1.7, accessible on the organization's website, http://www.djz.edu.my. The organization was founded in 1954.

22. *The Straits Times*, "More Malaysian Malays Studying in Chinese Primary Schools Today versus a Decade Ago", 11 November 2020.
23. The Chinese name of the organization is 董总, the short form of 马来西亚华校董事联合总会.
24. *60th Anniversary Souvenir Journal of the United Chinese Schools Committees' Association of Malaysia*, p. 1301, Table 1.16.
25. Ibid.
26. These figures were quoted from a presentation made by Dr Herman at a conference organized by the Confucius Institute at Universitas Sebelas Maret, in Surakata, Indonesia, on 27 October 2022. Herman is an Indonesian academic based at Universita, Universal, in Batam, Indonesia. He has generously allowed this author to use his research findings for this paper. His research was later published as "Yinni Gaoxiao Zhongwen Zhuanye Xiankuang Wenti ji Fazhan Yanjiu [Research on the current situation, problems and development of Chinese program graduate in Indonesia Universities]", by Tang Genji (Herman) and Ye Junjie (Chun Keat Yeap), in *Quanqiu Huayu (Global Chinese)* 9, no. 1 (2023): 159–80 (唐根基、叶俊杰《印尼高校中文专业现况、问题及发展研究》，载《全球华语》2023年第一期).
27. Knowledge of this historical episode was provided to this author by Stephanie Phanata, Director of the Confucius Institute at Universitas Sebelas Maret, in Surakata, Indonesia, via an interview in October 2022. She is a recipient of these Chinese scholarships, and through which had completed her BA and MA trainings at Jinan University (暨南大学) in Guangzhou, China.
28. See Muhammad Zulfikar Rakhmat, "Indonesia Tries to Embrace Chinese Language but Problems Persist", *Jakarta Post*, 19 August 2021.

References

American Association of University Professors. "On Partnerships with Foreign Governments: The Case of Confucius Institutes". https://www.aaup.org/report/confucius-institutes (accessed 16 January 2021).

Congressional Research Service. "Confucius Institutes in the United States: Selected Issues". Updated 20 May 2022. https://crsreports.congress.gov (accessed 30 August 2022).

Confucius Institute Headquarters *(Hanban)*. 2014. "Confucius Institute Annual Development Report 2014". Beijing: Confucius Institute Headquarters.

———. 2018. "Confucius Institute Annual Development Report 2018". Beijing: Confucius Institute Headquarters.

———. 2018. "学年度国家公派出国教师岗位汇总表 (孔子学院)" [Table of Overseas Teaching Positions Funded by the Government for 2018 at the Confucius Institutes 2018]".

———. 2019. "学年度孔子学院总部国家公派出国汉语教师岗位需求表 (孔子学院)" [Table of Overseas Teaching Positions Funded by the Government for 2019 at the Confucius Institutes 2019]".

Center for Language Education and Cooperation of the Ministry of Education (of China) (*Yuhe Zhongxin*). 2022. "年中方合作院校申报资助外派教师岗位需求汇总表" [Table of Overseas Teaching Positions Funded by the Government for 2022 at the Confucius Institutes 2022]".

Ding, Sheng, and Robert Saunders. 2006. "Talking Up China: An Analysis of China's Rising Cultural Power and Global Promotion of the Chinese Language". *East Asia* 23, no. 2: 3–33.

Gil, Jeffrey. 2008. "The Promotion of Chinese Language Learning and China's Soft Power". *Asian Social Science* 4, no. 10: 115–22.

———. 2009. "China's Confucius Institute Project: Language and Soft Power in World Politics". *Global Studies Journal* 2, no. 1: 59–72.

Hartig, Falk. 2015. "Communicating China to the World: Confucius Institutes and China's Strategic Narratives". *Politics* 35, no. 3–4: 245–58.

Hubbert, Jennifer. 2014. "Ambiguous States: Confucius Institutes and Chinese Soft Power in the U.S. Classroom". *PoLAR: Political & Legal Anthropology Review* 37, no. 2: 329–49.

———. 2019. *China in the World: An Anthropology of Confucius Institutes, Soft Power, and Globalization*. Honolulu: University of Hawai'i Press.

Kramsch, Claire. 2014. "Teaching Foreign Languages in an Era of Globalization: Introduction". *Modern Language Journal* 98, no. 1: 296–311.

Lee, Hock Guan, and Leo Suryadinata, eds. 2007. *Language, Nation and Development in Southeast Asia*. Singapore: Institute of Southeast Asian Studies.

Metzgar, Emily T., and Su Jing. 2016. "Friends from Afar? American Media Coverage of China's Confucius Institutes". *Journalism Practice* 11, no. 8: 1000–25.

Neo, Peng Fu. 2022. "Confucius Institute in Southeast Asia: An Overview". In *Rising China and New Chinese Migrants in Southeast Asia*, edited by Leo Suryadinata and Benjamin Loh, pp. 49–67. Singapore: ISEAS – Yusof Ishak Institute.

Paradise, James. 2009. "China and International Harmony: The Role of Confucius Institutes in Bolstering Beijing's Soft Power". *Asian Survey* 49, no. 4: 647–69.

Rakhmat, Zulfikar. 2021. "Indonesia Tries to Embrace Chinese Language but Problems Persist". *Jakarta Post*, 19 August 2021.

Sahlins, Marshall. 2013. "China U". *The Nation* 297, no. 20: 36–43.

———, and James Turk. 2014. "Confucius Institutes". *Anthropology Today* 30, no. 1: 27–28.

Schmidt, Heather. 2013. "China's Confucius Institutes and the 'Necessary White Body'". *Canadian Journey of Sociology* 38, no. 4: 647–68.

Stambach, Amy. 2014. *Confucius and Crisis in American Universities: Culture, Capital, and Diplomacy in U.S. Public Higher Education*. New York: Routledge.

Starr, Don. 2009. "Chinese Language Education in Europe: The Confucian Institutes". *European Journal of Education* 44, no. 1: 65–82.

The Straits Times. 2020. "More Malaysian Malays Studying in Chinese Primary Schools Today versus a Decade Ago". 11 November 2020.

United Chinese Schools Committees' Association of Malaysia (*Dong Zong*). *Dong Zong*

60 Nian Huiqing Tekan 董总60年会庆特刊 [60th Anniversary Souvenir Journal of the United Chinese Schools Committees' Association of Malaysia]. http://www.djz.edu.my (accessed 23 May 2023).

Wang, Danping, and Bob Adamson. 2015. "War and Peace: Perceptions of Confucius Institutes in China and USA". *Asia-Pacific Education Researcher* 24, no. 1: 225–34.

Wheeler, Anita. 2014. "Cultural Diplomacy, Language Planning, and the Case of the University of Nairobi Confucius Institute". *Journal of Asian and African Studies* 49, no. 1: 49–63.

Yang, Rui. 2010. "Soft Power and Higher Education: An Examination of China's Confucius Institutes". *Globalization, Societies and Education* 8, no. 2: 235–45.

Zhou, Xizhuang Michael. 2022. "Confucius Institute to the South Seas: A Case of Localization and Soft Power in Singapore". *China Review* 22, no. 1: 179–210.

Part II
CHINA'S SOFT POWER AND EDUCATION IN MAINLAND SOUTHEAST ASIA

CHINESE SOFT POWER IN THAILAND
The Influence of Chinese Education

Sivarin Lertpusit

Introduction

Beijing's global position was established in 2006 when President Hu Jintao stated that China relied on both hard power (the economy, science and technology, and military) and soft power (culture and language) (Huang and Jun 2019). The priority of Beijing's foreign policy has been the economic integration into the global economic system to promote a "peaceful rise" and "community with a shared future". In practice, China joined international organizations such as the World Trade Organization, APEC, and ASEAN+3, but also initiated economic institutions such as the Asian Infrastructure Investment Bank (AIIB) (Shambaugh 2015, pp. 109–20). Aside from economic tools, education and culture are important public diplomacy strategies to boost China's soft power at a time when the country is expanding its global influence. According to Joseph Nye, a political scientist at Harvard University, "soft power" is the ability to persuade others to support one's goals (Nye 2004). Nye identifies political values, foreign policy, and culture as the three spheres of soft power. Pop culture, public diplomacy, and coercive economics are just a few examples of the non-security-related areas where China is now extending soft power beyond Nye's definition (Zhu and Yang 2002).

In Southeast Asia, existing literature on Chinese education focuses mainly on soft power. Lan He and Wilkins' study on Chinese soft power in universities' branch campuses in Southeast Asia emphasizes the importance of the Chinese language and culture in transmitting soft power (Lan and Wilkins 2019, pp. 179–97). The campuses must follow the rules and regulations of the host countries to attain legitimacy. In another case, Zhu and Yang (2022) investigate the sources of China's soft power in higher education in Cambodia. The study identifies four emerging sources of Chinese soft power in modern society: science, technological advancement, educational reputation, and economic development model. The study points out that elites may be integrated into Chinese values through Chinese education; however, locals who have face-to-face contact with Chinese people and Chinese enterprises continue to express uncertain attitudes. As a result, the study suggests that non-state actors help Beijing implement its soft engagement strategy.

In the case of Thailand, studies on soft power in education focus on the emergence and the role of Confucius Institutes (CI). With sixteen Confucius Institutes (CI) and twenty-one Confucius Classrooms (CC), Thailand has the most CIs in Southeast Asia, demonstrating the country's close ties to China in education. According to Du Qiaohong (2017), the vigorous development of CIs in Thailand is due to the strong support of the Chinese and Thai governments. Wei, Jutaviriya and Pundhanamahakarune (2021) reaffirm and clarify Thai supporting policies, as well as Sino-Thai educational cooperation. Politically, Zhou (2021) explains that the role of CIs extends beyond education, with the full support of the Thai government, Thai royalty and local businesses. CIs, by integrating locally, also serve to strengthen the Sino-Thai relationship.

This chapter aims to demonstrate the Thai and Chinese government educational cooperation following the establishment of Sino-Thai diplomacy. Another objective is to evaluate the impact of Chinese education in Thailand, particularly among Chinese-educated Thais. The qualitative research method is used to gather information from a variety of sources, including academic articles, laws, regulations, official announcements, interviews, observation (between September and October 2022), and surveys. The author's poll focuses on the attitudes towards China by the following: Chinese graduates, those who have studied Chinese in Thailand, and those who have never attended Chinese language courses. In total, 161 questionnaires were returned. The chapter presents two findings: Firstly, China currently places a greater emphasis on vocational education in Thailand to support upcoming investments like the High-Speed Train project. Secondly, Sino-Thai cooperation has expanded from government-to-government and institutional connection to the individual level. Chinese-educated Thais are the key actors in promoting intercultural exchange and knowledge transmission between Thailand and China.

The History of Chinese Influence in Thai Education

The early twentieth century saw the introduction of Chinese influence on Thai education. Hua Eah School is the very first Chinese school in Siam, established in 1908 after the visit of Sun Yat Sen. The growth of Chinese schools, from 30 in 1920 to 271 in 1933, corresponded with the fostering of Chinese nationalism among Chinese ethnic groups through education (Skinner 1957; Kajadpai 1974; Penpisut 2007; Wasana 2008; Murashima and Worasak 1996; Watson 1976). By 1933, the ethnic Chinese have become the most powerful economic force in Siam, particularly in rice trading. From the political and nationalist movements of Chinese sojourners motivated by the Xinhai Revolution (1911) and the Japanese invasion of mainland China, Thai political leaders have expressed mistrust towards them since the 1920s. As the ethnic Chinese have grown to be Siam's most influential economic group and dominate the rice trade industry in Siam, Chinese merchants there responded to Japan's aggression by supporting coolies' strikes, boycotting Japanese products, and refusing to supply rice to Japan (Murashima and Worasak 1996; Chao 2021). The damage caused by the Chinese protests demoralized the Thai government and disrupted the Thai economy. To protect Siam's interests, the governors had to contend with the Chinese nationalist movement. Eventually, tensions between ethnic Chinese, Japanese, and the Thai government reached their peak in 1941, when Thailand and Japan formed an alliance.

Field Marshal Plaek Pibulsongkram, then Thai prime minister and also a nationalist politician, suggested a set of nationalist measures to counter the Chinese movement. State authorities viewed Chinese schools as the underground headquarters of Chinese political activists, promulgating laws and regulations to prohibit illegal activity in schools. The Private Schools Act of 1933, 1936 and 1948 established Thai language competency criteria for school instructors and limited Chinese language instruction hours. From the 1940s through the 1950s, strict enforcement culminated in the success of governmental control over Chinese schools in Thailand. Under Thailand's strong governmental opposition towards Chinese nationalism, attempts to spread Chinese political doctrines were unsuccessful. Fear of Communism and concern for Chinese nationalism prompted Thai governors to deport the leaders of Chinese activists, enforce laws to limit the movements of Chinese and begin to assimilate Chinese into Thai society.

In 1975, China and Thailand re-established diplomatic relations. To promote bilateral cooperation, both countries actively organized activities and collaborations in education. The scepticism towards Chinese schools and language had lessened, and Thai authorities later recognized that learning the Chinese language had economic benefits (Chinese Studies Centre, Chulalongkorn University 2008). The Chinese language is gradually implemented as a compulsory part of all levels of Thai education and is officially listed according to the National Education Act of 1999 (*Cabinet Resolution* 2022). From 2006 to 2010, the strategic plan to help Thai people learn Chinese included government financial support. Additionally, the prediction that 100,000 Chinese-speaking people would join the Thai labour market, reflected the importance of speaking Chinese (Wei, Keeratiporn and Thamtanet 2021).

In 1999, the two countries issued a declaration defining their cooperation strategy for the twenty-first century, which included collaboration in the field of education. China and Thailand reached an agreement to exchange teachers, teaching materials, training courses, and scholarships. Eventually, adjustments were made to the plans for fostering greater collaboration. The development of CIs and CCs demonstrates collaboration in the dissemination of Chinese language and cultural influence. Currently, there are sixteen CIs in Thai higher education institutions and twenty-one CCs in Thai elementary and secondary schools (Office of the Education Council 2016).

Thailand and China's educational cooperation has rapidly strengthened after the launch of the Lancang-Mekong Cooperation (LMC). The LMC was initiated by China with the goals of promoting regional economic development, enhancing human well-being and creating a peaceful and prosperous community among the countries of the Lancang-Mekong region (Lancang-Mekong Cooperation 2018). Under the Belt and Road Initiative (BRI), education is used to encourage South-South collaboration in the LMC. The Sino-Thai Vocational Collaboration signed in 2017 and the initiative to open the Thai-China Vocational College in 2020 are just two examples of the projects that are active under this project.

Aside from government-to-government cooperation, there have also been collaborations at the provincial and institutional levels. Yunnan and Guangxi have become important players on a regional scale due to the substantial number of Memoranda of Understanding (MOUs) established between Thai universities and these provinces (Chinese Studies Centre, Chulalongkorn University 2008). According to a survey conducted in 2016, 82 per cent of higher education institutions signed MOUs with Chinese colleges allowing for dual degree, joint degree, collaborative programmes such as 3+1 and 2+2 (years studying in home country and host country), internship projects, personnel exchanges, scholarships, and contributing teaching materials (Office of the Education Council 2016).

Recent Sino-Thai Cooperation in Education

The Thai Ministry of Education and the Ministry of Higher Education, Science, Research, and Innovation (MHESI) have been key in encouraging Sino-Thai educational cooperation. Recent memorandums of understanding (April 2022) were signed by the CLEC with three Thai organizations: The Ministry of Education, the Office of the Vocational Education Commission, and the Office of the Higher Education Commission (*TAP Magazine* 2022).

Previously, Sino-Thai cooperation was concentrated on language and cultural activities at all educational levels. Over 70 per cent of primary and secondary public schools in Thailand collaborated with the domestic Chinese language network such as Regional Teaching Chinese Private School Organizations. Aside from the local network, all Chinese language schools have also collaborated with *Hanban*, *Qiaoban*, CIs, and CCs (Office of the Education Council 2016a, 2016b). At the tertiary level, 82 per cent of institutes collaborate with Chinese organizations, most notably *Hanban* (Office of the Education Council 2016c). Aside from these organizations, the performance of associations such as the Chinese Teachers' Association of Thailand under the Royal Patronage of Her Royal Highness Princess Maha Chakri Sirindhorn significantly supports Chinese language study in Thailand.

Aside from the Chinese language curriculum, Thailand and China are currently focusing on technology and science. Thailand and China's Ministry of Science and Technology agreed to establish the Thailand-China Technology Transfer Center, the Talented Young Scientist Visiting Program, the Thailand-China Joint Research Center on Rail Systems, and the Space Technology Applications in 2019 (Hydro Informatics Institute 2020). China currently emphasizes vocational education to support prospective investments such as the Railway Cooperation between Thailand and China project. The project includes sister colleges between Thailand and China's vocational schools (2018) to create human resources in technology and techniques to serve the Thailand 4.0 project.[1] The Chinese Ministry of Education, Confucius Institutes for the Maritime Silkroad, the Office of the Vocational Education Commission, and the Thai Ministry of Education signed an MOU in 2020 to develop Chinese language learning centres, vocational teacher training centres and innovative training centres. The centre for the rail transportation system project was initiated from the cooperation between the Banpai Vocational School (Khon Kaen, Thailand) and the Wuhan Railway Vocational College of Technology (武汉铁路职业技术学院) from Hubei, China which lately established the Luban Highspeed Train Institute (高铁鲁班学院) in 2019 (Kamsoi 2021).

Crucially, knowledge from China is not limited to language. The prestige of Chinese science and technology education is increasingly being internationally acknowledged. Chinese education has now grown beyond language and cultural studies to include other subjects, particularly STEM (Science, Technology, Education and Mathematics). In Thailand, Thai institutions have been moving in the same direction. For instance, the Geo-Informatics and Space Technology Development Agency (GISDA), Burapa University and Wuhan University announced the launch of a new master's degree curriculum in Geo-Informatics and Space Technology under the supervision of the Sirindhorn Center for Geo-Informatics (SCGI). The curriculum permits students to pursue fundamental credits in Thailand for one year and practical courses in China for the following year. Eventually, two separate degree certificates from Burapa University and Wuhan University will be awarded to the students. A second example is the collaboration between the College of Arts, Media, and Technology at Chiang Mai University and the Chiang Mai University Confucius Institute to establish a master's degree in Thai-China digital technology e-commerce (*Thansettakij* 2022).

Extensive Cooperation: Government-Government and Institutional Connection to Individual Networks

Formerly, government agencies such as the CIs supported Sino-Thai educational collaboration. Later, the partnership was expanded to the institutional level, which facilitated the growth of student exchange programmes in both countries. Apart from technical support, institutional cooperation in the forms of dual degree and joint degree programmes has also been promoted. As a result of the continuous cooperation between the two governments, there is a greater acknowledgement of Mandarin as a competency skill in the Thai labour market and the recognition of China as an influential country.

Due to educational cooperation between the two countries, the interflows of knowledge and cultures have significantly advanced after five decades of Sino-Thai ties. Networks such as alumni associations have arisen, suggesting that these ties have reached the individual level. The growth of Thai students studying Mandarin in Thai institutions and China is a key indicator of this trend. In 2005, more than 226,000 students were learning Mandarin in domestic educational institutions. According to the Ministry of Education and the Office of Higher Education Commission, the number increased to 615,270 in 2009 (Office of the Higher Education Commission 2010). In terms of outbound students studying in China, it has climbed from 14,145 students in 2011 to 28,608 in 2018 (Thai Embassy in Beijing 2022). In accordance with data from the Ministry of Education of the People's Republic of China, Thai students represented the second-largest sending country after South Korea (490,000 international students in total).

Non-Government Networks and Associations as the Key Link for Chinese Soft Power

The educational system serves as an indirect means of transmitting Chinese culture, philosophies, practices and norms. The question is, what are the consequences of these transmissions to Thai society? Additionally, how does Chinese education work to increase the Chinese state's allure, persuasion, and appeal? To answer these questions, this paper relies on interviews with Chinese graduates, representatives of Chinese alumni associations, Chinese language lecturers, and Chinese studies experts to examine the impact of soft educational power. Furthermore, the author conducts a brief survey of people's attitudes towards China by analysing their educational backgrounds to map the general opinion.

The first query is about the extent to which Thai society has been impacted by people with Chinese education. Theoretically, experiencing social interactions in host countries is assumed to form a sense of belonging in the long term even after returning to home countries. Although there is no empirical evidence on the returns gained from investments in international students in China, however, the implication of education as a soft power tool has long been employed by countries (Maksimova 2022) such as the UK, the US and France. Focusing on Thailand, Chinese-graduated individuals contribute notable impact to Thai society in their fields including strengthening networks, embedding and leveraging the Chinese body of knowledge in Thai education and disseminating information from China's perspective.

Individuals' perception of *Guanxi* (关系, or connections), and the collective values of society in China are created over time. Hammond and Glenn (2004) state that social networking is a form of social stability, trust, and prescribed roles that generate predictability and cultivate positive human interactions. Experiencing the educational system in China, Chinese-graduated individuals frequently recognize the value of networking in China and continually apply the concept of networking in Thailand.

After the emergence of a trade war in 2018, networks of Chinese-educated students were progressively established with the assistance of Thai government institutions, particularly the MHESI. Active organizations include the Zhong Tai Education (ZTED) working group, the Chinese Students and Scholars Association in Thailand, the Thai-Chinese Student Association (TCSA), the Thai Alumni Association of Chinese Universities (TACU) and provincial associations. These alumni organizations engage in a variety of productive activities that strengthen connections between individuals and promote a better understanding of China.

The *Vit Mitri Thai-Jeen* (Thai-China Friendship in Science), a monthly journal that focuses on tertiary, science, research, innovation, and multifaceted information regarding China and Thailand, is one example of these alumni activities. The publication is published by the ZTED, founded in 2020 and funded by the Thai embassy in Beijing. Its purpose is to distribute information about studying in China. Additionally, the ZTED frequently organizes webinars on a range of topics, such as world politics, the trade war, Chinese culture, and Chinese linguistics. Another network is the TCSA, an organization that was established in 2021. The association is made up of Thai coordinators from each of China's twenty-seven provinces to foster strong cohesion among Thai students in China. Lastly, the TACU, a semi-open group, is actively developing initiatives such as the Chinese bridge project, which aims to promote and introduce a better understanding of "China".

The Amplification of Sinology in Thai Education

Chinese-educated individuals also play a significant role in promoting cooperation with China and the promotion of sinology studies in Thailand. Nithivadee Chanyaswas, PhD, who has over fifteen years of experience studying and working in China, is an example of an influential Chinese-educated individual in the educational profession. She addresses the nexus of intercultural engagement to gain an advantage when dealing with Chinese enterprises. At present, she serves as the Dean of Bangkok University's newly founded Chinese International College. The college has numerous MOUs with Chinese businesses, Chinese colleges, and Thai organizations to produce Chinese-speaking labourers with digital and future-oriented abilities.[2] Another notable case is that of Kanjanita Suchao-in, PhD, who earned her degree in Beijing. She is currently the Dean of the International Chinese College at Rangsit University, as well as the vice-president and secretary-general of the Thai Alumni Association of China's Universities.

People with experience in China play active roles in initiating cultural events in educational institutions. Muangphum, the president of the student organization in Nanjing (TACU-Nanjing), a PhD candidate at Nanjing University and an employee of the Alibaba group, arranged an innovative social media project in Thai universities. The project, funded by the National Research Council of Thailand, aims to foster understanding between China and Thailand through social media content. His network functions as a micro-bridging channel between universities in Thailand and China, demonstrating the potential of Chinese-educated networks.

Broader Publication of Chinese Information and Perspective

The above-mentioned connections, networks, and organizations have a significant impact on the development of Chinese intercultural communication and the spread of positive perspectives towards China. According to the results of the author's survey, positive attitude is correlated to the length of experience in China. The survey was disseminated via various online platforms and networks. Respondents include fifty-nine people who have never studied Mandarin, forty-two people who have taken courses in China, and fifty-eight people who have attended Chinese classes in Thailand. Among the graduates from China, twenty-two graduates have lived in China for less than a year, seventeen have stayed for between two and five years, and three have spent more than six years there. Nonetheless, the number of respondents who reported residing in China for a duration exceeding six years was only three individuals. Due to the limited representation of the informants, the author decided to withhold the findings obtained from the over-six years respondents.

The survey's findings reflect that those with extensive experience studying and working in China have positive opinions about China (see Table 4.1). The respondents who spent between two to five years showed

TABLE 4.1
Perceptions of China Categorized by Experiences

Experiences in China/ Perception	No Experience	Less Than 1 Year	2–5 Years
Culture and practices	4.2	4.5	4.3
Social behaviour (people-to-people)	3.0	3.2	3.6
Chinese pop culture	3.9	4.1	4.3
China is a high economic potential country	4.6	4.4	4.6
Thai and China are important trading partners	4.2	4.3	4.5
China is a great opportunity for the Thai economy (under a trade war)	4.2	4.0	4.4
China's domestic political system is suitable for Chinese society	3.7	3.9	4.2
Contentment on the role of China in ASEAN	3.7	3.8	4.0
Contentment on the role of China in Thailand	3.8	4.0	4.2
Contentment on the role of China in Myanmar	3.2	3.3	3.6
Contentment on the role of China in the South China Sea	3.2	3.5	3.8
Contentment on the role of China in the COVID-19 vaccine	3.4	3.5	3.6

Note: Scores reflected are average where 5 is "totally agree" and 1 is "totally disagree".
Source: Online survey conducted by the researcher in September 2022.

favourable sentiments regarding the country's position in international affairs. For example, in the case of Thailand-China relations, the group of 2–5 years reveal the most positive picture of China. When it comes to ASEAN and the South China Sea, those with 2–5 years of experience gave the highest score. Comparatively, the sentiments of respondents who had no experience in China had negative perceptions of China. The majority of their perceptions, such as culture and norms, social behaviour and satisfaction with China's presence on the world agenda are positioned near the bottom of the list.

Additionally, 63.5 per cent of all responses to the question of "whether China is a threat" show a moderate stance that cannot conclusively state whether they view China as a collaborative or a coercive partner. Thirty per cent of respondents consider China to be a friend. None of those who had lived in China for more than a year marked China as a threat, whereas those who identified China as a threat were non-Chinese-educated people and those who had attended classes in China for less than a year. The survey results thus confirm the hypothesis that Chinese education has a positive effect on Chinese-educated people.

In addition to the findings of the survey, numerous Chinese alumni members share information and viewpoints from a Chinese perspective. For example, Arm Tungniran, PhD, graduated from Peking University[3] is known as a China expert who frequently gives interviews about China. When he was chastised for being a pro-China scholar, Arm stated that his role as a Thai scholar is to provide an omni-perspective to balance the flow of information and to minimize social bias in order to point out "the national interest of Thailand". Aside from his public role, he is also the former director of the National Research Center's Sino-Thai strategic centre and the current director of Chulalongkorn University's Chinese Studies Center. His point of view on China, however, has had an impact on social attitudes and government strategic planning from his roles in academic institutions and government agencies.

Aside from academics, Chinese-educated personalities can be found in other areas, such as among reporters and social media influencers. Pravit Thangthaweesook, a TACU member, is the creator of the Facebook page *Tai Kam Jeen Kam* (*Thai-Chinese Talk*). The page typically educates followers about China and overseas Chinese culture using language and has more than 220,000 followers (*Thai-Chinese Talk* 2023). Nattapong Namsirikul, also known as Kru P'Pop, founded the page *Chinese Pop-up*, which is followed by 84,000 people. He currently hosts radio shows on Thinking Radio and Chinese Radio International. In addition, he hosts a programme titled "Chinese Club" for the Ministry of Education and works as a television show reporter for Tan Loke (Thai PBS) and ASEAN Plus (TNN news). These figures continuously promote the Chinese language, culture, values and knowledge to Thai society.

The aforementioned instances demonstrate the role of Chinese-educated individuals in spreading Chinese influence in Thai education. The majority of the interviewees admit that after spending time in China, they become accustomed to Chinese customs and begin to comprehend "China". Positive perceptions of China include its advanced technologies, organized administrative system, infrastructure, and cultural attitude. Aruni, a PhD candidate and member of the ZTED working group, asserts that China is distinct from the West; hence, evaluating China in accordance with Western ideals does not promote mutual understanding but rather criticism. For instance, the Chinese government must provide social security due to its geographical and population size; hence, individual rights and freedom are not the priority—values that run counter to Western ideals. Nitivadee emphasizes the importance of mutual cultural understanding in dealing with Chinese businessmen. Muangbhumi, a scholar of International Relations, clarifies that China has its own protocol and system, which liberals may fail to recognize. To educate the public, he organizes a cultural exchange project to promote Sino-Thai cultural understanding in order to convey information about China.[4]

Conclusion

Thailand enjoys positive economic, cultural and educational ties with China. Economic ties between the two countries generate demand for Chinese-speaking labour. As a result, in the 1990s, the Thai and Chinese governments began educational cooperation to propagate Chinese language and culture. The cooperation initially focuses on language studies at the postsecondary and elementary levels of education. Later, China became more renowned for its STEM (Science, Technology, Education and Math) and e-commerce programmes. These programmes have been extensively implemented in Thai vocational schools and universities. In addition, the Chinese educational reputation, employment possibilities, and scholarships attract a growing number of Thai international students.

Following the strengthening of linkages in education, Chinese-educated Thai individuals have actively applied and promoted China's image in Thailand. The survey and interview data clearly demonstrate the influence of soft power contributed by Chinese-educated individuals. Their perceptions of China are, on average, more favourable than those that were not educated in China.

Furthermore, they play an active role in delivering information and viewpoints from China's perspectives. For example, they develop Chinese know-how projects, provide additional knowledge of China, report Chinese news and inform the Thai public of China's strategy. They also replicate and strengthen Chinese networks within Thailand. In Thailand, education is thus a notable accomplishment of Chinese soft power.

Notes
1. The Thai government implemented the Thailand 4.0 programme as a new blueprint for transforming the country's economy into a value-based economy focusing on high-tech manufacturing such as electric vehicle and food processing industries. The objective is to strengthen the domestic economy and position the country as a regional trade and investment hub (supply chain hub). Bangkok, therefore, proposes the National Strategic Master Plan on Infrastructure, Logistics and Digital

(2018–37) to invest in new foundational infrastructures to boost competitiveness in order to accomplish the goals of the Thailand 4.0.
2. Interview, Dr Nithivadee Chanyaswad, Dean of Chinese International College, Bangkok University and Educational Committee of the TACU, 30 September 2022.
3. Arm's publications on China are, for instance, *Jeenkidyai Mongkarnklai* [The Vision of Mega China], *Jeen-America 3D* [3D Sino-US], *China Next Normal*, and *Eyes on China*.
4. Interview, Dr Nithivadee Chanyaswad, 30 September 2022; Muangphumi Harnsiripeth, a PhD student at Nanjing University, 30 September 2022; Supakitt Pannanukul, a Thai student representative of Hangzhou province, 22 September 2022; Arunee Anusuriya, a Thai student representative of Yunnan province, 24 September 2022; Arm Tungnirun, Director of China Study Center, Chulalongkorn University, 9 October 2022.

References

Cabinet Resolution. 2006. "แผนยุทธศาสตร์ส่งเสริมการเรียนการสอนภาษาจีนเพื่อเพิ่มขีดความสามารถในการแข่งขันของประเทศ พ.ศ.2549-2553" [Strategies on Chinese Learning for Advanced Competency 2006–2010]. Thailand Cabinet, 22 August 2006. http://soc.soc.go.th/SLK/showlist3.asp?pagecode=63807&pdate=2006/08/22&pno=1&pagegroup=1 (accessed 20 August 2022).

Chao Pongpichit. 2021. *ประวัติพรรคคอมมิวนิสต์แห่งประเทศไทย* [The History of Communist Party, Thailand]. Bangkok: Saengdao.

Chinese Studies Centre, Asian Studies Institute, Chulalongkorn University. 2008. *ความร่วมมือไทย-จีน ด้านการเรียนการสอนภาษาจีนในประเทศไทย* [Thai-China Cooperation on Chinese Language Learning in Thailand], p. 22. Bangkok: Ministry of Education.

Du, Qiaohong. 2017. "Study on Chinese Cultural Activity of Confucius Institute in Thailand". Cited in Wei, Fan, Keeratiporn Jutawiriya, and Thamtanet Punnatanamahakarun. 2021. "นโยบาย ของจีนในการส่งเสริมการพัฒนาสถาบันขงจื๊อสู่ประเทศไทย" [Chinese Policy on Promoting the Development of Confucius Institute to Thailand]. *Political Science and Public Administration Journal*, Khon Kaen University 6, no. 1: 1–30.

Hammond, Scott, and Lowell Glenn. 2004. "The Ancient Practice of Chinese Social Networking: *Guanxi* and Social Network Theory". *E:CO Special Double Issue* 6, no 1–2: 24–31.

Huang, Wei-Hao, and Jun Xiang. 2019. "Pursuing Soft Power through the Confucius Institute: A Large-N Analysis". *Journal of Chinese Political Science* 24: 249–66.

Hydro Informatics Institute. 2020. "Sino-Thai Cooperation". 6 May 2020 https://shorturl.at/hwH23 (accessed 12 July 2023).

Kajadpai Burudpat. 1974. *ชาวจีนในประเทศไทย* [Chinese People in Thailand]. Bangkok: Praewittaya.

Kamsoi, Annie. 2021. "'Sino-Thai Vocational Cooperation' in Thailand 4.0 Era: The Case of Collaboration in Chinese-Thai Rail Transport System between Banpai

College and Wuhan Railway Vocational College of Technology". *Sinology Journal* 15, no. 1: 57–86.

Lan, He, and Stephen Wilkins. 2018. "Achieving Legitimacy in Cross-border Higher Education: Institutional Influences on Chinese International Branch Campuses in Southeast Asia". *Journal of Studies in International Education* 22, no. 3: 179–97.

Lancang-Mekong Cooperation. 2018. "Five-year Plan of Action on Lancang-Mekong Cooperation (2018–2022)". 12 January 2018. http://www.lmcchina.org/eng/2018-01/12/content_41449786.html (accessed 28 September 2022).

Maksimova, Angelina. 2021. "Soft Power as a Policy Rationale for International Education in China". *Politica-China*, 4 March 2021, https://politica-china.org/areas/politica-exterior/soft-power-as-a-policy-rationale-for-international-education-in-china (accessed 20 December 2022)

Murashima, Eiji, and Worasak Mahattanobon. 1996. การเมืองจีนสยาม [Chinese-Siam Politics: The Political Movement of Overseas Chinese in Thailand 1924–1941]", Bangkok: Chulalongkorn University.

Nye, Joseph. 2004. *Soft Power: The Means to Success in World Politics*. New York: Public Affairs.

Office of the Education Council, Ministry of Education. 2016a. "รายงานการวิจัยเพื่อพัฒนาระบบการจัดการเรียนการสอนภาษาจีนในประเทศไทย ระดับมัธยมศึกษา" [Research on Chinese Language Learning in Thailand: Secondary Education Level], pp. 80–84. Report.

———. 2016b. "รายงานการวิจัยเพื่อพัฒนาระบบการจัดการเรียนการสอนภาษาจีนในประเทศไทย ระดับประถมศึกษา" [Research on Chinese Language Learning in Thailand: Primary Education Level]. Report.

———. 2016c. รายงานการวิจัยเพื่อพัฒนาระบบการจัดการเรียนการสอนภาษาจีนในประเทศไทย ระดับอุดมศึกษา" [Research on Chinese Language Learning in Thailand: Higher Education Level], pp. 41–48. Report.

Office of the Higher Education Commission. 2010. "ยุทธศาสตร์ส่งเสริมการเรียนการสอนภาษาจีนในประเทศไทย" [Strategies in Chinese Language Learning in Thailand], p. 3. Report.

Penpisut Intornpirom. 2007. "การควบรวมโรงเรียนจีนของรัฐไทยตั้งแต่เปลี่ยนแปลงการปกครองถึงสมัยจอมพล ป. พิบูลสงคราม 2475–2487" [The Thai State Control over Chinese Schools since the Political Revolution to Marshal P. Pibulsongkram 1932–1944]. *Journal of History, Srinakarin Wirot University*: 100–18.

SCGI Master Program. Sirindhorn Center for Geo-Informatics. https://scgi.gistda.or.th/ (accessed 25 July 2023).

Shambaugh, David. 2015. "China's Soft-Power Push: The Search of Respect". *Foreign Affairs* 94: 99–107.

Skinner, William G. 1957. *Chinese Society in Thailand: An Analytical History*. Cornell University Press.

TAP Magazine. 2002. "ไทย-จีน ลงนามความร่วมมือด้านการศึกษา พัฒนาบุคลากร-การเรียนการสอนภาษาจีน" [Thai-China signed MOU on Chinese Language Learning and Teacher Training]. *Thai-ASEAN Panorama*. 20 April 2022 https://www.tap-magazine.net/blog-th/edu71 (accessed 22 August 2022).

Thai Embassy in Beijing. 2021. "วิทย์ไมตรีไทย-จีน" [Thai-Sino Friendship in Science]. https://

www.mhesi.go.th/images/Pusit2021/pdfs/THA-CHN-Feb2564.pdf (accessed 2 December 2022).

Thai-Chinese Talk. 2019. "ไทยคำจีนคำ" [Thai-Chinese Talk]. Facebook. 1 August 2019. https://www.facebook.com/thaichinesetalk?locale=th_TH (accessed 24 July 2023).

Thansettakij. 2022. "มช.จับมือสถาบันขงจื๊อเปิดปริญญาโท "อี-คอมเมิร์ซไทยจีน" [Chiang Mai University Cope with Chiang Mai University Confucius Institute in Opening a Master Degree on Thai-China E-commerce]. 28 February 2022. https://www.thansettakij.com/economy/515538 (accessed 3 October 2022).

Wasana Wongsurawat. 2008. "Contending for a Claim on Civilization: The Sino-Siamese Struggle to Control Overseas Chinese Education in Siam". *Journal of Chinese Overseas* 4, no. 2: 161–82.

Watson, J.K.P. 1976. "A Conflict of Nationalism: The Chinese and Education in Thailand, 1900–1960". *Paedagogica Historica* 16, no. 2:429–51.

Wei, Fan, Keeratiporn Jutawiriya, and Thamtanet Punnatanamahakarun. 2021. "นโยบายของจีนในการส่งเสริมการพัฒนาสถาบันขงจื๊อสู่ประเทศไทย" [Chinese Policy on Promoting the Development of Confucius Institute to Thailand]. *Political Science and Public Administration Journal, Khon Kaen University* 6, no. 1: 1–30.

Y. Zhou. 2021. "Confucius Institute in the Sino-Thai relations: A Display of China's Soft Power". *Asian Journal of Social Science* 40, no. 4: 234–43.

Zhu, Kejin, and Rui Yang. 2022. "Emerging Resources of China's Soft Power: A Case Study of Cambodian Participants from Chinese Higher Education Programs". *Higher Education Policy* 36: 633–55.

UNDERSTANDING CHINA'S EDUCATIONAL SOFT POWER FROM RECIPIENTS' PERSPECTIVES
A Case Study of the Yunnanese Chinese in Northern Thailand

Aranya Siriphon

Introduction

Over the past two decades, the People's Republic of China (PRC) has increasingly implemented soft power strategies through *Qiaoban*, the Overseas Chinese Affairs Office (OCAO), an administrative office which assists the Chinese government in handling *Qiaowu*, or Overseas Chinese affairs, and other official and non-governmental organizations. While the PRC has recently restructured *Qiaoban* and other PRC-backed institutional organs working in the field of overseas Chinese affairs into the United Front Work Department (UFWD) (Aranya and Li 2021, pp. 289–304), however, *Qiaoban* and its various institutional organs remain the most prominent institutions in gaining attention from overseas Chinese communities in Thailand. *Qiaoban* exports its brand of Chinese education and culture through collaboration with schools and colleges to establish educational programmes in several levels of formal Thai education. The assistance provided to overseas Chinese groups includes curricula and educational materials both for Chinese-language study and for other subjects, such as mathematics, history and geography. This is intended to unify the curricula of Chinese schools, to promote the simplified characters used in mainland China and to support Chinese-language education overseas (Xing 2008, p. 370, cited in Nyíri 2012, pp. 369–97).

While China's educational soft power strategies appear to be effective with overseas Chinese communities in Thailand, the Yunnanese Chinese in northern Thailand face the dilemma of receiving educational support from China. As many of the Yunnanese Chinese are former soldiers and supporters of the Chinese Nationalist Party (Kuomintang, or KMT), they have to contend with the appropriate way to receive support from China. Hence, the Yunnanese Chinese are at a crossroads in determining if they should follow the rise of China, stay loyal to their ancestors' support of Taiwan, or seek an alternative strategy to deal with this situation.

This paper looks at the Chinese schools of the Yunnanese Chinese community. Some of these Chinese schools are preferential to Beijing and have been receiving China's education support, applying the model of their teaching system including extended university networks. Whereas other Chinese schools with pro-Taipei sentiment continue to uphold Taiwan's Chinese education, such as the use of traditional Chinese characters, curricula and teaching systems under the Taiwan model. Through examining local points of view, this paper attempts to address the multiple perspectives and responses towards educational soft power from China and Taiwan. In doing so, this paper provides an illuminating analysis of Chinese education among the Yunnanese Chinese and a thought-provoking reflection on how the Chinese educational desire of the Yunnanese Chinese can reflect the relationship between culture, sentiment, and structural force in which family and Chinese norms are tied. Today, Yunnanese Chinese parents in northern Thailand value Chinese education due to their hopes that their children can maintain Chinese norms and values despite possessing Thai citizenship and attending Thai schools under the Thai educational system.

Qualitative methods were applied to this study, including fieldwork conducted recently in 2022 by revisiting Arunothai, a KMT village in Chiang Mai province. This village is prominent as it was the main centre of the Third Field Army under the command of General Li Wen Huan from Taiwan and was the first refugee village established together with a Chinese school along the Thai border in the 1960s. Primary sources consist of formal and informal interviews with school directors, staff and teachers working for the schools, directors of the Yunnanese Chinese Association in Chiang Mai and Chiang Rai, and several parents and respondents. Interviewees' names are kept anonymous for privacy protection. It also included observation of cultural activities in Chinese schools established by Yunnanese Chinese. Secondary sources mainly included relevant academic literature as well as news and other documents.

This paper found that although China's educational soft power appears to have a positive influence on Thailand's overseas Chinese communities, China's soft power deployed to the Yunnanese Chinese in northern Thailand remained constrained. This is due to several conditions, such as lingering sentiment towards Taiwan, difficulty in gaining trust and incommensurable education quality regarding Confucian values provided by China. Consequently, pro-Taipei schools and their students today are still more influential than those supported by China. Even so, the constraints in additional budgeting and education support from the Taipei government may impact the sustainability of pro-Taipei schools of the Yunnanese Chinese in the long run. Hence, this paper contributes to understanding the complexities of multiple recipients located within a particular history and locality, where soft power from China and Taiwan is translated, utilized and negotiated differently to serve the Yunnanese Chinese's goals.

Literature Review on China's Soft Power

Many scholars during the past two decades have been studying China's soft power in multiple dimensions such as resources of power, usage strategies, and its outcomes. Coined by Nye (1990, 2004), soft power refers to the power of attraction in which actors have the ability to shape preferences and attract international audiences to their favour. Kurlantzick (2008), the first scholar who coined the term "charm offensive" for usage strategies of China's soft power, pointed out that China worked inclusively through diplomacy, trade incentives, cultural and educational exchange opportunities, and other techniques to project a benign national image, thereby positioning itself as a model of social and economic success to develop stronger international alliances. Echoed by other scholars later (Liu 2018; d'Hooghe 2015; Zhu 2013), China is viewed as a recent rising power attempting to bargain her power in Southeast Asia vis-à-vis the United States (Lum and Morrison 2008). Shambaugh (2015) and Wong (2016) note that China could exercise soft power through her strongest suit, economic power. For example, economic aid through regional trade agreements and expanding Official Development Assistance (ODA) towards cooperation.

Recently, Yıldırım and Aslan (2020, pp. 141–71) argued that more elements of China's soft power strategies should be looked at. They observe that China is performing two kinds of offensive and defensive soft power strategies towards developing and developed countries. The charm offensive aspect aims to get other countries to do their bidding by consolidating comprehensive power through a developmental model, such as aid, investment, traditional culture, foreign policy and international broadcasting in developing countries. The defensive aspect occurs from softening the rise of China by introducing appealing parts of Chinese culture through investments and international broadcasting to Western countries. This defensive aspect is also implemented through the acquisition of media outlets and via the entertainment sector and gaming industry by Chinese-owned companies. However, if failure occurs a defensive stance in developing countries can be taken (ibid.). Taking the cases of public diplomacy on masks and vaccine aid during the COVID-19 pandemic, Carminati (2020) echoes this view, contending that China's effective expansion of soft power reflects the responsible and helpful international image built by helping other countries through economic aid and assistance.

When focusing on China's soft power in exporting Chinese education, some researchers have emphasized the role of *Hanban* and extensive Confucius Institutes (CIs) (Ding and Saunders 2006, pp. 3–33; Ding 2008, pp. 193–213; Hartig 2015, pp. 245–58; Paradise 2009, pp. 647–69; Liu 2017, pp. 233–46). Others view education as a major source of China's influence (Raimzhanova 2017), impacts and outcomes of CIs (Yang 2010, pp. 235–45). Some scholars evaluate the tensions and paradoxes in the CI project by analysing the dilemmas in the exercise of power strategies in the global age (Lo and Pan 2016, pp. 512–32). Zhou and Luk (2016, pp. 628–42) also note that China's soft power is not attractive in the eyes of receivers because the establishment of CIs has triggered another version of the "China threat", leading to worldwide criticism. As a result, China's soft power is marred by controversies and concerns over CIs, poor record of respecting political and social rights; a lack of political transparency, rule of law, and independence of the media and artists; and over moral decay (Lai and Lu 2012, pp. 83–102).

Regarding expansion, China today has more than 500 CIs and Confucius Classes (CCs). Although some have been closed down following concerns about academic freedom on university campuses, most developing countries welcome them, considering that they teach an increasingly useful language and offer scholarships to study in China. Thailand is an example where China's soft power and CI strategy appear effective when observed through the proliferation of CIs and the acceptance of Chinese-affiliated schools and universities throughout Thailand (Wang 2019, pp. 99–113; Li 2020). The three main reasons for this success are identified as the existing historical background of Sino-Thai relations; Thailand's openness towards China motivated by economic interests; and the role of ethnic Chinese communities in Thailand in helping to propagate international collaboration via trade, economy, and culture (Kornphanat 2016, pp. 151–73).

Yunnanese Chinese Communities in Northern Thailand: Historical Context to Present Day

General Background of Yunnanese Chinese in Northern Thailand
The Yunnanese Chinese generally live in the mountainous areas of the northern Thai borderlands. Categorized as "overland Chinese", or "overland Yunnanese" which mostly migrated by land from the south and southwest China (Forbes 2007; Chang 2014, pp. 3–4), the Yunnanese Chinese is a remarkable ethnic Chinese group differentiated from those who migrated overseas from China, like Hokkien, Hakka, Teochew or Hainanese in Thailand. In northern mainland Southeast Asia, the Yunnanese Chinese are historically highly mobile, using horses and mules for short- and long-distance caravan trading along overland routes through mountainous areas (Suthep 1997; Hill 1998).

The term Yunnanese Chinese is differentiated into two main ethnic Yunnanese—the Hui and the Han (Huang 2010, p. 6). They are relatively distinct in their ethnicity, histories of overland migration, religious attachment and identities. The Hui comprise two main groups split according to religious identity. The first is the descendants of the Hui refugees and ex-soldiers, especially Muslim caravan traders who engaged in long-distance caravan trade in mountainous areas of the upper Mekong Region for hundreds of years. The second is the non-Muslim ethnic group who fought against the Manchu rulers of the Qing dynasty in Southwestern Yunnan Province during the nineteenth century. The Han refers to the descendants of the pioneer settlers of KMT Army troops. The Han's migratory history was related to a political movement after losing the 1949 Civil War in China. This loss saw them flee from Yunnan province into Myanmar and later northern Thailand after the Chinese Communists took power in China in the 1950s. Both the Hui and the Han are locally called Ho, Haw, Chin Ho, Cin-Ho or Chin Haw by the Thais and others in Thailand (Hill 1998; Forbes and Henley 1997).

The Political History of the KMT Han Chinese
Historically, the KMT Han Chinese were caught within the circumstances of the Cold War associated with the anti-Communist Western bloc, and

the forced relationship between Taiwanese and Thai governments due to international pressure. From 1953 to 1954 and in 1961, the Taiwanese government evacuated the KMT Han Chinese stationed in Burma back to Taiwan. However, around 3,300 KMT Chinese of the two units (the Third and Fifth Field Army), including former soldiers and their families as well as refugees, decided to retreat to the northern Thai border instead of evacuating to Taiwan. While approximately 1,500 troops of the Fifth Field Army under the command of General Tuan Shi Wen settled in Doi Mae Salong, the mountainous area in Chiang Rai Province, approximately 1,700 troops of the Third Field Army led by General Li Wen Huan settled around the villages near to the mountainous area of Fang District in Chiang Mai Province where the Third Field army established refugee villages in the 1960s (Huang 2010, pp. 6–12; Chang 1999, 2001).

The Third and Fifth KMT Armies in the 1960s helped the Thai government fight communism along the northern Thai border while continuing to receive informal financial assistance from the Taiwanese government. After the unrest ended in the 1970s, the Thai government through the Supreme Command Headquarters, requested for the KMT units to disarm in exchange for Thai citizenship and agricultural land. This exchange was a reward for their 1963–67 victories in the battles with Communist guerrillas of the Communist Party of Thailand (CPT) operating in the mountainous areas (Chang 1999, pp. 68–69). This reward allowed them to make a living from farming in northern Thailand (Kanchana 1994, 2004) and is meant to stop their overland trade in opium and narcotic drugs, perceived by the Thai government as a threat to Thai national security along the borders (Chang 1999; Wang 2006, pp. 337–58). Subsequently, the KMT leaders and elderly members established villages and schools, making their living, and sustaining traditional Chinese culture along the northern Thai border.

Regardless of whether they are Hui or Han, the Thai government has seen Yunnanese Chinese as one among other hill tribe groups derived from a so-called "hill-tribe discourse" for the past three decades (Pinkaew 1998, pp. 92–135). The discourse associated mountainous people with unstable population movements and regarded them as opium cultivators that increased narcotic drug use and drug-related violence. These mountainous people were also susceptible to communist infiltration, deforestation and underdevelopment. Adhering to this discourse, the Thai government implemented assimilation policies and measures to integrate these hill tribe groups into Thai culture and society. The main measures included granting more Thai citizenship to ethnic children, providing

Thai education through Thai schooling, and endorsing state-sponsored Theravada Buddhism. While the Thai government enforced the assimilation policy, the Taiwanese government and state-sponsored non-government organizations (NGOs) continued to provide financial and technological assistance to help increase the economic and social development of KMT Chinese communities.

Today, the number of Yunnanese Chinese descendants in northern Thailand is approximately 200,000. Most possess Thai citizenship and inhabit 108 villages in three main provinces: Chiang Rai, Chiang Mai and Mae Hong Son. Some of the younger Yunnanese Chinese moved to the urban cities of Bangkok, Phuket and other cities of Thailand for work. There are at least four Yunnanese Chinese Associations today located in Bangkok, Chiang Rai, Chiang Mai, and Phuket representing the Yunnanese Chinese, including the Thai-Taiwan Business Association (TTBA).

The KMT Chinese Education in Northern Thailand
In the 1970s, while the Ministry of Education of Thailand established the *rongrian chao thai phu chao*, or the Thai hill tribe schools under the Thai assimilation policy, the KMT troops of the two military units and refugee village leaders established Chinese schools following the model of Taiwan's Chinese teaching system. The early schools established are the Guang Huo School established in 1968 located in Wiang Haeng district, Chiang Mai Province, and the Hua Xing School established in 1971 located in the Arunothai village of Chiang Mai Province where General Li, the former commander of the Third Field Army settled.

At these Chinese schools, they taught Confucian orthodoxy and other subjects that cultivated a sense of anti-Communism towards mainland China and the righteousness of the Taiwan Republic and KMT. The Chinese writing system also followed traditional Chinese characters retained in Taiwan, Hong Kong, Macau and among overseas Chinese communities. Teachers in these schools usually included KMT ex-soldiers and scholars. Textbooks, educational materials, and other facilities were sent from Taiwan at the request of KMT leaders and community members in Thailand. The schools provided Chinese education not only to children of KMT Chinese but also to other ethnic students, for example, Shan, Lahu and Akha, from within the village and surrounding villages.

While Thai schools in the 1980s were continually used as a political tool in the border regions to assimilate Yunnanese Chinese and other ethnic children into the Thai body politic, the KMT Chinese leaders continued to provide a patriotic sense of Chinese identity tied to the history of the

KMT through their own schools. The education was supported by political leaders in Taipei, through unofficial means such as the Free China Relief Association (FCRA), a semi-official organization working closely with the Nationalist Party in Taiwan that arrived in northern Thailand in 1982 (Chang 1999, 2001). The FCRA not only provided aid to the KMT Chinese in northern Thailand but also actively promoted a sense of pro-Taipei loyalty by fostering the image that Taiwan is the motherland of the KMT Chinese in Thailand (Chang 1999, pp. 132–34). The Yunnanese Chinese Association (YCA) in Chiang Rai province, a KMT local organization established in 1981 by the KMT ex-general, collaborated with the FCRA to help provide financial aid and promote Taiwan's Chinese curricula for Chinese schooling. This included the provision of images of Sun Yat Sen and Chiang Kai-shek for the communities to pay respect, as well as providing patriotic music tapes for distribution in the community to the schools (Chang 1999, p. 137). They also paid frequent visits to the communities to provide education assistance, offering full scholarships for children to study in Taiwanese curricula-based schools and further their studies in Taiwan.

However, by the end of 1994, FCRA's agricultural technology and education support projects were not completed due to funding cuts and changing political priorities in Taiwan. This was because Southeast Asia was experiencing a period of growing stability, and the Thai government shifted their focus to economic development in which economic opportunities uplifted as insurgencies melted away and conflicts came to an end. Although there was no more Taipei-supported funding, the schools continued to operate extensively through the Taiwan-based schooling model, teaching Confucian orthodoxy with traditional Chinese characters and emphasizing the distinctiveness of traditional Chinese culture. This persistence in operating on a Taiwan-based schooling model reflects the goodwill of the community towards Taiwan, all of which are geared towards a residual anti-communist ideal.

At the end of the 1990s, under Deng Xiaoping's leadership, China adopted the Western free-market economy and opened China's border to connect with the Upper Mekong borders for a more cooperative trade economy. At this point, the Thai national education policy intensively implemented by the Ministry of Education required ethnic children living at the borders, including Yunnanese Chinese, to receive a formal Thai elementary education. This meant that ethnic children were required to follow the Thai national curriculum by going to Thai schools every day from eight in the morning to four in the afternoon during weekdays using

Thai as the medium language. This education policy could not stop KMT children from going to their Chinese teaching schools rescheduled to operate during weekends or weekdays early mornings or evenings. Hence, from the 2000s, approximately 110 Chinese schools established within 108 Yunnanese Chinese villages in northern Thailand continue to provide Chinese education from primary to high school levels. These schools follow Thai national law by registering officially with the Ministry of Education as a type of private school known as "Tutoring School" following the Private School Act B.E. 2007.

Registered as a "Tutoring School" licensed under the Private Education Commission of the Thai Ministry of Education, these schools today teach multiple subjects in Chinese language during weekday evenings and provide Chinese education to Yunnanese children and other ethnic groups who live in surrounding villages. The schools continue the model of Taiwan's Chinese teaching system, teaching subjects such as Mathematics, Chinese History and Global History, Geography, and Chinese calligraphy in traditional Chinese characters. Textbooks were brought in from Taiwan, except for History where textbooks are revised by KMT teachers with emphasis on the ancient historical period of China to the Republic of China, KMT migratory history and Thailand history, omitting the history of the 1949 Civil War, noting that children should learn knowledge close to their local lives and ancestral roots (Aranya and Sunanta 2018, pp. 69–82). Additionally, hanging images of Sun Yat Sen and other Kuomintang leaders at schools have been maintained continually (see Figure 5.1). There is also a parade each year on "Memorial Day" prepared by teachers and students to celebrate the National Day of the Republic of China, Sun Yat Sen, the 1912 founding father of the Republic of China and the Confucian worship ceremony held on 28 September.

Today, the Department of Overseas Compatriot Education Affairs of Overseas Community Affair Council (OCAC) of Taiwan considers these Yunnanese Chinese schools in northern Thailand as part of "overseas compatriot schools". The department's purpose is to provide overseas compatriot education, endeavouring to promote Taiwan's diverse cultures and cultivate overseas younger generations through partially subsidized education. In 2021, 1,054 schools utilized Taiwan-based education (of which 41.27 per cent in Asia, 45.45 per cent in the Americas, 6.36 per cent in Europe and less than 6.92 per cent in other areas). There are around fifty Overseas Compatriot School Associations affiliated with Taiwan which continue to introduce Taiwan's Chinese teaching system and its diverse cultures to the world (OCAC 2021).

FIGURE 5.1
Photos of Sun Yat Sen Along with Thai-Taiwan Flags and Thai Kings and Queens Adorn the Walls of Hua Xing School (Both Old and New) and Other Taiwanese-based Chinese Schools

Source: Photos taken by Aranya Siriphon on 17 September 2022.

The Yunnanese Chinese Schools at a Crossroad

In the 2000s, Taiwan witnessed a political shift when the government changed from the Chinese Nationalist Party (KMT) to the Democratic Progressive Party (DPP). As the interest of DPP is opposite of KMT, the Yunnanese Chinese in Thailand were affected. Additionally, China's soft power approach to education through *Qiaoban* and its affiliated institutions, such as the Chinese consulate in Chiang Mai, began to reconnect with diverse overseas Chinese communities in Thailand (Aranya 2016, pp. 1–17). The reduction in support from Taipei presented a challenge for Yunnanese schools in continuing their operations, resulting in difficulty in retaining the loyalty of younger generations towards Taiwan.

The Arunothai village is a prominent example in which second/third-generation leaders and the Chiang Mai Chinese Language Teachers Association (CLTA) tried to solve the shortage of teachers, textbooks, and other resources due to an immediate lack of Taipei's support. In 2004, they visited the Chinese Consulate General in Chiang Mai to seek assistance in running the schools. In 2009, a response arrived from the Consul General in the form of student scholarships and textbooks during his visit. The visitation and educational assistance raised tensions among elderly and younger leaders in the Arunothai village (Sosing and Chatkrit 2020, pp. 39–41). As a result of the tension caused, the leaders ended up establishing Jiaolian School in 2011, a new Chinese school in Arunothai village with the financial support of the Chinese consulate in Chiang Mai and the *Qiaoban*. Jiaolian School was registered under the Thai National Education Law as a "Tutoring School", licensed under the Private Education Commission of the Thai Ministry of Education. Apart from the school registration, the Jiaolian Foundation was registered officially to build education networks and to receive monetary donations from China and other forms of support from external organizations. During Jiaolian School's operational processes, polarized sentiments between older and younger generations were evident in the village. One interviewee complained about "betray[ing] our ancestors who [are loyal toward] Taiwan by receiving assistance from communists".[1]

Despite tensions in Arunothai village since 2012, Jiaolian School has continued to receive the PRC's support. The school adopted standard Mandarin, used simplified characters for teaching and imported Chinese textbooks from China to provide Chinese education from kindergarten to high school and teach multiple subjects: Mathematics, English, Geography (Global and Chinese Geography), and History (Global and Chinese). China's soft power strategy via education is reflected in how it operated at Arunothai village. Free textbooks, stationery and study materials are not only provided for every student enrolled at Jiaolian School but eight to ten Chinese language teachers from China are also sent to the school every year to train local teachers, both in the school and affiliated schools, in standard Mandarin for four to twelve months. Additionally, the Chinese consulate in Chiang Mai and other Chinese universities also provide scholarships for students pursuing Higher Education in China through academic networks. For students who are unable to apply for a Thai passport as they do not possess a Thai identification card, the Chinese consulate grants overseas Chinese passes to allow them to enter China for education (Aranya 2022, pp. 1–11).

Multiple Perspectives towards Beijing and Taipei via Yunnanese Chinese Schools

Pro-Beijing Perspectives among the Yunnanese Chinese

Jiaolian School has shown some Yunnanese Chinese parents how China's educational assistance may be fruitful for their children. For example, since 2010, the school succeeded in providing 300 graduating students with Chinese scholarships for tertiary education. The school's education network in China has been extended to include Chinese universities, contributing to student mobility both during students' enrolment and after their graduation. Some leaders recently said, "Jiaolian School is going in the right direction, growing the future along with a rising China".[2] Apart from that, other parents and younger leaders have seen no differences between using Taiwan-based curricula and China-based curricula. Some parents stated that the China-based curricula possess higher technological and innovative knowledge. Additionally, there are concerns that children may waste their time practising traditional Chinese writing through the Taiwan-based curricula, as "simplified Chinese writing is used by over a thousand million Chinese in China today".[3]

Today, approximately 1,000 students living in Arunothai village, and the surrounding area enrol at Jiaolian School every year. Around forty Yunnanese schools have decided to follow Jiaolian School in receiving PRC's educational support.[4]

Pro-Taipei Perspectives Among the Yunnanese Chinese

While approximately forty Yunnanese schools have followed Jiaolian School, currently seventy Yunnanese schools continue to use the Taiwanese model of Chinese education and schooling. An old school established in the 1960s, the Hua Xing School retains the Taiwanese traditional writing system and quality assurance evaluation from Taiwan. The curriculum has been modified to incorporate both Thailand-based issues and the history of Yunnanese Chinese. Hua Xing School is still the headquarters of pro-Taipei perspectives among the Yunnanese Chinese due to its strong connection with the Taipei Economic and Cultural Office in Thailand, Taiwanese business companies and religious associations of Taiwan. Although the Taiwanese government is unable to provide financial assistance to Yunnanese schools, the roles of non-government organizations (NGOs) and private companies have filled the role by providing education assistance, such as scholarships, funding for educational materials and building schools. Some examples of NGOs from Taiwan and Thailand contributing to the Yunnanese schools include the Overseas Chinese Association in Taiwan, the Rotary Club of Taichung, Taiwan and the Ming-Ai Catholic Association in Taiwan. Recently, these voluntary institutions and companies from Taiwan donated money to Hua Xing School to build a new 40,000 m^2 school amounting to US$4 million. The new school planned to complete in 2025 aims to "facilitate students from kindergarten to high school with a projected enrollment of 1,700 students every year."[5]

The pro-Taipei perspective is tied to comparisons with the Beijing model of Chinese education, firstly, the difference in writing systems and learning of Confucian values, and secondly, unpleasant experiences in negotiating with donors from Beijing. Firstly, the new textbooks used in the classrooms include three writing systems—the traditional, simplified and *hanyu pinyin*, the official romanization system for teaching standard Mandarin Chinese in Mainland China, Taiwan and Singapore. By combining these writing systems, the pro-Taipei schools think that there will be more opportunities for ethnic Chinese students to master the language in both old and new scripts while maintaining the traditional Chinese culture.

In terms of Confucian thought and values, pro-Taipei parents noted that pro-Beijing schools like the Jiaolian School only promoted Confucianism in a modern style of interpretation, saying that the Jiaolian School does not focus on devotion to family, parents and respect, good moral behaviour, and the virtue of humanity. Although "Confucius" was the name given to the *Hanban*'s overseas language and cultural institution, Confucius Institute, Confucian thoughts and philosophy were rarely found in its textbooks used at Jiaolian School. Additionally, Jiaolian School teaches general Chinese history, culture and geography as supplement classes, presenting Confucius as one of the key figures in Chinese history.

By contrast, pro-Taipei schools like the Hua Xing School claim that Confucian thought and values are a source of moral and ideological support for traditional Chinese culture. At schools, elements of Confucian values are always added by teachers while reading textbooks or practising in everyday life. For example, the Chinese textbook in several grades possesses several chapters on Confucius' teachings, teaching students to be diligent and dutiful members of the community, practise family ethics through learning the roles of parents and children and emphasizing Confucius as the ideal of knowledge and virtue. Through textbooks and schooling practices, Confucian principles are maintained through traditional interpretations. "Through interactions at school, the Confucian process of self-cultivation, respect, discipline and sympathy towards others are cultivated in the students."[6]

Echoed by two parents and one leader, the primary concern is that "modern PRC teaching styles by pro-Beijing schools do not sufficiently focus on Confucian ethics or traditional Chinese customs and cultures."[7]

Confucian values are also maintained by pro-Taipei schools through Confucius worship ceremonies held on his birthday on 28 September every year. The ceremony is dedicated to Confucius to reconnect with Taiwan and their networks. The worship ceremony is usually organized by the Yunnanese Chinese School Network in Chiang Mai and Chiang Rai. Representatives from main financial supporters and donors, mainly the Culture Center of Taipei Economic and Cultural Office (TECO), the Taiwanese Business Association (TBA) and the Overseas Chinese Association of Taiwan, usually attend the ceremony together with the representatives of the Yunnanese Chinese schools of Chiang Mai, Chiang Rai and other provinces. See Figure 5.2.

Secondly, unpleasant former experiences with pro-Beijing donors led pro-Taipei schools to prefer Taiwanese support. The hesitation in receiving China's educational support is not due to loyalty but from the disappointing experience with pro-Beijing donors. In 2014, the Cultural Department of Yunnan Province, the official Yunnan provincial government of China, sent an official letter to the Yunnanese Chinese Association in Chiang Rai, offering to donate computers, laptops, textbooks, and youth volunteers to Yunnanese Chinese schools in Chiang Rai. However, this offer came with a condition, requesting Yunnanese Chinese schools change their traditional writing system to the official simplified writing system of Mainland China (Aranya 2015, pp. 147–66). Instead, pro-Taipei donors, for the Yunnanese Chinese, are preferred because they never mentioned a debt of gratitude.

> No conditions are required when talking to our donors from Taiwan. They are happy to help our children. But, for either Chinese companies or government, we are not sure what they want in return when offering

FIGURE 5.2
A Confucian Worship Ceremony Is Held on September 28 Every Year, Attended by School Members of Pro-Taipei Schools

Source: Photos reproduced with permission of Worrapimook Intrasan.

help. They may say now they don't need any repayment but we have already been indebted to gratitude. We yet know when they will ask for a debt of gratitude which we may be difficult to work with.[8]

Other Perspectives Towards Choosing China or Taiwan

Apart from pro-Taipei and pro-Beijing sentiment, the third group of parents and leaders among the Yunnanese in northern Thailand possess the perspective that regardless if it is China or Taiwan if they benefit the local economy and children, then they are welcome. Such sentiment prioritizes the local economy and children, thus appearing to take a balanced view of the situation. Villagers today regularly watch CCTV (China Central Television) in the Chinese language and are more exposed to China than before. Chinese media and China's social media are additional vessels that the current generation has been utilizing daily. Signboards in the village have also switched from using traditional characters to simplified characters.

At the institutional level, even though the Yunnan Association of Chiang Mai and the Chinese Language Teaching School Club—the two main organizations representing Yunnanese Chinese in Chiang Mai—keep in touch with Taiwan through regular meetings with representatives of the Culture Center of Taipei Economic and Cultural Office (TECO) located in Thailand, they also invited the Chinese Consulate in Chiang Mai to visit the associations to develop Chinese education in Yunnanese Chinese schools.

According to the former Chairman of the Yunnan Association,

> We should stop taking sides today since China and Taiwan are our siblings. Although Taiwan may feel unhappy and some KMT leaders may respond negatively, we should consider our children and engage with China and the modern world. Students and their families have other attractive opportunities to consider, such as scholarships, cheap tuition and affordable dormitories sponsored by the PRC. If it serves well for our children and our economy, then we should welcome them. I think parents are forward-thinking and future-oriented in wanting their children to be exposed to well-established networks within Chinese universities.[9]

THE FUTURE OF THE YUNNANESE CHINESE SCHOOLS

Compared with other Chinese schools established in Thailand, the case study of the pro-Taipei and pro-Beijing education in Yunnanese Chinese schools in northern Thailand is a unique situation. Two main considerations arise in assessing the future of Yunnanese Chinese schools. Firstly, the administrative structure of school registration under Thai education laws. Secondly, schooling objectives and their subsequent outcomes.

First, 110 Yunnanese Chinese schools in northern Thailand have been renewing their non-formal school licence under "Tutoring School". This license is officially provided by the Ministry of Education following the Private School Act B.E. 2550 (2007) and 2554 (2011) and regulated by the Private Education Commission of the Thai Ministry of Education. Under this licence, the Yunnanese Chinese schools have more flexibility in determining the type of curricula and subjects that can serve their main cultural objectives, such as preserving traditional Chinese cultures and Confucian thought via teaching. The flexibility in schooling is also reflected in the methods of providing education, period of study, and measurement and evaluation for graduation. The schools can teach multiple disciplines and subjects of Chinese education in Chinese language during weekday evenings and weekends, providing Chinese education to Yunnanese children and other ethnic groups living in surrounding villages. Similar to Islamic schools, for example, the Po Noh schools in southern Thailand, which sustain the Islamic culture via religious school teaching, the licence allows Yunnanese Chinese schools to provide Chinese education to sustain Chinese culture.

This current trajectory of licensing might change soon. Jiaolian School and Hua Xing School, the two headquarters of pro-Taipei and pro-Beijing schools, are planning to change their licence from a non-formal school licence to a formal school licence. By registering as "Formal School" following the Private School Act (No. 1 and 2) B.E. 2550 (2007) and 2554 (2011), both Yunnanese Chinese schools will shift their licence to the category of "International School". By changing the licence, the schools will align with the other Chinese schools in Thailand today, for example, the Thai-Chinese International School (TCIS), Thai-Singapore International School (TSIS) located in Samutprakarn, Kwong Chow School in Bangkok and Chiangmai Tzu Chi School in Chiang Mai. To gain a formal school licence, the schools are required to meet the qualifications of school settings under the current Private School Act of Thailand. This means that requirements including land acquisition, the schooling investment budget and human resources need to be accounted for. As such, time is needed for the two headquarters of pro-Taipei and pro-Beijing schools to accumulate land and budget to meet the licensing requirements.

Secondly, the schools are keeping the medium of instruction in the Chinese language as part of sustaining their Chinese culture. The pro-

Taipei schools of the Yunnanese Chinese have been adhering to their methods of instruction to sustain Chinese culture and ethics, planning to open summer schools for short-term exchange programmes with Taiwan. Additionally, more textbooks are planned for revision to include the three writing systems so that more students can master the language. For these plans to take effect, educational funding is required. The school hopes to link with more donors, such as Taiwanese businesspeople and companies, or Taiwanese-Thai associations as well as Overseas Chinese Associations in Taiwan. Today, the Yunnanese Chinese leaders who run the pro-Taipei schools have been getting in touch personally with Taiwanese donors to help provide scholarships for students to further their studies in Taiwan and support budgets for the plans stated above.

The headquarters of pro-Beijing schools of the Yunnanese Chinese, the Jiaolian School, have expanded their networks from the consulate and embassy in Thailand to Chinese universities in China. These networks aided in sending promising students on scholarships or exchange programmes to China. Although the pro-Taipei and pro-Beijing schools face differing challenges in funding, they plan to expand their education to serve their own objectives and outcomes for providing students with better opportunities. Regardless of financial support from China or Taiwan, the Yunnanese Chinese schools continue to survive economically and culturally, maintaining Chinese culture and tradition for their children. However, being registered as a formal international school will result in administrative changes in managing Chinese schools.

Conclusion

Through the case study of the Yunnanese Chinese, an ethnic Chinese group living in northern Thailand, this paper addresses the perspectives of ethnic Chinese in Thailand, and their responses towards Chinese educational soft power from China and Taiwan. While China's soft power strategy appears to have been effective, particularly with overseas Chinese communities in Thailand, the Yunnanese Chinese in northern Thailand have to contend with issues of conducting Chinese education.

The Yunnanese Chinese in northern Thailand illustrated how China's soft power is limited due to lingering loyalties to Taiwan, undesirable interactions with pro-Beijing donors and incommensurable education quality regarding Confucian values. The pro-Taipei school and their students today are still larger in number than those of pro-Beijing schools and are still more influential than pro-Beijing schools in northern Thailand.

This paper showed how pro-Taipei schools still sustain their sentiments, perspectives, and close networks with Taipei, even though there is an increase in pro-Beijing schools. Nevertheless, the limitation of donations and educational support from Taiwan may impact the number of pro-Taipei schools under the Taiwan model. This paper has contributed to an understanding of China's education soft power, particularly from the perspective of the recipients, the overland ethnic Chinese in northern Thailand and their Chinese sentiments.

Notes

1. Interview with the former director of the Chiang Mai Yunnanese Chinese Association, 10 March 2022.
2. Interview with an elderly leader at Arunothai village, 13 March 2022.
3. Interview with a mother who sends her two kids to Jiaolian School, 17 September 2022.
4. Interview with the current director of Jiaolian School, 13 March 2022.
5. Interview with the current director of Hua Xing School, 17 September 2022.
6. Ibid.
7. Interview with two parents and one leader who visited Hua Xing School, 17 September 2022.
8. Interview with the current director of a Yunnanese Chinese school near Arunothai village, 17 September 2022.
9. Interview with the former Chairman of one among four Yunnanese Chinese Association in Thailand, 12 April 2022.

References

Aranya Siriphon. 2015. "'*Xinyimin*', New Chinese Migrants and the Influence of the People's Republic of China (PRC) and Taiwan on the Northern Thai Border". In *Impact of China's Rise on the Mekong Region*, edited by Yos Santasombat, pp. 147–66. New York: Palgrave Macmillan.

———. 2016. "The *Qiaoban*, the PRC Influence and Nationalist Chinese in the Northern Thailand". *International Journal of Asian Studies* 13, no. 1: 1–17.

———. 2022. "Between Taipei and Beijing: Education Options among the Yunnanese Chinese of Northern Thailand". *ISEAS Perspective*, no. 2022/78, 4 August 2022, pp. 1–11.

———, and Sunanta Yamthap. 2018. "Contesting 'Chinese' Education: Schooling in the Kuomintang Chinese Diaspora in Northern Thailand, 1975–2015". In *Southeast Asian Education in Modern History: Schools, Manipulation, and Contest*, edited by Pia M. Jolliffe and Thomas R. Bruce, pp. 69–82. London: Routledge.

———, and Jiangyu Li. 2021. "Chinese Dream, Emerging Statecraft, and Chinese Influence in the Mekong Region". *International Journal of Asian Studies* 18: 289–304.

Carminati, Daniele. 2020. "The State of China's Soft Power in 2020". *E-International*

Relations. 3 July 2020 https://www.e-ir.info/2020/07/03/the-state-of-chinas-soft-power-in-2020/ (accessed 1 October 2022).

Chang, Wen-Chin. 1999. "The Kuomintang Yunnanese Chinese of Northern Thailand". In *The Dynamic of Emerging Ethnicities*, edited by Johan Leman, pp. 35–55. Frankfurt am Main: Peter Lang.

———. 2001. "From War Refugees to Immigrants: The Case of the KMT Yunnanese Chinese in Northern Thailand". *International Migration Review* 35, no. 4: 1086–105.

———. 2014. *Beyond Borders: Stories of Yunnanese Chinese Migrants of Burma*. Ithaca, New York: Cornell University Press.

d'Hooghe, Ingrid. 2015. *China's Public Diplomacy*. Leiden: Brill Nijhoff.

Ding, Sheng. 2008. "To Build a 'Harmonious World': China's Soft Power Wielding in the Global South". *Journal of Chinese Political Science* 13, no. 2: 193–213.

———, and Robert Saunders. 2006. "Talking up China: An Analysis of China's Rising Cultural Power and Global Promotion of the Chinese Language". *East Asia* 23: 3–33.

Forbes, Andrew. 2007. "The "Čin-Hō" (Yunnanese Chinese) Muslims of North Thailand". *Journal of Institute of Muslim Minority Affairs* 7, no. 1: 173–86.

———, and David Henley. 1997. *The Haw: Traders of the Golden Triangle*. Bangkok: Amarin Printing and Publishing Company.

Hartig, Falk. 2015. "Communicating China to the World: Confucius Institutes and China's Strategic Narratives". *Politics* 35, no. 3-4: 245–58.

Hill, A. Maxwell. 1998. *Merchants and Migrants: Ethnicity and Trade amongst Yunnanese Chinese in Southeast Asia*. New Haven: Yale University Press.

Huang, Shu-Min. 2010. *Reproducing Chinese Culture in Diaspora: Sustainable Agriculture & Petrified Culture in Highland Northern Thailand*. Maryland: Lexington Books.

Kanchana Prakatwuttisan. 1994. *Brigade 93 Kuomintang Chinese Nationalist Immigrants in Doi Pa Tang* (in Thai). Chiang Mai: Siamratta Printing.

———. 2004. *Kuomintang Chinese Nationalists left in Northern Thailand* (in Thai). Chiang Mai: Siamratta Printing.

Kornphanat Tungkeunkunt. 2016. "Culture and Commerce: China's Soft Power in Thailand". *International Journal of China Studies* 7, no. 2: 151–73.

Kurlantzick, Joshua. 2008. *Charm Offensive: How China's Soft Power Is Transforming the World*. New Haven: Yale University Press.

Lai, Hongyi, and Yiyi Lu, eds. 2012. *China's Soft Power and International Relations*. London and New York: Routledge.

Li, Jiangyu. 2020. "Practicing 'Nation-State Work' Abroad: International Chinese Teachers of Confucius Institutes in Thailand". PhD dissertation, Faculty of Social Sciences, Chiang Mai University.

Liu, T. Tony. 2017. "Exporting Culture: the Confucius Institute and China's Smart Power Strategy". In *the Routledge Handbook of Global Culture Policy*, edited by Dave O'Brien, Toby Miller and Victoria Durrer, pp. 233–46. New York: Routledge.

———. 2018. "Public Diplomacy: China's Newest Charm Offensive". *E-International Relations*. 30 December 2018. https://www.e-ir.info/2018/12/30/public-diplomacy-chinas-newest-charm-offensive/ (accessed 1 October 2022).

Lo, J. Tin-yau, and Suyan Pan. 2016. "Confucius Institutes and China's Soft Power: Practices and Paradoxes". *Compare: A Journal of Comparative and International Education* 46, no. 4: 512–32.

Lum, Thomas, and Wayne Morrison. 2008. "China's "Soft Power" in Southeast Asia". Paper Prepared for Members and Committees of Congress (Congressional Research Service – CRS report for Congress). Order code RL 34310.

Nye, Joseph. 1990. *Bound to Lead: The Changing Nature of American Power*. New York: Basic Books.

———. 2004. *The Means to Success in World Politics*. New York: Public Affairs.

Nyíri, Pál. 2012. "Investors, Managers, Brokers, and Culture Workers: How the 'New' Chinese Are Changing the Meaning of Chineseness in Cambodia". *Cross-Currents: East Asian History and Culture Review* 1, no. 2: 369–97.

OCAC (Overseas Community Affair Council, Republic of China, Taiwan). 2021. "Department of Overseas Compatriot Education Affairs". https://english.ocac.gov.tw/OCAC/Eng/Pages/VDetail.aspx?nodeid=420&pid=1130 (accessed 5 October 2022).

Paradise, James F. 2009. "China and International Harmony: The Role of Confucius Institutes in Bolstering Beijing's Soft Power". *Asian Survey* 49, no. 4: 647–69.

Pinkaew Laungaramsri. 1998. "Hill Tribe Discourse" (in Thai). *Journal of Social Sciences, Chiang Mai University* 11, no. 1: 92–135.

Raimzhanova, Aigerim. 2017. *Hard, Soft, and Smart Power: Education as a Power Resource*. Germany: Peter Lang.

Shambaugh, David. 2015. "China's Soft-Power Push: The Search for Respect". *Foreign Affairs*. 16 June 2015 https://www.foreignaffairs.com/articles/china/2015-06-16/chinas-soft-power-push (accessed 1 October 2022).

Sosing Methatarnkul, and Chatkrit Ruenjitt. 2020. *A Final Report: Adaptation and Change of Chinese Schools in Chinese Community in Northern Thailand under the Context of China as Superpower: A Comparison between Huaxing School and Jiaolian Language School in Arunothai Village, Chiang Dao District, Chiang Mai*. Chiang Rai: Mae Fah Luang University.

Suthep Soonthornpasuch. 1977. "Islamic Identity in Chiang Mai City: A Historical and Structural Comparison of Two Communities". PhD dissertation, University of California, Berkeley.

Wang, Liulan. 2006. "Hui Yunnanese Migratory History in Relation to the Han Yunnanese and Ethnic Resurgence in Northern Thailand". *Southeast Asian Studies* 44, no. 3: 337–58.

Wang, Yujiao. 2019. "Confucius Institutes in Thailand: Revealing the Multi-dimensionality of China's Public Diplomacy". *Journal of the Graduate School of Asia-Pacific Studies* 37, no. 3: 99–113.

Wong, John. 2016. "China's Rising Economic Soft Power". *The Asia Dialogue*. 25 March

2016. https://theasiadialogue.com/2016/03/25/chinas-rising-economic-soft-power/ (accessed 1 October 2022).

Yang, Rui. 2010. "Soft Power and Higher Education: An Examination of China's Confucius Institutes". *Globalisation, Societies and Education* 8, no. 2: 235–45.

Yıldırım, Nilgün, and Mesut Aslan. 2020. "China's Charm Defensive: Image Protection by Acquiring Mass Entertainment". *Pacific Focus* 35, no. 1: 141–71.

Zhou, Ying, and Sabrina Luk. 2016. "Establishing Confucius Institutes: A Tool for Promoting China's Soft Power?". *Journal of Contemporary China* 25, no. 100: 628–42.

Zhu, Zhiqun. 2013. *China's New Diplomacy: Rationale, Strategies and Significance.* Farnham: Ashgate.

6

CHINA'S SOFT POWER IN LAOS, WITH SPECIAL REFERENCE TO CHINESE EDUCATION AND CHINESE LANGUAGE TEACHING

Lim Boon Hock

INTRODUCTION

This paper seeks to examine China's soft power in the Lao People's Democratic Republic (Laos), with special reference to Chinese education and Chinese language teaching. To understand the extent of China's "soft power" or multifaceted socio-economic and cultural influence in Laos, it is pertinent to trace the socio-historical background of the relationships between China and her neighbours bordering the southern parts of China. One might ask why Chinese businessmen are investing aggressively in Laos and many parts of the world at large. The active Chinese investment overseas was a response to the call of the Chinese government's "Go Out Strategy" (走出去战略) initiated in 1999 by the China Council for the Promotion of International Trade (CCPIT).

Unlike most countries that strategized policies on attracting inward foreign investment and inactively supporting outward investment, China encourages its enterprises to invest overseas as well. The main reason for "going out" was to counter the response to the opening up of the domestic market due to the open-door policy when China became a member of the World Trade Organization in December 2001. Over the years, China has emerged gradually as a challenging economic force to be reckoned with, given her vast geographical size, growing wealth, huge population and economic transformation such that her market has become larger than that of Japan, Germany, the United Kingdom and India combined.

Today, the business potential in China is still attracting world-class businesses to invest in the country; hence, domestic firms need to equip themselves with international business acumen to remain competitive with foreign investments. Many Chinese businessmen tap on business opportunities in countries along the Belt and Road markets by "going out" to look for brands, technologies and resources to boost competitiveness back into developing the Chinese markets.

The Belt and Road Initiative (BRI) covers the entire geographical area of the historic Silk Road trade route. In the case of Laos, the first BRI project was the China-Lao railway, which started its construction in December 2016 and was completed in December 2021, as scheduled, and has been in operation since then. The railway section in Laos starts from Boten, located at the Lao-China border in the northern district, running 414 kilometres to the capital, Vientiane, in the southern district of Laos.

In November 2017, Xi Jinping made an official visit to Laos, the first visit in eleven years by a Chinese head of state and the Communist Party of China (CPC). Leaders of the two countries agreed to strengthen economic ties and cultural exchanges, pushing forward China's reform and the opening up of Laos. The two countries reaffirmed their friendship and mutual support to accelerate the synergy of the BRI and Lao's strategy of turning itself from a land-locked to a land-linked country. In April 2023 in Beijing, Wang Yi, a member of the Political Bureau of the CPC Central Committee and Director of the Central Commission for Foreign Affairs met with Saleumxay Kommasith, a member of the Political Bureau of the Lao People's Revolutionary Party (LPRP) Central Committee, Deputy Prime Minister and Minister of Foreign Affairs. Wang Yi pointed out that China and Laos are both socialist countries led by communist parties with shared ideas, beliefs and aspirations. Saleumxay presented in his speech that Laos and China have similar development philosophies and political systems that follow the way of socialism.

In recent years, the desire to learn the Chinese language has developed rapidly, causing the quality of education to improve. A wave of Chinese language institutions of different scales emerged, ranging from kindergarten, primary, secondary, high school, and tertiary institutions to language centres and Confucius Institutes. Some governmental institutions in Laos also conduct Chinese language courses for selected staff. Through giving an overview of the Chinese language education in Laos, this paper examines the impact of Chinese soft power in Laos and presents Laotians' experience of learning the Chinese language, their perceptions of the influx of Chinese nationals in the country and their degree of acceptance on Lao-China relationships. Empirical data was collected in fieldwork interviews with eighty Laotian residents, to support the analysis and implications drawn on the future developments of Chinese education in Laos.

China's Soft Power: Growing Demand in the Learning of Chinese Language in Laos

Soft power is China's diplomatic tool to catch up with the bandwagon of cultural globalization. Establishing Confucius Institutes in other countries to promote and teach Chinese culture and language is one example of the Chinese government's exertion of soft power.

The year 2021 marks the sixtieth anniversary of diplomatic relations between China and Laos. The Chinese President announced that bilateral ties and trade relations will enter the stage of building on past successes for future advancement. This implies that the China-Laos bilateral relations are growing stronger, particularly with the opportunities in trade and cultural exchanges that come with the opening of the China-Lao Railway on 3 December 2021. The rapid sprouting of Chinese enterprises and business establishments in Laos implies that Laotians who are proficient in Chinese and Laotian languages will be perceived as in-demand and high-calibre workers. Such heightened interests in Chinese language teaching and learning will directly shape the characteristics of the local labour market in the time to come.

China's investments in Southeast Asian countries have brought about job opportunities for the locals. In 2003, Chinese investment in Laos was barely 1.5 per cent. But in 2018, it accounted for 79 per cent in the country. The strong growth in Chinese investment has prompted job seekers to view proficiency in the Chinese language as an essential skill and a social mobility opportunity to advance themselves for a brighter future. With the increased interest in learning the Chinese language, many high-school graduates flock to study Chinese as a major in university. Chinese language proficiency has become one of the prerequisites in job hunting in Chinese companies.

In 2018, there were a total of 492,185 foreign students from 196 countries pursuing their studies in 1,004 educational institutions in China's thirty-one provinces. A large number of Laotian youths have gone to the extent of studying the Chinese language or taking degree courses in China too. According to the statistics of the Ministry of Education of China, in 2018, there were 14,645 Laotian students in China, ranking third in population after Thailand and Indonesia in ASEAN; and eighth among students of all

TABLE 6.1
Population of Foreign Students in China in 2018

Rank	Country	Number
1	South Korea	50,600
2	Thailand	28,608
3	Pakistan	28,023
4	India	23,198
5	United States	20,996
6	Russia	19,239
7	Indonesia	15,050
8	Lao PDR	14,645

Source: http://en.moe.gov.cn/documents/reports/201904/t20190418_378692.html

other countries residing in China (see Table 6.1). There were 63,041 foreign students (12.81 per cent) receiving Chinese government scholarships and 429,144 (87.19 per cent) were self-funded.

A Brief Historical Overview of the Teaching of Chinese Language and Chinese Culture in Laos

Overseas Chinese have a long history of living in Laos and their dialect origins are mainly from Guangdong, Fujian and Chaozhou. Currently, they are mostly distributed in Vientiane, Luangphabang, Pakse, Savannakhet and Thakhek. In the 1930s, overseas Chinese established private schools to teach Chinese language to Laotians of Chinese descent. The French colonial government at that time did not interfere with this, allowing for the inheritance and development of the language. In 1954, after Laos' independence and with the establishment of diplomatic relations between China and Laos, Chinese schools gradually expanded and flourished.

According to the Ministry of Education and Sports of Laos, school education includes early childhood education, general education and vocational education. In early childhood education, children are required to master listening, speaking, reading and writing. General education (GE) has three stages—primary, junior high (secondary) and high school. The total number of years in GE is 12 years, which is a 5+4+3 model. Article 17 of the Lao Education law stipulated that primary school is compulsory education. The Lao government places great importance on the teaching of foreign languages. As stated in Article 17, foreign languages were included in the curriculum of primary three students. Although foreign languages are either English or French in public schools, Chinese language is an additional subject taught in Chinese schools, and they receive Chinese volunteer teachers and teaching material support from the Chinese government.

In promoting Chinese education in Laos, academic institutions involved in the teaching of Chinese language and culture include Chinese schools and private training institutions teaching the Chinese language at all levels. Many of these academic institutions are built under the initiative of the Chinese government and other private Chinese voluntary associations, one of which is the China Foundation for Peace and Development (中国和平发展基金会)—a strategic international cooperation in the educational sector in Laos.

Founded in Beijing in January 2011, the China Foundation for Peace and Development (CFPD) is a charitable organization under the umbrella of the Ministry of Civil Affairs, International Department of the Communist Party of China (CPC) Central Committee. The foundation receives special consultation from the United Nations Economic and Social Council, and its objective is to disseminate the concept of peace and development through carrying out international public welfare projects, and people-to-people exchange activities and to support Chinese social organizations in participating in international exchanges.

Since its founding, CFPD has carried out about eighty charitable projects in thirty-four countries especially in those along the BRI route such as Laos, Cambodia, Myanmar, Mongolia, the Philippines, Tajikistan, Pakistan, Nepal, Sudan, Zambia and Tanzania, with accumulated investments of over 200 million yuan (RMB). CFPD has also hosted a large number of events and activities for international exchanges, such as the "Peace and Development Forum and Friends of the Silk Road Dialogue". Delegations from countries around the world have been invited to China for exchanges and discussions on various topics including social governance, news media, modern agriculture and sustainable development.

There were several educational projects funded by the CFPD in Laos. One of them in Laos was Lao-zhong Nongbing Village Primary School (老中农冰村小学). When it was first built in 1965 by villagers, the former Nongbing Village Primary School had six classrooms and six teachers, and can only enrol 125 students, far from meeting the growing demand of youths in the village. In June 2012, after conducting several field visits and feasibility studies, the CFPD decided to reconstruct the primary school on a plot of 800 m² land in Champaburi County, Vientiane. In less than a year, the old, dilapidated and dark classroom was replaced by a new two-storey building, two teacher dormitories, and classrooms with desks, chairs, blackboards and fans. The school currently accommodates more than 500 students.

The school was then renamed Lao-Zhong Nongbing Village Primary School (LZNVS).[1] In March 2013, to further improve the quality of LZNVS, the CFPD dispatched qualified volunteer teachers to teach the Chinese language and increased the supply of teaching aids to the school. Besides Chinese-language lessons, the school also offers a variety of Chinese cultural classes such as paper cutting, calligraphy, song, ink painting, shuttlecock games and dumpling culinary. In 2017, students from the school were invited to sing on the China Central Radio and Television (中央广播电视) programme, *Silk Road: Jasmine Flower* (丝绸之路: 茉莉花).

The year 2019 marked the fifty-eighth anniversary of diplomatic relations between Laos and China. In a speech by the Chinese ambassador to Laos, Jiang Zaidong said,

> In recent years, China-Laos cooperation has continued to be tilted towards people's livelihood and poverty-stricken areas, and specific projects have covered many aspects such as infrastructure, public services, farmers' livelihoods, and poverty alleviation. As a close friend of the Lao people, Chinese people always pay attention to the development of education in Laos and are willing to provide help within their capacity.[2]

Chinese Education in Vientiane

This section will look at the spread of Chinese education in the Laotian society. In-depth interviews were conducted with leaders of selected schools, education institutes and universities that are actively involved in the teaching of Chinese language and culture in Vientiane, the capital city of Laos. Field observations and focus group discussions were also conducted during visits to several Chinese educational institutions, including the Confucius Institute (孔子学院), Mulan Education Center (木兰私塾), Liaodu Public School (寮都公学) and Lao Soochow University (老挝苏州大学) to document the impact of China's soft power in the country.

Confucius Institute (孔子学院)

The Confucius Institute (CI) was jointly established in 2010 by the National University of Laos (NUOL) and China's Guangxi University for Nationalities (广西民族大学) to promote and teach Chinese language and culture in Vientiane. This was due to the high demand for the learning of Chinese language as the increase in Beijing's investment in Laos has prompted university students and the public to see proficiency in the Chinese language as an important asset in their job hunting. Face-to-face interviews conducted with university admission officers revealed that the Chinese language was the most popular major for new students enrolling in the 2021/22 school year, with close to 1,000 students taking the Chinese department's entrance examination. The popularity of the Chinese language major has outweighed other popular majors such as Economics, followed by Business Management and Banking/Finance.

CI conducted various forms of training in the Chinese language and even tailored training programmes to meet the needs of different types of students. There are morning classes, afternoon classes and evening classes from Monday to Thursday. During the weekends, morning and afternoon classes are offered. For the public, beginner and intermediate courses are offered, while teachers from NUOL are offered teacher training courses. As of September 2019, CI has trained 20,470 students including 277 civil servants from the Prime Minister's Office, Vientiane Municipality Office and Lao Academy for Politics and Public Administration.

An interview conducted with an associate professor in the CI revealed that due to the increasing demand for enrolment in his department, they accepted 240 students in the fiscal year 2021/22, as compared to the 200 students accepted in the previous academic year. He further shared that Chinese investment in Laos will require Laotians who can speak Mandarin. A Chinese major student pointed out that fresh high school graduates are racing to choose Chinese as a major because they perceive that it will help them secure a high-paying job in Chinese-owned companies. Graduates with a major in Chinese studies can earn a salary between 5–6 million kip (US$300 to 350) per month if they work for Chinese companies, about two times the salary of those working for Laotian employers.

In July 2018, a second CI was established at Souphanouvong University[3] in Luangphabang, near the Chinese town of Mohan. See Table 6.2. In October 2018, the School of Economics and Tourism started a Chinese language elective course for 200 students in four classes.

The reconstruction of a new CI building in NUOL was initiated in late 2016 and completed in April 2019, before being officially handed over to the university president, Professor Somsy Gnophanxay. The ceremony was attended by the then Lao Minister of Education and Sports, Sengdeuane Lachanthaboun, Chinese Ambassador to Laos, Jiang Zaidong and former Chief Executive Officer of Confucius Institute Headquarters,

TABLE 6.2
Cumulated Data of Student Population at Confucius Institute over Five Years

Year Established	Confucius Institute	Location	Graduates
2010	National University of Laos	Vientiane	13,388
2018	Souphanouvong University	Luangphabang	2,592
Total			15,980

Source: Chinese Embassy in Laos, November 2020. 老挝华文学校概况统计, 2020年11月.

Xu Lin. The CI building has three stories with dormitories for lecturers and students and covers an area of 15,600 m². It took 20 months to construct the building, and the cost incurred in the construction was estimated to be more than 97 billion kip or RMB76,900,000, supported by grant assistance from the Chinese government. In terms of educational assistance, the Chinese government has been providing scholarships each year to Laotian students to study in universities in China. Beginning in 2016, Confucius Day which falls on 28 September is celebrated annually in the two universities in Laos.

Department of Chinese Studies at the National University of Laos

The Chinese Embassy in Laos helped to build the Department of Chinese Studies in the NUOL in 2003. The department offers courses in Chinese Studies at the undergraduate level and works strictly in accordance with the regulations of the Ministry of Education and Sports of Laos.

Currently, the department has fourteen teachers, four of whom are volunteer teachers dispatched by the Office of Chinese Language Council International, also known as *Hanban* (国家汉语国际推广领导小组办公室-简称: 汉办). As shown in their weekly timetable, NUOL undergraduates have to attend twenty-two classes in the Chinese language, four in the English language and six Laotian subjects such as culture, literature, political science and Lao grammar. Table 6.3 shows some Chinese textbooks used by the Department of Chinese Studies in the NUOL.

Lao National Defense Academy and Vientiane Police College

In 2004, the Vientiane Police College established a four-year Chinese major course for police cadets while the Lao National Defense Academy started a Chinese degree course for soldiers from various arms of the army in 2009. Trainees need to fulfil a 2+2 curriculum mode where they study for two years at the Lao National Defense Academy and another two years

TABLE 6.3
Chinese Textbooks Used for Teaching in the Department by Different Publishers

	Subjects	Publishers
1	Conversational Chinese 301*	Beijing Language and Culture University Press
2	Intermediate spoken Chinese	Peking University Press
3	Survival Chinese 101	Foreign Language Teaching and Research Press
4	Practical modern Chinese grammar	Commercial Press
5	Chinese culture and business	NUOL Press

Note: * An intensive, well-thought-out two-volume beginning course for adult learners. The lessons develop an 800-word vocabulary and 301 basic conversational sentence patterns. On completion, the student should be able to carry on simple conversations and will have acquired a solid foundation for further study.
Source: Fieldwork data.

at the Kunming Campus of the Chinese Army's Institute of Border and Coastal Defense. In each batch, there are twenty trainees aged between 20 and 35 years old. Upon graduation, the trainees will receive a bachelor's degree and be promoted to the rank of lieutenant. The objectives are to equip police and soldiers with Chinese communication skills to ensure that they are capable enough to undertake Chinese-Lao military exchange and cooperation projects; and to be responsible for the translation of official documents related to China's military assistance.

Mulan Education Center (木兰私塾)
In a focus group discussion with eight Chinese major undergraduates of NUOL who are taking night classes on Chinese language at Mulan Education Center, five strongly agreed that their country's future lies with Beijing, while the rest agreed to a certain extent.[4] Another suggested that the Laotian government should consider including the Chinese language in public schools, instead of teaching mainly Laotian and English languages.[5]

The Mulan Education Center is one of such in the city's more popular Chinese language centres opened in February 2019. The school inauguration was attended by many high-ranking government officers including the Vice Ministers of Finance and Foreign Affairs. Mulan started with about 300 students enrolled in classes catering from kindergarten students to working adults. In 2020, one year after its establishment, the enrolment exceeded

TABLE 6.4
Cumulation of Examinees of the Three Designated HSK Test Centers Till 2021

Venue	Initiated in	Examinees
National University of Laos	2011	8,506
Lao Soochow University	2012	8,174
Souphanouvong University	2019	1,475
Total		18,155

Source: 汉语考试服务网 (www.chinesetest.cn) 2022年11月.

700. A member of staff expressed his confidence that their enrolment numbers will double or triple in the next three to four years. One of Mulan's strategic moves was to help graduates who pass the Chinese Proficiency Test (汉语水平考试) HSK level IV examination secure employment in Chinese firms in the country.[6] See Table 6.4.

While many Chinese language centres have sprouted in Vientiane, many small Chinese language centres are being set up in public schools in Luang Namtha, Oudomxay and Bokeo provinces in the north of Laos that are in close proximity to China.

Liaodu Public School (寮都公学)
Liaodu Public School was founded in 1937 by the Overseas Chinese in Vientiane. It has kindergartens, elementary schools, junior high schools and high schools. In 2021, it was said to be ranked the fourth-best school in Laos and top among the nine Chinese schools in the country. It is the largest full-day school with more than 2,800 students in total. Chinese language is ranked the most important subject taught in the school and the language is also used for teaching Chinese history, mathematics and science subjects. Textbooks were imported from Jinan University Press (暨南大学出版社), Zhejiang People's Fine Arts Publishing House (浙江人民美术出版社) and Chenguang Publisher Yunnan (晨光出版社).

Unlike kindergartens in Laos with three-year programmes, Liaodu's kindergarten programme is designed for two years. This means that students of Liaodu will be promoted to Primary One when they are 6 years old. Primary schools in Laos have five years of compulsory education but the textbooks that were recommended for teaching by Hanban (汉办)[7] are for six years of study. Hence, in Liaodu, lower primary classes and upper primary classes take three years each to complete. Secondary school takes four years while high school takes two years. High school graduates can further their studies in local colleges or universities. Those who graduate from high school and have obtained HSK Level IV and above pass will stand a high chance of getting the Chinese government's scholarship to study in China for a bachelor's degree, mainly at Huaqiao University (华侨大学) located in Xiamen and Quanzhou, Fujian province for three years. With the strengthening of China and Laos bilateral ties, China has offered scholarships to young Laotians in recent years. Over 1,300 Laotians have been granted fully funded Chinese government scholarships (CGS) between 1990 and 2016, a figure that exceeds all other ASEAN countries.[8]

In Liaodu, with a class size of about fifty students, all Chinese subjects are conducted in the morning and Laotian and English language classes are taught in the afternoon. Students start to attend English language classes only when they are promoted to upper primary—from Primary Four onwards. Besides getting the endorsement and accreditation from *Hanban's* Confucius Institute, Liaodu also gets manpower support from the People's Republic of China's Overseas Chinese Affairs Bureau, known as *Qiaoban* (侨办), where Chinese volunteer teachers from China are posted to teach Chinese language and culture in the school. An average of between twenty-two and twenty-three Chinese teachers are posted to Liaodu Public School every year to teach the Chinese language to help raise the standard of the language. These Chinese teachers are mainly from Yunnan, Guangxi and Sichuan and most of them are experienced teachers in secondary and high schools.

In the past, students of Chinese descent formed the majority of the student population in Liaodu, but now, Laotian students make up about 75 per cent of the total number of students in the school. This is partly due to the overall increase in the population of the country as well as the infiltration of ethnic Chinese into the Laotian society over time. Many parents of Laotian students in Liaodu are politicians and businessmen. The school plans to include vocational training in its curriculum in the near future to meet the need for Chinese language proficiency among workers in blue-collar jobs when Chinese investments in Laos continue to increase.

Chinese cultural influences are visible on the school campus in Liaodu. For example, a Confucius statue was imported from Shandong and erected in the garden of Liaodu School. Many banners are also seen hanging on the walls with Chinese slogans such as "普及普通话，四海是一家。说好普通话，朋友遍天下", clearly conveying the school's mission in the teaching of

Chinese language and culture. The school bookshop was named 中华乡愁书院 to remind students of the significance of the Chinese origins among ethnic Chinese in Laos. Liaodu celebrates most of the Chinese festivals year-round as well as the National Day of China on 1 October.

Chinese Universities Established in Laos
China has always been actively encouraging Sino-foreign joint programmes to help develop and internationalize the education system in China. More recently, the government also encouraged the establishment of Sino-foreign cooperation in education outside of China. Under the policy on Chinese public educational institutions established overseas, funding has to rely on private investment or in partnership with local or foreign enterprises.

In Asia, according to China's Ministry of Education (MOE) 2003 Interim Measures, the MOE had approved four Chinese universities to build educational institutions overseas. One of these Chinese universities is the Laos Soochow University.

Laos Soochow University was the first overseas university to be established outside of China. As the forerunner of Chinese higher education's "Go Out Strategy", it has evolved from one rarely heard-of institution to a widely known university in Laos. Laos Soochow University campus was included in the proposal in 2007 when China and Laos agreed to jointly construct a Special Economic Zone (SEZ) where the management of Soochow Industrial Park in China was offered to undertake the design and construction project.

Laos Soochow University has been playing a 'go-between' role in Laos as it is an official contact point for potential Chinese entrepreneurs to understand the economic and social development outlook of Laos and Southeast Asia. It provides orientation on the country, helps to carry out market surveys and arranges guided tours to relevant government departments. Two special courses offered on International Economy and Trade and Finance were approved by the Lao MOE in July 2012. Two more courses that were subsequently approved in 2013 were "Chinese Language" and "Computer Science". The university adopts the "1+3" mode where undergraduates study general subjects designated by Lao MOE and the Laotian language in Lao in the first year and continue from the second to fourth year to study at Soochow University in China. Graduates are conferred dual degrees from Soochow University in both China and Laos.

Survey on the Perception of Chinese Education in Laotian Society

In the previous section, this paper looked at the range of Chinese education available in Vientiane, Laos. This section will look at the sentiments and reactions among Laotians towards China and her economic and socio-cultural relationships. A survey was conducted in the capital city Vientiane from January to April 2023, to find out how people in Laos feel about learning the Chinese language and Chinese education in general, as well as their experiences and perception of China and her presence or "soft power" in Laos. The survey solicited the opinions from a sample of eighty respondents, selected from a convenience sampling[9] design. Each survey respondent was approached personally and invited to participate in the survey. Prospective respondents were provided with an online link to the survey questionnaire which was designed using Google Forms.

Of the 80 respondents, 82.5 per cent were Laotians, 10.0 per cent were Chinese Laotians and 7.6 per cent were people from other countries currently living in Laos (Figure 6.1).

In terms of age distribution, among those who reported their age (sixty-two out of eighty respondents), the majority were between 30 and less than 40 years old (61.3 per cent). With an average age of 33.06 years, the respondents were mostly young adults, many of whom were aware of the significance and relevance of learning the Chinese language to their career progression (Figure 6.2).

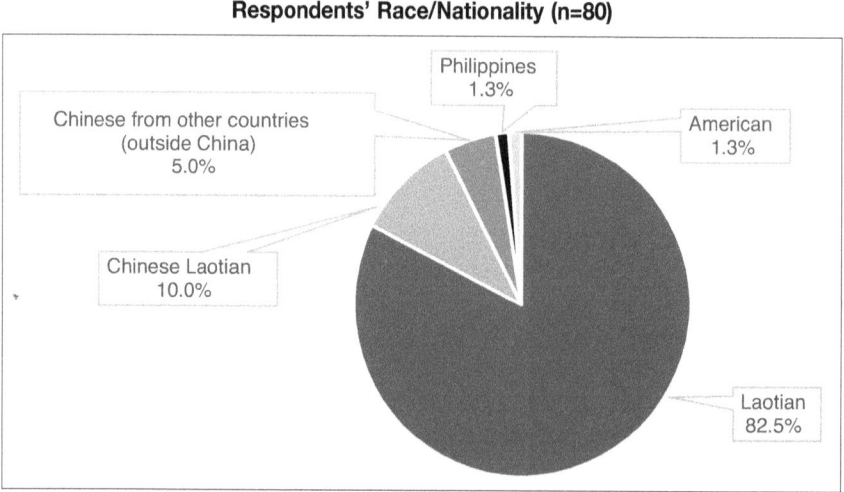

FIGURE 6.1
Respondents' Race/Nationality (n=80)

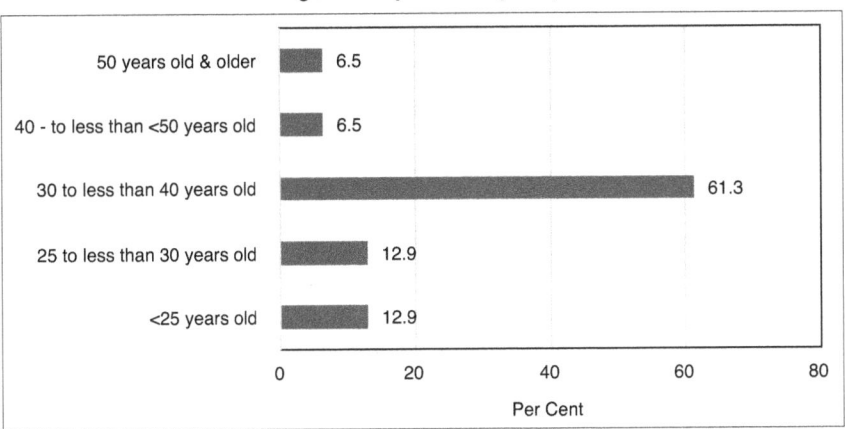

**FIGURE 6.2
Age of Respondents (n=62)**

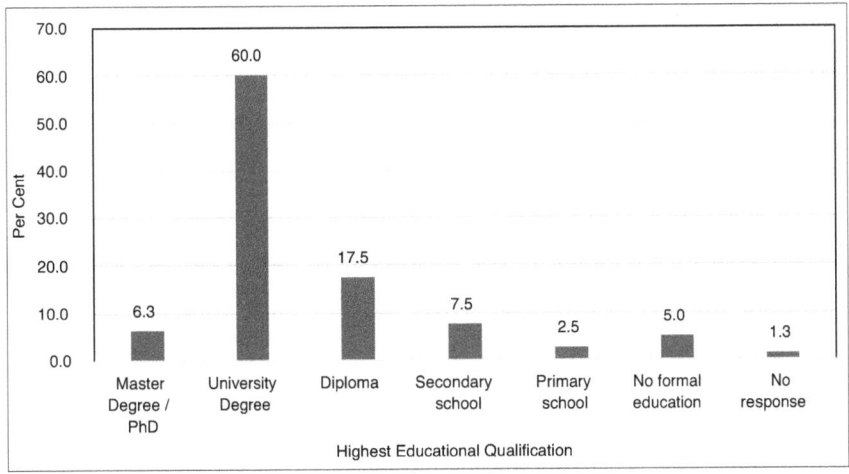

**FIGURE 6.3
Respondents' Highest Educational Qualification (n=80)**

Figure 6.3 shows that at least six in ten respondents were university graduates, while the remaining reported their highest educational qualifications as ranging from "no formal education" to a "diploma".

This tilt in the educational background of respondents who leaned towards tertiary education qualifications seems to reflect the unspoken reality in Laotian society that the interest in learning the Chinese language appears to be greater and better appreciated among the higher-educated people in Laos. This was evident in Figure 6.4 which shows almost all or

FIGURE 6.4
Respondents' Report Level of Interest in Learning the Chinese Language (n=80)

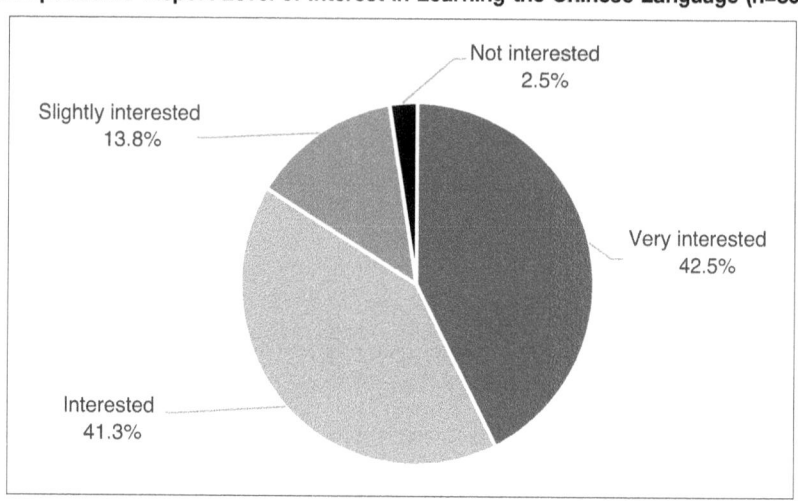

97.5 per cent of the respondents expressing varying degrees of interest in learning the Chinese language.

When asked about their reasons for expressing interest in learning the Chinese language, almost four in ten respondents cited that they "need to read and understand Chinese documents in (their) work" (38.5 per cent) as the reason, while close to a quarter of the respondents "(wanted) to get a job in Chinese companies in Laos" (23.1 per cent). 9.0 per cent of the respondents reported that they "(needed) to write Chinese letters and documents in (their) work" and 10.3 per cent expressed that they "hope to work in China in future" (Figure 6.5).

These survey results clearly reflect the growing importance and relevance of Chinese literacy in the workplaces in Laos. Other reasons that were not directly related to work, but implied the growing impact and prevalence of China's soft power in the social lives of Laotians, include "I want to talk to my Chinese friends in Chinese" (19.2 per cent), "I want to make friends with Chinese people" (15.4 per cent), "I am interested in Chinese culture" (11.5 per cent) and "I want to travel in China" (16.7 per cent).

Among those who reported having learned the Chinese language before, about four in ten or 41.8 per cent of them learned it on their own without attending formal lessons and 17.9 per cent learned it through their social interactions with Chinese friends and at the workplaces while interacting with Chinese colleagues and/or work contacts. The rest attended classes

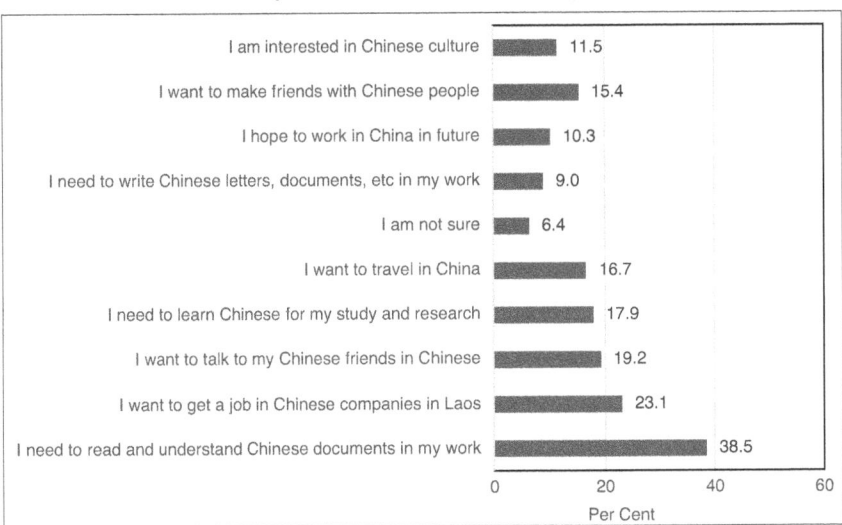

FIGURE 6.5
Reasons for Respondents' Interest in Learning Chinese (n=78)

TABLE 6.5
Medium Through Which Respondents Learn the Chinese Language

	Number	%
Learn on my own/self-study	28	41.8
Through my interactions with Chinese friends/work contacts	12	17.9
Attended classes in a language centre in Laos	11	16.4
Through compulsory or elective courses at school	7	10.4
Attended Chinese language courses in China	5	7.5
Through an online Chinese language training institution	3	4.5
Private tuition	1	1.5
Total	67	100.0

in the Chinese language, either voluntarily or as compulsory electives in school (Table 6.5).

Respondents were asked to share their opinions about the importance of the Chinese language in their everyday lives. The majority revealed that it was "important" for them to "speak Mandarin" (53.8 per cent), "read Chinese text" (53.7 per cent) and "write in Chinese" (53.8 per cent) in their daily lives and a substantial proportion even felt that it was "very important" for them to "speak Mandarin" (35.9 per cent), "read Chinese text" (22.4 per cent) and "write in Chinese" (18.5 per cent) (Table 6.6).

As shown in Figure 6.6 while the majority or 38.9 per cent had teachers who came from China, there was also a noticeable proportion of respondents (26.4 per cent) who did not know the nationality of their Chinese language teachers. The rest of them had Chinese language teachers who were Chinese Laotians (18.1 per cent), Chinese from Asian countries outside China (9.7 per cent) and other non-Chinese (6.9 per cent) residing in Laos.

Figure 6.7 shows the growth potential of Chinese language education with nine in ten of the respondents expressing that they "will definitely

TABLE 6.6
Respondents' Opinion on the Importance of Chinese Language in their Daily Lives

In your daily life, how important is it for you to be able to...	... speak Mandarin?		... read Chinese text?		... write in Chinese?	
	Number	%	Number	%	Number	%
Very important	28	35.9	15	22.4	12	18.5
Important	42	53.8	36	53.7	35	53.8
Not important	8	10.3	16	23.9	18	27.7
Total	78	100.0	67	100.0	65	100.0

Source: Fieldwork data.

FIGURE 6.6
Nationality of Chinese Teacher (n=72)

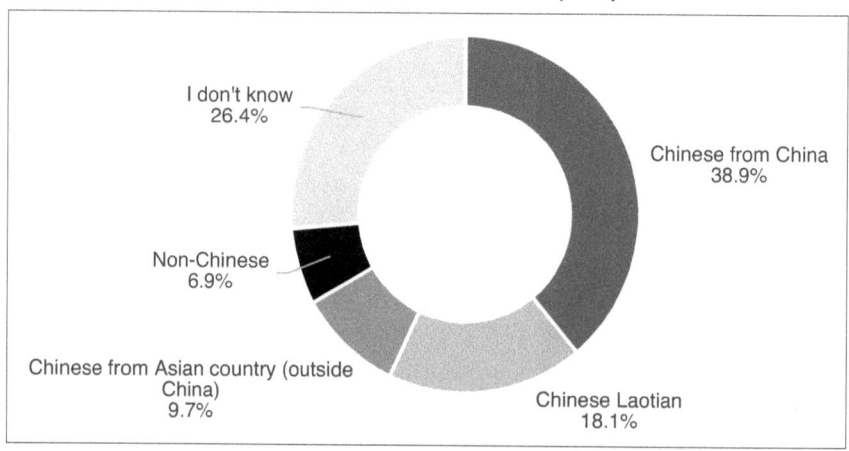

FIGURE 6.7
Whether Respondents Would Consider Attending a University in China (n=80)

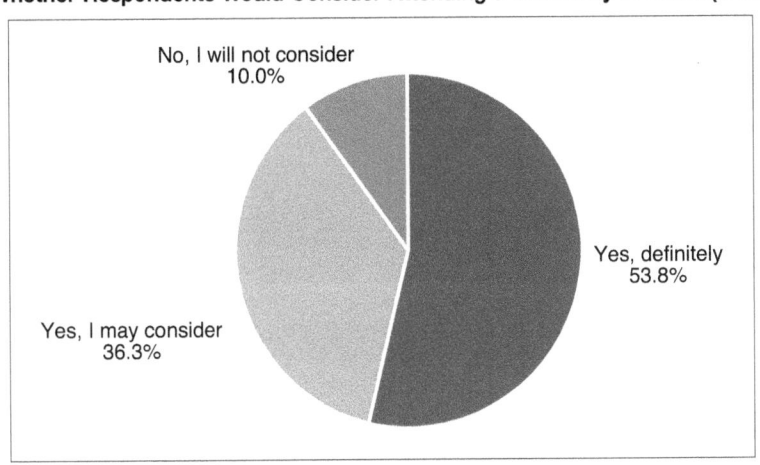

consider" (53.8 per cent) or "they may consider" (36.3 per cent) attending a university in China if they were given a choice to do so.

Some of the reasons given by the respondents on why they would consider attending a university in China included their concerns about the importance of the "language learning environment" and their awareness of the important role played by China in the economic development of Laos. Others cited patriotic reasons like "I want to study in China, learn new ideas and come back to build Laos" and pragmatic reasons like "I want to know the Chinese culture and language and get the opportunity to work in China".

The survey also revealed the opinions and impressions of the Laotian people towards Lao-China relations, in terms of the economic and sociocultural impacts of China's influence in Laos. Questions were posed on how important respondents would see "China's investments in Laos", "China's cultural influence in Laotian society", "China's support in Laos' economic development", "work opportunities in China" and "Chinese education for Laotian children". From the survey, it is apparent that the respondents generally have more positive perceptions about the Lao-China relations, as shown in Table 6.7.

Approximately four in five of the respondents who expressed their opinions showed varying degrees of importance in their ratings on the various aspects of the relationship between Laos and China, ranging from China's investments, cultural influence, economic support, work and Chinese education in Laos.

TABLE 6.7
Respondents' Opinions about Lao-China Relations

In your opinion, how important is ...	... China's investments in Laos?		... China's cultural influence on Laotian society?		... China's support in Laos' economic development?		... work opportunities in China?		... Chinese education for Laotian children?	
	No.	%	No.	%	No.	%	No.	%	No.	%
Very important	12	16.4	7	10.4	13	18.6	8	12.3	16	22.9
Important	21	28.8	20	29.9	20	28.6	16	24.6	16	22.9
Slightly important	26	35.6	25	37.3	21	30.0	17	26.2	26	37.1
Not important	5	6.8	3	4.5	3	4.3	9	13.8	4	5.7
Not sure	9	12.3	12	17.9	13	18.6	15	23.1	8	11.4
Total	73	100.0	67	100.0	70	100.0	65	100.0	70	100.0

Source: Fieldwork data.

Most respondents appreciated the support provided by China in terms of investments in Laos and in boosting Laos' economic developments, with 80.8 per cent and 77.2 per cent, respectively, expressing these support measures as at least "slightly important", if not, "very important" to Laos.

China's "soft power" in terms of its cultural influences on Laotian society was also found to be important in varying degrees by 77.6 per cent of those who voiced their opinions. While the BRI was cited as a contributing factor to China's support for the development of the Lao economy, some respondents also explained that "Lao and China have a significant longstanding relationship and economic ties throughout history", and "China can help Laos to change from a land-locked country to a land-linked country".

Notwithstanding the above survey findings, respondents appeared to be relatively less certain about the importance of having work opportunities in China, with 23.1 per cent feeling unsure in their responses, and 13.8 per cent expressing that "work opportunities in China" is "not important". This could be attributed to the fact that many Laotians were optimistic about the work opportunities in Laos and in their country's economic growth potential, which was already visibly felt with the opening of the China-Lao railway. The railway opened the doors for Laos to tap into the forces of globalization in terms of trade and work opportunities overseas. On the other hand, respondents who expressed their uncertainties or doubts about the importance of work opportunities in China could possibly be experiencing a cultural lag and the lack of adequate exposure to the world outside their home country, which could render some uncertain and/or apprehensive about venturing out of their country to work in China.

What is noteworthy from the survey results is that "Chinese education for Laotian children" was viewed as a significant impetus and promising opportunity for Laotians to improve their quality of life and as a means for them to facilitate upward social mobility for their children. Almost half of the respondents felt that making Chinese education accessible for Laotian children was either "very important" or "important" (45.8 per cent) and 37.1 per cent felt this was "slightly important".

In the survey, respondents were asked whether they would consider sending their children to Chinese schools and universities, in Laos and China. As much as Laotians would like their children to be educated in Chinese schools or universities in China, the reality is they may face constraints in the opportunity structures and financial means to support their children's Chinese education overseas in China. It is therefore not surprising that, realistically, a large majority, or 63.8 per cent of the respondents opted to

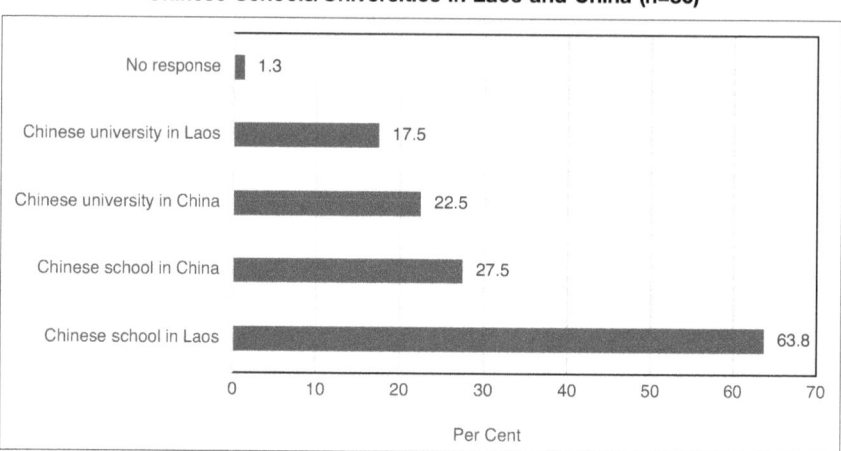

FIGURE 6.8
Respondents' Preference in Sending Their Children to
Chinese Schools/Universities in Laos and China (n=80)

send their children to Chinese schools in Laos, instead of in China. The reasons for wanting to send their children to Chinese schools in Laos were cited as "convenient for parents to monitor their children" and "affordability" reasons. Those who preferred to send their children to China for their studies explained that their children would be able to "learn Chinese language more systematically" and "have the opportunity to understand and use the Chinese language better" (Figure 6.8).

Conclusion

In Laos, Chinese education is not just a course in the new era, but it also symbolizes the desired outcome of China's Belt and Road Initiative. China's soft power is manifested in her active participation in the Greater Mekong Subregion (GMS) through economic cooperation and cultural exchanges with her fellow GMS member countries. This proactive "Go Out" strategy is in sync with her political initiatives to promote regional development and world peace. Through building and strengthening bilateral ties with neighbouring countries like Laos, new economic activities and opportunities will continue to be created for both countries and these will, in turn, help in the opening up and development of China's less developed provinces and rural regions. Laos plays an important role, especially after the completion and operation of China-Lao Railway, to serve as China's gateway to enable China to continue its investment outreach in Southeast Asian countries. The growing manpower demand for Laotians with Chinese language proficiency will continue to grow and it has directly shaped the developmental directions of the local labour market. However, the journey is still long because of the inadequate supply of qualified native-speaking Chinese teachers, overpopulated class sizes and insufficient teaching facilities, faced by Chinese schools in Laos like in the case of Liaodu Public School. Another problem is the use of Chinese textbooks recommended by *Hanban*, which lacks the localization of contents to make them more relevant to the Laotian society so that students in Laos can better identify with them.

The desirable outcomes of China's soft power in creating and sustaining a multifaceted "win-win" relationship between China and Laos are yet to be seen. What is more certain is the impetus that her Belt and Road Initiative has already created in the current unprecedented and heightened interest in the learning of the Chinese language in local schools in Laos and the perception that acquiring Chinese language proficiency promises upward social mobility opportunities which is seen as a stepping-stone to a brighter future.

Notes

1. China Foundation for Peace and Development, "A Letter from General Secretary Xi Jinping Replied to All the Teachers and Students of China-Laos Friendship Nongping Primary School", *Annual report 2019*, p. 4, http://www.cfpd.org.cn/News/536/2434.htm
2. Some other China-aided schools reported in several annual reports of CFPD were China-Laos "Friends of the Silk Road", Smart Campus Project (中老友好 "丝路之友" 智慧校园项目) in September 2018, Five Schools of Sino-Laos Friendship, "Friends of the Silk Road" (中老友好 "丝路之友" 五所学校的建设) in the same period, Sino-Laos Friendship Vientiane City Meng Nuo School (中老友好万象市孟诺学校的建设) in May 2017 and China-Laos Friendship Pan Sai Village Secondary School (中老友好潘赛村中学) in December 2013.
3. One of the five national universities in Lao PDR.
4. One of the participants, who requested anonymity, commented that "most investors in Laos are Chinese and they are giant companies compared with investors from other nationals".
5. Another participant commented that "In the past in Vientiane, many language schools were teaching only English with a handful of them offering French. Today, most of them have included Chinese language in their language courses because of its popularity".
6. One student shared that "attending Mulan school at night to improve my spoken Chinese language so that I can get a better pay job in a Chinese firm".
7. Also known as Confucius Institute Headquarters (and originally known as the China National Office for Teaching Chinese as a Foreign Language).

8. Convenience sampling design was used largely because Laotians generally do not respond readily to surveys unless they are being approached by personal contacts like friends, colleagues or relatives as a favour to participate in surveys.
9. One respondent wrote "Whilst foreign investment can be beneficial, it also has to be managed appropriately which I myself am not sure".

References

Asian Development Bank. 2018. "Lao People's Democratic Republic: Development Effectiveness Brief (Lao Translation)". https://www.adb.org/lo/publications/lao-pdr-development-effectiveness-brief

He, Zhouyan. 2019. "BRI Explainer: What Is the Belt and Road". *People's Daily*, 23 April 2019, version 17.

Radio Free Asia's Lao Service. 2021. "Chinese Investment in Laos Sparks Chinese-Language Learning Boom", translated by Max Avary. Written in English by Eugene Whong. 23 February 2021. https://www.rfa.org/english/news/laos/chinese-02232021191135.html#:~:text=A%20Chinese%20language%20education%20boom,sources%20in%20Laos%20told%20RFA

Yap, Jasmina. 2017. "China Invests in Lao Students". *The Laotian Times*, 15 November 2017. https://laotiantimes.com/2017/11/15/china-invests-lao-students/

Zhou, Ying, and Sabrina Luk. 2016. "Establishing Confucius Institutes: A Tool for Promoting China's Soft Power?". *Journal of Contemporary China* 25, no. 100: 628–42. https://doi.org/10.1080/10670564.2015.1132961

7

CHINESE EDUCATION AND EDUCATING CHINESE IN A POST-CONFLICTED STATE
Mandarin Education Systems in Cambodia

Shihlun Allen Chen

INTRODUCTION

As a post-conflict country with long years of civil war, Cambodia has a unique experience in education and cultural reconstruction due to its intense political changes and post-war international reconstruction experience. Having gone through seven regimes since the first half of the twentieth century, the nation has been trapped as a divided nation at war since 1970. It was only in December 1998 when the last Khmer Rouge guerrillas surrendered to the royal government of Hun Sen Administration,[1] when the nation was truly unified. Based on such congenital construction deficiency and constant political disorder, a stable national education system in modern Cambodia is absent. The limited colonial education for the elites, Buddhist monasteries' enlightenment education and the ethnic Chinese primary education associated with the local Chinese communities are the three most significant systems for de-literate sources (Chen 2015).

Through examining the Chinese impacts and influences on education in Cambodia, this chapter aims to profile Chinese education in Cambodia into three periods: ethnic Chinese education, local Chinese education and foreign Chinese education. These periods will be elaborated through a combination of my long-term ethnographical fieldwork in Cambodia's Chinese communities (2009–18) with research reflections on Cambodia's foreign policy and aid dependency in the past two decades. In conclusion, this chapter argues that the case of various Mandarin education systems in Cambodian demonstrates that foreign language education in a post-conflicted and under-reconstructing state tends to be a domestic-oriented pragmatic and economically rational choice, rather than a politized and strategized power rationality driven by geo-politics.

Chinese Education Systems in Contemporary Cambodia

Current Chinese education in Cambodia can be understood through two-way communications in three major periods: incoming and outgoing flows of traditional ethnic Chinese education, emerging foreign Chinese education, and developing domestic Chinese education in Cambodia.

The Traditional Ethnic Chinese Education System

Chinese Cambodians or ethnic Chinese community refer to the Chinese descendants that arrived in Cambodia since the earliest record of Chinese settlement by Zhou Daguan in 1296 (Zhou 2017). They are different from the new Chinese immigrants or so-called *xin yi min* (新移民). After the Paris Peace Agreement was promulgated in 1991, it was determined that the New Kingdom government would be established through a new general election held in 1993. The then Cambodian People's Party (CPP) leaders Hun Sen and Heng Samrin summoned eleven business leaders from the Cambodian Chinese community to express the ruling party's community's support for the reconstruction and real estate redemption of the Chinese community. As the former Chairman Yang Qi-qiu of the Association of Chinese in Cambodia (ACC, 柬华理事总会), the leading organization of the Chinese Cambodian community, recalled in our interview, Heng Samrin promised to restore all the Chinese community's pre-war properties, including all *Huiguan* (会馆) buildings, Chinese school campuses and temples.

At the same time, the leaders of the Chinese community were asked to support the CPP in the coming general election. After the new Administration was established, ACC and its affiliated five hometowns *Huiguan*, twelve surname organizations and more than thirty provincial branches were all reconstructed. With the new government's support, most of the temples and local Chinese schools were repurchased by Chinese businessmen from the wartime occupiers and rebuilt on the spot. These temples and schools are the main operations of all *Huiguan* and provincial ACC branches. As Chairman Yang Qi-qiu further elaborated, "Other than routine reception and farewell activities (送往迎来 *Song wang ying lai*) and seasonal temple worship activities, half of the business (ACC) are all Chinese school operations and fundraising." Hence the repurchasing and rebuilding of these entities were of paramount importance.

Up to mid-2022, ACC and its affiliated five *huiguan* and fifty-seven local branches have six major communal Chinese schools in Phnom Penh and fifty-two local Chinese schools in provinces across Cambodia. The rapid rehabilitation of these communal Chinese schools in Cambodia in the early 1990s also filled the absence of public educational resources in the early reconstruction of the New Kingdom. It became the main source of labour for the influx of overseas Chinese capital investment from Hong Kong, Taiwan, and nearby Southeast Asian countries. However, while Chinese-speaking teachers may be easy to find in peaceful Phnom Penh, essential materials such as chalk, desks, chairs, paper and textbooks were not available. This meant local Chinese schools had to heavily rely on foreign aid and private donations. Unable to be self-sufficient, most ACC-affiliated Chinese schools were unable to meet the end balance of all expenses. The two ACC Chairmen (Yang Qi-qiu, in office from 1996 to 2016; Pung Kheav Se, 2016–present) and deputy Chairmans of ACC noted that their major commitment and mission were to cover or find the support for necessary funding to ensure all affiliated schools can maintain their operation.

Therefore, it is understandable that the development of ACC-affiliated Chinese schools had to rely heavily on foreign resources when the entire country's national budget was 100 per cent dependent on the foreign government's official development assistance from the international community until 1998. This development assistance declined to over 10 per cent in 2018. The development of ACC-affiliated schools can be divided into three phases. The first phase is from 1991 to 1997, with the import of Chinese materials from different countries to supply the demand for Chinese education in Cambodia. In 1987, Taiwanese businessmen were among the earliest foreign merchants that came to Cambodia. Their early engagement with penniless Cambodian officials and local brokers gave them a great advantage not only in business but also in strong connections with local ethnic Chinese merchants. The short-lived Phnom Penh Taipei Economic and Trade Representative Office also brought in all necessary educational materials to Cambodia, such as professional teachers, colourful textbooks, and even copy machines and precious paper. However, the demand for Chinese education in Cambodia then far exceeded the supply of materials provided by Taiwan. To fulfil this demand, textbooks (in both simplified and traditional Mandarin), and related educational materials from mainland China, Hong Kong, and Malaysia were also brought into Cambodia.

ACC-affiliated schools are usually considered supplementary cram schools in the Chinese language. Students only attend half-day classes for some years at the same time as Khmer public schools or English private schools. Almost all provincial schools of ACC affiliation only provide a six-year primary level curriculum, but only Duanhua School in Cambodia (柬埔寨端华学校, 1914–present), offers a three-year junior school and two-year secondary school curriculum. Therefore, it is still difficult for ACC-affiliated school graduates to extend their education to local or foreign high schools or universities due to the dependency on foreign aid materials and difficulties in maintaining further education for students.

During this period, both mainland China and Taiwan invited Cambodian school administrators and teachers to attend training courses at Jinan University, Guangzhou or at Taiwan Normal University, Taipei. In the second half of 1997, China's Jinan University and its edition of textbooks became the main teaching material for all ACC-affiliated schools. Only some private primary schools and I-Kuan Tao Buddhist halls (一贯道佛堂) that also provided basic Chinese lessons still used materials distributed by Taiwanese publishers outside the ACC school system. Till today, Taiwan-originated I-Kuan Tao Buddhist halls give free Chinese courses to support their internal worship services and attract local believers. With more than ninety locations in Cambodia, they are the only few educators in the country who still teach traditional Chinese and *Zhuyin*. However, these courses given by I-Kuan Tao Buddhist hall's volunteers do not provide any certification of members' Chinese proficiency, therefore most students consider this Chinese language training course as supplementary resources along with other formal channels like ACC schools.

The second phase from 1997 to 2008 saw the wartime generation challenge the pre-war generation of Chinese community leaders in ACC. The wartime generation is made up of young professionals headed by the principal of Fujian Huiguan Minsheng School (福建会馆民生学校) and some young school administrators eager to improve the profitability of urban Chinese schools. These young administrators seek to open ACC to an English-Chinese-Khmer trilingual curriculum and include new courses such as computer, accounting and software usage, which challenge the older generation's traditional approach of using Chinese schools as a platform for inheritance and maintenance of ethnic and cultural identities. However, while they seek to improve the autonomy of the curriculum and localization of teaching materials, the heavy dependency on China for teaching materials, resources, and teaching aids (援教师资) hinders their resolve. They cannot ignore China's financial support through ACC to increase teacher salaries and subsidies.

My informants and fieldwork experiences of overseas Chinese affairs in Cambodia and cross-straits showed that overseas Mandarin education was seen as the last battlefield in defining Chinese culture during this period. Taiwan lost the representative office in Phnom Penh in 1997 after compressing the function and budget of the Overseas Community Affairs Council in charge of sponsoring Chinese education overseas. Since President Chen Shuibian, overseas Chinese education affairs were moved to the newly established Ministry of Culture. These are all signs that Taiwan's attention has shifted to cross-strait relations and domestic affairs. Taiwan's withdrawal from overseas Chinese affairs, network connection with ethnic organizations and overseas Chinese education market since 2000 has made Taiwan lose its economic advantage, making the competition for cultural influence unbalanced. In the meantime, China's booming economy provided more energy and resources to invest more in geopolitics, diplomatic relations, and its overseas ethnic network. ACC is one of the beneficiaries of China's investment in overseas Chinese in Cambodia, with China's aid to Cambodia growing more than 10 times, and its trade amount more than 9.3 times from 1997 to 2008 (Chen 2018, p. 374). The ACC graduate will go on to be a major source of Chinese-spoken labour for Cambodia's labour-intensive light and service industries. The singularity of incoming aid—from multiple countries to just China—has profoundly changed the operative nature and curriculum of Cambodia's ethnic Chinese education system and reflects the improvement and strengthening of relations between China and Cambodia.

The third phase takes place from 2008 to 2020 with the explosive demand for Chinese-speaking labour, skilled administrators and trustworthy interpreters in Cambodia. This is due to China's Outgoing Strategy in 2008 and later the One Belt and One Road (OBOR) Initiative launched in 2013. After more than twenty years of reconstruction, Cambodia's public education system has gradually been restored in most areas, although private education from pre-K to K-12 is still the default choice for families who can afford it. The price of private education ranges from US$120 to US$1,800 per month, while household income grew to US$1,547.51 per capita (World Bank 2020). Privatization of education and its English orientation has become the centre of debate on social equity, nationalism, and cultural crisis in Cambodia (Chansopheak 2009; Brehm and Silova 2014; Heng and

Sol 2021). With the popularity of mobile phones, social media, and digital publications, Cambodia's young elites and baby boomers—those who were born after 1991—are living in a divided trilingual world of information sources in English, daily conversation in Khmer and business in Chinese or Teochew. Socio-economic elites and young urban professionals are used to working in English, socializing in Khmer, and getting rich in Chinese. Trilingualism therefore is considered as the perfect professional background and skillset for the highest paid jobs in Cambodia.

This rationale of pragmatic multiculturalism soon faced a direct impact after the OBOR Initiative was launched in late 2013, as Cambodia is seen as China's most steadfast development partner in the region. Chinese citizens in Cambodia allegedly grew from 12,000 in 2012 to 700,000 in 2019 (Luo and Un 2020, p. 2). The explosive growth rate of the new immigrant population has far exceeded the development of the government's governing and local living capacity. The emotion of dissatisfaction and the wish for economic prosperity has become a new dilemma for Cambodians. Elder ACC leaders who mostly were born before wartime and young elite Chinese descendants who control most professional and industrial organizations such as the Cambodia Chamber of Commerce are fully aware of their awkward position and generational gaps. On the one hand, both their personal wealth and community have gained great benefit from the closed Cambodia-China bilateral relations. On the other hand, many consciously feel the challenges these circumstances present to their Cambodian national identity.

Although China's economic and political influences in Cambodia have dramatically increased in the last ten years, Cambodia's education system and ethnic education have both begun to reflect and review their distance and approach to acquiring and utilizing Chinese resources. According to my field engagement with five memoranda of understanding (MOUs) signed by bilateral universities or educational institutes from 2016 to 2023, recent Cambodian administrators have paid more attention to the practical actions, reciprocal rights and obligations between bilateral cooperation than how the MOU was practised among institutes before 2016. Educators, scholars and administrators still appreciate all possible resources any foreign stakeholders can bring in but also pay great attention to the conditions, backgrounds, and intentions behind all those checks and proposals.

My field trips between 2009–13 and 2014–18 support the changing atmosphere of this cooperation, and the declining enrolment of ACC-affiliated schools has forced ACC leaders to consider a more open and practical approach to redesigning their curriculums. ACC's ageing members and affiliated school staff began to focus on internal development and connection with local enterprises during this period, rather than fostering employees from the school gate to factory gates for Chinese employers. ACC-affiliated schools are now more open to professional skill training and non-Mandarin materials and most ACC organizations established youth factions that use English, Khmer or ethnic dialects, other than Mandarin.

At the same time, the new ACC Chairman, Pung Kheav Se who is also a leading banking tycoon in Cambodia has committed to establishing the "Chinese Cambodian's own university" (柬华日报 2019), referring to the Cambodia University of Technology and Science, or generally called Cam Tech University since 2016. The concept of Cam Tech gradually obtained China's support and was officially established in 2018 along with three additional educational aid projects to support the royal government's plan to open higher education institutes in rural and remote provinces like Kratie, Banteay Meanchey and the Kampong Speu province. These educational aid projects included hardware infrastructures like the campus and building construction and a partial budget for early operation with designated Chinese universities as cooperative partners in school development. Cam Tech's location in the capital and the full support of the local capital are also the reasons why China once considered the necessity of involvement.

Due to the travel restrictions of the pandemic, most Chinese aid teachers and volunteer teachers cannot travel to Cambodia from mid-2020 to early 2023. Hence, the ACC-Teacher Training programme was established in 2021 to deal with the sudden teaching vacancies. Along with the new affiliated University opening in 2018, the current ACC administration consciously creates a more self-sufficient and less dependent operating model for their education programmes. However, some local universities that have tried not to rely on the Confucius Institute (CI) system and attempted to hire and train their own Chinese instructors since 2019 all eventually compromised and embraced the sponsorship. It is then understandable that Cambodia will still need Chinese volunteer teachers and educational aids until the local education system and Cambodian scholarship recipients returning from China can fully self-nurse local Chinese instructors.

To sum up the three phases of ethnic Chinese education in Cambodia, it is fair to say that the first phase of ethnic Chinese education in the kingdom was a big reconstruction project to build from ground zero. Since the 1990s, ethnic Chinese education has played an extremely crucial function in Cambodia since this system has rebuilt rapidly with all available materials from all ways to appease the absence of public education and unaffordable English private education. In the second phase, China's fast-growing investments, aid and trade with Cambodia have profoundly rooted this economic rationality to utilize Chinese language and ethnic education as professional skill training for better income jobs. Cambodia's ethnic Chinese education system developed its aid dependency on Chinese resources to enhance its market competitiveness along with China's growing influence in Cambodia. However, such dependency on China's personnel, funds and materials has reduced in the third phase mainly due to the local government, ethnic Chinese tycoons, and community leaders having grown enough wealth to self-sustain their own path of development, while the royal government of Cambodia has developed better infrastructure and governing capabilities over the years.

Foreign Chinese Education in Cambodia

As mentioned above, the ups and downs of cross-strait competition on the patronage of local ethnic education before 2000 had a great impact on the early development of Cambodia's ethnic Chinese education reconstruction. The contents and methods of these materialistic educational aid sponsorships from cross-straits were still indirect and passive until the local establishment of Phnom Penh's CI in 2009, representing the Chinese state's direct involvement in furthering Chinese culture and language in Cambodia. Under the support of China's National Office for Teaching Chinese as a Foreign Language (国家汉语国际推广领导小组办公室, Hanban 国家汉办), the CI at the Royal Academy of Cambodia (CI-RAC) is the second institute of its kind in the world. Based on the intensive and considerable bilateral communication and full investment of its Chinese partner college, Jiujiang University (九江学院), CI-RAC offered courses for more than 3,000 primary students and seven Confucius Classrooms in seven different public units or higher education institutes in Phnom Penh and Siem Reap from 2012 to 2014 (Chen 2015, pp. 173–74). Unlike ACC-affiliated schools which mostly provide courses in primary education, CI-RCA aims to offer courses for both short and long terms, youths and adults, beginners and advanced levels, all with affordable pricing and various event support.

Therefore, CI-RCA was the leading brand of Mandarin education in Cambodia, even though its suburban location has been the main obstacle to its expansion. Its leading position has since been challenged by the private cram schools that flourished after the Cambodian gold rush driven by the OBOR Initiative. More than 300,000 Chinese citizens and investors swarmed into Cambodia after 2016 due to the initiative (Luo and Un 2020, p. 3). They created a huge demand for Chinese-speaking employees and interpreters, especially when the Chinese capital and business attention started to shift from Phnom Penh and Siem Reap to Sihanoukville, where residents grew ten times in three years (Po and Heng 2019). International criticism against CI since 2013 and the reducing demands of CI sponsorship in universities have also limited CI-RAC's development and challenged CI's operation mode around the world. Therefore, private Mandarin cram schools and many private schools began to offer both Mandarin and Khmer courses. The flexibility and practicality of these after-school/work programmes are more suitable for job seekers who are looking for low-cost, short-term, low-requirement and easy-access courses. The difficulties in the operation of the CI and the call for the reform of all CI's modes of operation have made things different since 2018 (中央深改组 2018). CI-RCA as one of the earliest units of this global layout as well as Cambodia being China's iron friend and development partner, has then played a crucial and exemplary role in exploring CI's new operation mode overseas.

The reform of the CI is almost in sync with the internationalization of China's vocational and technical education, although this was temporarily suspended because of the COVID-19 epidemic. However, Cambodia's CI soon started to bring in further partnerships between Chinese vocational institutes and local colleges, including the Cambodia Wenzhou Polytechnic Yalong Silk Road College (2018) established by the Wenzhou Polytechnic College; the Guilin University of Electronic Technology at the National University of Battambang (2019); and the Nanjing Vocational University of Industry Technology at the newly established Cam Tech University (2022). Instead of CI's state-involved and university-operated operation, the newly established programme, Luban Workshop (鲁班工坊), is of keen interest. The Luban Workshop aims to integrate bilateral education resources and industry needs, paying attention to shifting preferences on both sides. CI's language training with Luban workshops may be the solution for Cambodia's need for labour quality improvement, and China's need to ease its international image and its domestic pressure of the declining birth rate and negative population growth since 2022 have also increased the demands of China's education institutes to explore the overseas market. It can be argued that China's state behaviour and willpower to ameliorate its international image and cultural influence in Cambodia through Mandarin education is not a success due to CI-RCA's limited locations, student capacity and the scale of the project in urban areas. Although their student numbers may be far less than the needs of Cambodia's domestic market and their contribution is incompatible with ACC-affiliated schools in primary education, an authoritative language institution in higher education, CI-RCA provides complete and systematic language training for undergraduate students and professionals in need, particularly for students who look forward to obtaining China's governmental scholarships and studying in China.

Other than state-involved institutes, non-state actors such as private sectors, non-government organizations, religious organizations, private tutors, and training programmes within Chinese state-owned enterprises also play key roles in Cambodia's Mandarin education. This is especially so for construction projects, plantations, and long-term construction sites in remote and isolated areas. Instead of hiring new graduates, most Chinese enterprise owners and aid construction site managers would instead train their staff or "borrow" someone from finishing projects. Graduates from formal Mandarin education programmes can fulfil the basic communication requirements of Cambodia's major industries like hospitality, shopkeeping, reception and tourism. However, experienced employees with on-site corporative training can serve in any managerial position and professional communication workplace. I could always run into Cambodian staff who spoke fluent Mandarin and often switched from site to site, project to project. They are normally ethnic Chinese descendants who later became middlemen capable of subcontracting or collaborating with Chinese enterprises in the following years.

Cambodia's other key foreign-involved Mandarin acquisition approach are non-governmental educational institutes, including those of religious, charitable and social assistance. In the absence of any official space for activities, since 1997, a large number of non-governmental organizations and non-profit organizations in Taiwan have begun to carry out philanthropic activities in Cambodia with financial support from public donations and governmental support in Taiwan, such as the Field Relief Agency of Taiwan (知風草協會), Formosa Budding Hope Association (台灣希望之芽協會), and TEP Culture and Education Association's Cambodia-Taiwan Education Program (德普文教協會). All take Mandarin teaching as a key method for anti-poverty and job skill training for remote villages. I-Kuan Tao had great success because Buddhist monastery education has been a significant part of Cambodian culture (陳春滿 2019; 楊蔚齡 2022). This NGO approach to promoting traditional Chinese education in Cambodia not only provides a non-governmental and depoliticized alternative option that strives for room to manoeuvre Cambodia's adherence to the one-China policy. But it also satisfies the language, religion, ethics, rituals and life philosophy needed for ethnic Chinese identity construction other than traditional Khmer Theravada Buddhism monastery education in rural areas. Overall, there are multiple choices of approaches towards foreign-directed Mandarin education in Cambodia.

Domestic Mandarin Education in Cambodia
The new kingdom's Chinese language education is relatively young compared to the traditional ethnic Chinese education and China's official Chinese education foray into Cambodia. With faculty support from three Yunnan universities, the earliest Chinese language courses given in Cambodia's public schools can be dated back to 2007 in the Royal University of Phnom Penh (RUPP), known as the best university in Cambodia. These language courses soon became a formal MOE-recognized academic department of Chinese Studies in the Institute of Foreign Languages, with three full-time local instructors and two part-time Chinese instructors who are exchange graduate students from China. On the other hand, Asia Euro University, a private college owned by an ethnic Chinese claims to be the first institute that has started to offer Chinese language courses since 2006. My records show that among seventy-eight colleges in Cambodia, only RUPP, Asia Euro University and Life University provided regular and stable Mandarin courses before COVID-19 broke out, and seven institutes offered introductive courses on China Studies, mostly cultural, historical and political courses. Up till 2022, only the Royal Academy of Cambodia and RUPP provided bachelor's and master's degree-awarded programmes in Chinese or China Studies. Asia Euro University, which has the most Chinese language student enrolments in Cambodia, however, only provides a bachelor's degree programme. When comparing the size and significance of ethnic Chinese education in Cambodia, the amount of Mandarin and China Studies courses in Cambodia is relatively underdeveloped. Ethnic Chinese education is still the major channel for Cambodians to access systemized Mandarin acquisition, although most ACC-affiliated schools only provide courses from pre-K to K-6 (only Duanhwa school provides K9 to K10), Mandarin was not an option to any kindergarten-level local public school until 2022. ACC-affiliated schools do supply the basic Mandarin education to cope with the flourishing Chinese capital development. However, the cultivation of professional and academic Chinese talents in Cambodia's higher education is obviously not sufficient to reflect China's economic and political influence in Cambodia, in comparison to mainstream English-oriented higher education.

We can further understand this development gap from Cambodian youth's choices of language acquisition, studying abroad destinations and international scholarships. Despite all kinds of untraceable bilateral governmental or non-governmental training programmes that may have more participants than those of degree-oriented educational programmes,[2] Cambodian students have been awarded governmental scholarships to study higher educational degrees in China since 1995 with the numbers of scholarship recipients remaining limited but stable. According to public records, the Chinese government granted more than 3,000 scholarships for Cambodian students at undergraduate and postgraduate levels in 2020. China's formal Ambassador to Cambodia Wang Wentian stated that the Chinese government has offered 500 scholarships to Cambodian students every year for five consecutive years from 2016 to 2021. Yet, according to the Chinese embassy in Cambodia, the number of scholarships awarded to Cambodian students remained around 181 to 185 between 2017 to 2020. Records from China's Cambodia Embassy summarized that more than 400 Cambodian students were studying in China between 2000 and 2010; the accumulative number went up to 3,000 in 2020, and a total of 625 Cambodian students registered in higher-education level programmes up to the first semester of 2021–22 academic year during the epidemic travel restriction. This is to say, the annual flow roughly grew from 40 students per year in the 2000s, and 260 students per year in the 2010s. My read is that around 69.23 per cent (180 out of 260) students were awarded China's governmental scholarship, while the remaining are self-funded or with other sources. The numbers and ratio of Cambodian students studying in China with and without scholarships are in line with the Chinese Ministry of Education's record of the total number and ratio of international students studying in China. At the same time, the number of Cambodian students studying in Taiwan grew from eight students in 2016 to sixty-eight students in 2021.[3]

Chinese governmental scholarships require certified Mandarin skills like the score on the Chinese proficiency test (*Hanyu Shuiping Kaoshi*, HSK), which is not common and not compulsory in senior high school or most college curricula in Cambodia. Needless to mention, applicants who pass the language test soon find that there are not many English-teaching programmes and teachers in China to assist them in completing their undergraduate or junior postgraduate education. Not only that, but they may also lose their governmental scholarships in the middle of the degree and are only limited to extending their further education in China. This is why, even though the Chinese government does provide more scholarships than real applicants, both the quality and quantity of prospective students are lower than expected.

During Premier Li Keqiang's state visit to Cambodia in January 2018, the bilateral governments agreed to collaborate on vocational education and professional training programmes to support the construction of Cambodia's vocational and technical education in K9–K12 levels and above. Wenzhou Polytechnic College and Yalong Intelligent Equipment Group collaborated to establish the first Chinese vocational school in Phnom Penh, Cambodia Wenzhou Polytechnic Yalong Silk Road College in July 2018. Directed by the Yalong group, this school-industry collaboration opened two more new Silk Road Colleges with Chongqing Industry and Trade Polytechnic and Liaoning Mechatronics in 2019. Many vocational schools are eager to establish branch joint units in Cambodia; hence, a national federation of China-Cambodia Vocational Education Alliance was founded in 2019 to coordinate this cross-national education cooperation. Up to 2022, thirty-six MOUs have been signed by bilateral Chinese vocational institutes and Cambodia's provincial institutes. On 11 November 2022, after the ASEAN Annual Leader Summit in Phnom Penh, bilateral governments announced that Mandarin would be included in Cambodia's public education curriculum. As language is a key barrier for both sides, Khmer major students and programmes in China have correspondingly increased since 2021, while Mandarin will be introduced at the middle level of public education in Cambodia.

Mandarin will become one of four foreign languages, alongside English, French and Korean that are taught in Cambodia's public education curriculum while many predict Mandarin will soon spread and make a direct impact on Cambodian society. The concern is on the possibility and the duration required for Mandarin to challenge English as the predominant language among the Cambodian elite and urban professionals. It is doubtful that Chinese education can challenge the current Khmer-English dual system, especially with Cambodia's dual currency system (US dollar and Cambodian riel) Indeed, foreign language education in Cambodia is not new. There were French before wartime, and Russian and Vietnamese under Vietnamese occupation. As comparative linguist Kimmo Kosonen and education expert Thomas Clayton addressed, Cambodia's open and hybrid system to adapt foreign languages and materials in Cambodia's education system has shaped its young generation's bilingual mentality of work in English and life in Khmer. Will Brehm further argued that the bottom-up privatization approach in Cambodia's education (Brehm 2021, pp. 9–10) has changed every student's everyday life to an extent of economic rationality, "everything is—or can be—for sale". In this regard, if English predomination is a natural result of globalization and internationalization for any small market and weak state, adding one more alternative language choice in reflecting the reality of changing geopolitical order and domestic economic structure to empower citizens' professional skills and career options seems rational and practical.

Conclusion

This is a new narrative on the development of Chinese education over three periods based on the author's field works and currently available literature stressing the availability of written sources. Through assessing the three facets of Chinese education in Cambodia—ethnic Chinese education, foreign Chinese education and domestic Chinese education, this paper tracks the development of Chinese education alongside the progress of the Cambodian state.

In the early days of ethnic Chinese education, materials were sought from many countries through foreign aid as the demand for Chinese education was high. The countries from which Cambodia sought foreign aid to bolster Chinese education eventually consolidated into one country—China. However, ethnic Chinese education was limited to external courses for youths and did not offer further Chinese education beyond primary school, with one exception that offered courses till secondary school. Therefore, ethnic Chinese education remains limited.

China's relationship with Cambodia strengthened over the years, and eventually gave rise to the entry of foreign Chinese education, where China introduced CIs through *Hanban* in Cambodia. This saw positive demand, as these institutes not only offered courses for the primary level but also for adults who sought to improve their Mandarin for economic opportunities. Other forms of foreign Chinese education include independent training from Chinese companies working in remote regions and Taiwan's non-profit organizations offering Chinese education under Buddhist monastery education.

The final facet saw Cambodia building up their domestic Chinese education with the aid of Chinese universities. Chinese became part of the public school curriculum, alongside Khmer, English and French. However, even with the increase in scholarships to China, the number of students that head to China for higher learning remains low. Hence, through examining the three facets of Chinese education in Cambodia, it is evident that the demand for Chinese education in Cambodia is not only dependent on the economic opportunities generated through close Cambodian-Chinese ties but also on the limitations that this relationship presents to Cambodians.

Notes

1. AP News, "Last of Khmer Rouge Surrenders", https://apnews.com/article/8f2215595183d49de73c196803ad0523 (accessed 4 August 2022).
2. Before COVID, these training programmes/projects organized by State-owned enterprises, various levels of governmental organizations, and educational institutes may have more students and delegates than regular degree-oriented study abroad programmes between China and Cambodia. However, such short-term and technological/operational training programmes have not been studied/researched systemically. So related information and situations are not recorded or traceable as another kind of educational communication between two countries.
3. 中华民国教育部統計處.全臺灣大專校院境外學生人數統計2014–2021.https://data.gov.tw/dataset/6289 (accessed 3 October 2022).

References

Brehm, W. 2021. *Cambodia for Sale: Everyday Privatization in Education and Beyond*. Routledge.
Brehm, William C., and Iveta Silova. 2014. "Hidden Privatization of Public Education in Cambodia: Equity Implications of Private Tutoring". *Journal for Educational Research Online* 6, no. 1: 94–116.
Baumann, Peter, and Gisela Cramer. 2017. "Power, Soft or Deep? An Attempt at Constructive Criticism". *Las Torres de Lucca: Revista Internacional de Filosofía Política* 6, no. 10: 177–214.
Burgos, Sigfrido, and Sophal Ear. 2010. "China's Strategic Interests in Cambodia: Influence and Resources". *Asian Survey* 50, no. 3: 615–39.
Chansopheak, Keng. 2009. "Basic Education in Cambodia: Quality and Equity". In *The Political Economy of Educational Reforms and Capacity Development in Southeast Asia*, edited by Yasushi Hirosato and Yuto Kitamura, pp. 131–52. Springer Dordrecht.
Chen, Shihlun Allen. 2015. "Socializing Chineseness: Cambodia's Ethnic Chinese Communities as a Method". PhD dissertation, University of Hawai'i at Manoa.
———. 2018. "The Development of Cambodia-China Relation and Its Transition Under the OBOR Initiative". *The Chinese Economy* 51, no. 4: 370–82.
Heng, Kimkong, and Koemhong Sol. 2021. "Academic Research in Cambodia: Progress, Challenges, and Ways Forward". *Cambodian Journal of Educational Research* 1, no. 2: 6–23.
Hsiao, Hsin-Huang Michael, and Alan Hao Yang. 2014. "Differentiating the Politics of Dependency: Confucius Institutes in Cambodia and Myanmar". *Issues and Studies* 50, no. 4.

Luo, Jing Jing, and Kheung Un. 2020. "Cambodia: Hard Landing for China's Soft Power?". *ISEAS Perspective* 2020/111, 6 October 2020.

Mathews, Gordon. 2019. "China in the World: An Anthropology of Confucius Institutes Soft Power and Globalization". *Asian Anthropology* 20: 290–92.

Nye Jr., Joseph S. 2008. "Public Diplomacy and Soft Power". *Annals of the American Academy of Political and Social Science* 616, no. 1: 94–109.

Po, Sovinda. 2017. "The Limits of China's Influence in Cambodia: A Soft Power Perspective". *University of Cambodia Occasional Paper Series* 1, no. 2: 61–75.

———, and Heng Kimkong. 2019. "Assessing the Impacts of Chinese Investments in Cambodia: The Case of Preah Sihanoukville Province". *Pacific Forum Issues & Insights* 19: 1–19.

Wojciuk, Anna, Maciej Michałek, and Marta Stormowska. 2015. "Education as a Source and Tool of Soft Power in International Relations". *European Political Science* 14: 298–317.

World Bank Group. 2020. *Cambodia Economic Update*. World Bank Group.

Zhou, Daguan. 2007. *A Record of Cambodia: The Land and its People*. Chiang Mai: Silkworm Books.

Zhu, Kejin, and Rui Yang. 2022. "Emerging Resources of China's Soft Power: A Case Study of Cambodian Participants from Chinese Higher Education Programs". *Higher Education Policy* 1–23.

陳春滿. 2019. "一貫道傳播模式研究: 以寶光建德柬埔寨道場為例". 碩士論文, 一貫道天皇學院一貫道學研究所.

林志忠. 2008. "近百年來柬埔寨華校教育發展之探討". 臺灣東南亞學刊 5, no. 2: 3–34.

林志忠. 2012. "柬埔寨高等教育市場化改革之評析". 教育科學期刊 11, no. 2: 1–21.

劉芯吟. 2015. "一貫道發一崇德宗教傳播與華語文教學之結合–以柬埔寨金邊師德佛堂為例". 碩士論文, 國立臺灣師範大學應用華語文學系.

罗杨. 2021. "华性的历史层累与结构重写, 柬埔寨华文教育的人类学考察". 南洋問題研究 1: 101–12.

楊蔚齡. 2022. "柬埔寨僧院之教育扶貧及社會參與". 博士論文, 國立暨南國際大學東南亞學系.

野泽知弘, 乔云. 2012. "柬埔寨的华人社会—华文教育的复兴与发展". 南洋资料译丛 3: 66–80.

柬华日报. 2019. "柬华理事总会召开2019年会员代表大会". 11 March 2019 https://jianhuadaily.com/20190311/47535 (accessed 25 April 2023).

中央深改组. 2018. "教育部对十三届全国人大一次会议第1825号建议的答复". 关于推进孔子学院改革发展的指导意. http://www.moe.gov.cn/jyb_xxgk/xxgk_jyta/jyta_xwb/201812/t20181221_364339.html. (accessed 25 April 2023).

Part III

CHINA'S SOFT POWER AND EDUCATION IN MARITIME SOUTHEAST ASIA

8

CHINA'S EDUCATIONAL SOFT POWER
A View from Malaysia

Ngeow Chow Bing and Fan Pik Shy

INTRODUCTION

Ever since the concept of "soft power" has become a popular term in international relations, scholars, government officials, and think-tank analysts have devoted a considerable amount of energy to researching and analysing what constitutes soft power in its various dimensions and manifestations, such as popular culture, media, scientific achievements, language, and of course, education. Education, in particular higher education, is an effective "soft power" resource (Wojciuk, Michalek, and Stormowska 2015), but only if countries are blessed with a well-developed higher education sector and able to utilize it well. The United States is a prime example in this regard. The massive appeal of its excellent universities and colleges adds substantially to the prestige and soft power of the United States.

China is aware that its higher education sector can also be harnessed for "soft power" purposes. Beijing has invested a tremendous amount of resources into its elite universities in an effort to make them on par with the best in the world, while at the same time also providing a large amount of scholarship or other forms of financial assistance to attract students from all over the world to study in China. In addition, the Chinese government has also invested in many short-term training programmes for foreign participants, which are also a kind of exercise in educational soft power. The most notable governmental exercise of "soft power" by China, the Confucius Institute project, also involves collaboration between China's universities and the hosting institutions in other countries. Although not directed by Beijing, more and more of China's universities are also bringing the brand of Chinese education physically abroad in the form of an international branch campus or what is termed as *jingwai banxue* (境外办学), which has soft power implications as well (He and Wilkin 2019; Ngeow 2022).

This paper examines China's educational soft power as it pertains to Malaysia. In particular, it explores such questions as who are the "China-educated Malaysians", how large is this group of people, what fields of knowledge China offers that attract Malaysian students to study there, how influential are the China-educated Malaysians in Malaysian society and in what way, and how they perceive China. Here, the notion of China-educated Malaysians is a broad one, including those who have received China-provided education within Malaysia. Hence, broadly speaking, China-educated Malaysians can be grouped into the following categories: (1) Malaysian students receiving university education in China; (2) Malaysians undertaking short-term course participation in China; (3) Malaysians receiving basic language training within Malaysia (Confucius Institutes); (4) Malaysian students receiving China's university education within Malaysia (Xiamen University Malaysia).[1] The source materials of this chapter include news articles, government reports, reports or commemorative volumes of relevant organizations, and interviews (both focus group and individual interviews).

University Education in China

China has emerged as a major choice for Malaysian students since the late 2000s. In 2009 and 2011, the Malaysian and Chinese governments signed two memoranda of agreement (MOUs) on higher education cooperation respectively. The latter MOU, in particular, established the basis for mutual recognition of each country's legitimate higher education degrees, paving the way for greater acceptance of the validity of China's degrees by the Malaysian public sector.

Table 8.1 presents data on the number of Malaysian students studying in China's universities in recent years. There are discrepancies between the data provided by Malaysia's Ministry of Higher Education and China's Ministry of Education (in some years the numbers provided by both countries differ by a wide margin, and in other cases, the numbers match but appear in different years). Overall, the data provided by China seem to be more reliable and realistic, as the data indicate a consistent pattern of steady growth since the mid-2000s, while the wide fluctuations as shown in Malaysia's data (for example, between the years 2011 and 2012, 2015 and 2016, 2018 and 2019) suggest that the data may not be very accurate.

TABLE 8.1
Malaysian Students Studying in China's Universities

Year	Statistics from Malaysia			Statistics from China
	Sponsored	Self-sponsored	Total	
1999	—	—	—	454
2000	—	—	—	490
2001	—	—	—	632
2002	—	—	—	840
2003	—	—	—	841
2004	—	—	—	1,241
2005	—	—	—	1,589
2006	—	—	—	1,743
2007	—	—	—	1,908
2008	28	1,715	1,743	2,114
2009	—	—	2,114	2,792
2010	119	2,673	2,792	3,885
2011	—	—	2,252	4,259
2012	245	544	789	6,045
2013	389	543	932	6,126
2014	254	210	464	6,645
2015	490	324	814	6,650
2016	420	6,230	6,650	6,880
2017	614	6,266	6,880	7,948
2018	623	7,325	7,948	9,479
2019	922	1,310	2,232	9,500
2020	3,820	953	4,773	—
2021	—	—	11,920	—
2022	187	5,854	6,041	

Sources: For Malaysian statistics, the annual volumes of *Statistik Pendidikan Tinggi*, available at: https://www.mohe.gov.my/muat-turun/statistik; for Chinese statistics, compiled from various sources including China's Ministry of Education and China Association for International Education.

The Malaysian data, however, interestingly display two categories: "sponsored" and "self-sponsored". There is no definition of the "sponsored" category in any of the annual volumes of *Statistik Pendidikan Tinggi* (*Higher Education Statistics*). Presumably, this category primarily includes governmental (including the government, government-owned companies, and public universities) sponsorships, but could also include private sector sponsorships that have been reported to the Ministry of Higher Education.

Regardless, this indicates how much the Malaysian public (and possibly also the private) sector, which often prioritizes sponsoring scholarships at Western or Japanese universities, has now been increasingly willing to finance Malaysian students to undertake higher education in China. It underscores the growing recognition of China as an emerging power and the rising standard of China's universities.

However, the accuracy of Malaysian governmental data on the "non-sponsored" category is highly questionable. It is reasonable to assume that this category predominantly comprises students from the Chinese-educated ethnic Chinese Malaysian community. Malaysia is a multi-ethnic country with a sizeable ethnic Chinese population (22.4 per cent according to the latest census, which equates to roughly 7.4 million people). For decades, this ethnic Chinese community has preserved its own Chinese education system, which encompasses Chinese schools from primary to tertiary levels. The entire system is usually referred to as *huajiao* (华教) in Malaysia, built and run independently by the ethnic Chinese community of Malaysia (the Malaysian government does include the primary level as part of the national education system). Hence, there are many ethnic Chinese Malaysians who are Chinese-educated and natural Chinese speakers. In the 1980s and 1990s, Taiwan was the preferred destination for Chinese-educated Malaysians intending to pursue Chinese-language higher education, until the option of studying in mainland Chinese universities became viable in the late 1990s.[2]

Roughly speaking, the Malaysian students who are under the "sponsored" category generally—but not exclusively—come from a non-Chinese-educated background, in contrast to the students under the 'non-sponsored' category which overwhelmingly consist of the Chinese-educated ethnic Chinese Malaysians. Hence, among the Malaysian students receiving higher education in China, there is a clear distinction between two different streams or circles (see Table 8.2).

The non-Chinese-educated circle comprises mainly ethnic Malays and is small in numbers compared to the Chinese-educated one. They are mostly funded under the programmes initiated by the Malaysian government. There are two notable government programmes managed by the Ministry of Education called "Program Penghantaran Pelajar Cemerlang ke Universiti Terkemuka Luar Negara (PRC)" (Programme of Sending Excellent Students to Leading Universities Abroad [PRC]) and "Program Penghantaran Pelajar ke China untuk Pembelajaran Bahasa Mandarin dalam Kalangan Pentutur Jati ke Arah 1 Malaysia" (Program of Sending Students to China to Learn Mandarin Among Native Speakers Towards 1Malaysia), initiated in 2007

TABLE 8.2
Non-Chinese-Educated and Chinese-Educated Malaysian Students Studying in China

	Non-Chinese Educated	Chinese-Educated
Financing	• Public and private sector sponsorship.	• Self-sponsorship; • Community sponsorship.
Size	• Small, a few hundred at most.	• Large, at least in the thousands.
Ethnicity	• Mostly Malays.	• Overwhelmingly ethnic Chinese (Chinese-educated and Chinese-speaking).
Fields of Study	• Basic Chinese language training; • Teaching Chinese to Speakers of Other Languages (TCSOL); • Economics and business-related.	• Diverse fields; • Popular majors: Chinese Studies/Chinese Literature (中文系), Journalism, Business, Engineering, International Relations, Natural Sciences, Medicine.
Universities	• Mostly concentrated in these universities: Beijing Foreign Studies University (BFSU) and Beijing Language and Culture University (BLCU).	• More diverse and in different cities: Beijing, Shanghai, Guangzhou, Xiamen, Hangzhou, etc.
Social Organization and Connections	• Informal connections and circles among graduates of BFSU and BLCU; • Limited social impacts.	• Associations of Graduates from Universities and Colleges in China, Malaysia; • Various alumni organizations (Jinan, Peking, Tsinghua, Huaqiao, Xiamen, Fudan, Zhejiang, etc.); • Vibrant participation in community affairs as Chinese community organizations; • Alumni bodies' continuous engagement with the Chinese government's "overseas Chinese affairs system" (侨务系统).
Career prospects	• Mostly public sector; • Government schools; • Chinese language teaching centres.	• Mostly private sector; • Chinese schools.

and 2009 respectively. In addition, the government-linked Yayasan Pelajaran MARA (MARA Education Foundation) also began to sponsor and dispatch Malay students to China in 2008. Before these programmes were initiated, the likelihood of Malay students studying in China was very rare.

Under these programmes, students mostly study at Beijing Foreign Studies University (BFSU) and, since 2011, also at Beijing Language and Culture University (BLCU). At BFSU, from 2007 to 2021, a total of 422 students were enrolled on these programmes, with 396 of them having graduated with a bachelor's degree (Wang 2022, pp. 8-9). These programmes are meant for non-Chinese-educated students to learn the Chinese language as a second language and also to specialize in an academic major known as "Teaching Chinese to Speakers of Other Languages" (TCSOL, *guoji zhongwen jiaoyu* 国际中文教育).[3] The goal is to train Chinese language teachers to serve in Malaysia's national primary and secondary schools (but not the Chinese language schools of Malaysia). Some of these students also undertake advanced training (master's or even doctoral training in the TCSOL discipline). The students with postgraduate TCSOL degrees will often come back to teach at public universities, in particular Universiti Teknologi Mara, the premier higher education institution reserved for the Malay ethnic group.

Not all Malay graduates who have completed their TCSOL studies in China will pursue their careers in government institutions. Some of them are more inclined towards entrepreneurship and establish Chinese language teaching businesses that target non-native Chinese speakers in Malaysia as their main prospective clientele.[4] Despite the multilingual/multicultural environment in Malaysia with many Chinese schools, it is very difficult for non-native Chinese speakers to learn Chinese, because the Chinese schools in Malaysia only cater for native speakers. Here, the TCSOL-trained graduates fulfil a critical niche market. The emergence and apparent popularity of the Chinese language teaching businesses testify to the positive impacts of these China-trained Malays in spreading Chinese language education among non-Chinese-speaking communities in Malaysia.

In addition, not all Malays studying in China focus on learning the Chinese language or majoring in TCSOL only. Some of them are able to learn the Chinese language at the undergraduate level and then pursue postgraduate studies in natural sciences, social sciences, or business studies in China.

Generally speaking, these Malay students who have studied in China tend to maintain a positive view of China. In a Zoom focus group interview with five former/current students at BLCU, students/graduates noted how the importance and prominence of the Chinese language has grown alongside China's rise.[5] Proficiency in the Chinese language has become an essential skill for graduates seeking employment at China's enterprises investing in Malaysia and other places. One student's comment encapsulated the prevalent sentiment regarding the utility of learning Chinese: "As more Chinese enterprises investing (*sic*) in Malaysia, our employees need to be equipped with the Chinese language. In the past it was English, but now learning Chinese is important." Some also appreciated the Chinese language as a window to understanding Chinese culture better. A master's student at BLCU highlighted the significance of studying the Chinese language in the context of domestic ethnic relations, whereby he felt that by learning the Chinese language and culture, more Malays will appreciate the culture of their fellow ethnic Malaysian Chinese citizens and can improve national harmony.

The size of this circle of Malay students, while growing, remains relatively small. Currently, there are only loose and informal connections among the graduates and alumni. For instance, the BFSU alumni association exists informally, not as a registered body, but through a WhatsApp chat group. The lack of a formal organization has limited the social impact of these China-educated Malay students. Moreover, after their return to Malaysia, most of these students tend to revert to predominantly Malay-speaking social circles and environments, reducing their chances of using the Chinese language. As expressed by some students in the focus group interview, they are concerned that their Chinese language capabilities could stagnate or even decline, notwithstanding their positions as teachers of Chinese language to non-native speakers.[6]

The Chinese-educated circle, as mentioned, is overwhelmingly ethnic Chinese. They are mostly self-funded or funded by the community such as clan associations. Due to their natural Chinese language ability, many of these students are exempted from taking the Chinese language standard test in the admission process in China's universities.[7] Since the learning of the Chinese language is unnecessary, the fields of study pursued by Chinese-educated Malaysians are much more varied. While Chinese Studies/Chinese Literature (中文系) has always been popular, many Chinese-educated Malaysian students study social sciences, natural sciences, journalism, business, engineering and even medicine in China. Unlike the non-Chinese-educated circle, many of the graduates in the Chinese-educated circle end up working in the private sector.

Another notable and important aspect of this circle is its active alumni network. There are several alumni organizations formed among the graduates of various China's universities (Peking, Xiamen, Fudan, Jinan, etc.), and there is also the umbrella organization known as the Associations of Graduates from Universities and Colleges in China, Malaysia (马来西亚留华同学会, commonly known as *Liu Hua* 留华).[8] *Liu Hua*, in particular, has emerged as a lively and important Chinese community organization (*huatuan* 华团) in Malaysia.

Liu Hua is actively involved in Chinese community affairs in Malaysia, especially those pertaining to Chinese education (*huajiao* 华教) issues. In fact, in the introductory forward to *A Special Commemorative Volume of Ten Years of Associations of Graduates from Universities and Colleges in China, Malaysia, 2005–2015*, the founding president of *Liu Hua* regarded *Liu Hua* as a Malaysian civil society organization, ready to participate in and contribute to the debate of national public policy issues, in particular on issues related to education and ethnic relations (*Malaixiya Liuhua Tongxuehui* 2015, p. 24). On the other hand, *Liu Hua* has played a major role in maintaining and advancing people-to-people ties between China and Malaysia. It is the main organizer of the "China Winter Camp" (*donglingying* 冬令营) activity, which brings thousands of ethnic Chinese youth in Malaysia to visit China, especially their ancestral hometowns. *Liu Hua* actively promotes universities in China to Chinese-educated Malaysians and is one of the most active organizations lobbying for the recognition of Chinese university degrees by the Malaysian government. It also plays a role in connecting the Malaysian educational sector to its Chinese counterparts, for example, by organizing field trips for Malaysia's education officials, school officials (headmasters) and school board members to China for educational exchanges and collaboration. Several teachers' training programmes are also conducted under the coordinating role of *Liu Hua*. Moreover, *Liu Hua* maintains a productive working relationship with the Overseas Chinese affairs organizations of China, including the State Council's Overseas Chinese Affairs Office, the provincial Overseas Chinese Affairs offices, and the Zhigong Party. It collaborates with these entities in educational, cultural and youth activities.[9]

Among the various university alumni organizations, the Peking University Alumni Association of Malaysia (founded in 2013) has been one of the most vigorous ones. Through its efforts it has brought many well-known professors of Peking University, such as Justin Lin Yifu, to provide public lectures in Malaysia. Before the pandemic, it collaborated with the International Islamic University of Malaysia in organizing the Confucian-Islamic Youth Civilization Forum. The forum was first held in Shandong in 2016, followed by the second forum in 2019 in Kuala

Lumpur, notably with the attendance by the Timbalan Yang di-Pertuan Agong (Deputy Supreme Head of Malaysia) Sultan Nazrin Shah of Perak. Due to the outstanding work of the Peking University Alumni Association of Malaysia, its president was awarded the Distinguished Alumnus Award by Peking University in 2017 and elected as a committee member of its global alumni association.[10]

Like their Malay student counterparts, students within this circle also generally have positive views of China, although some do notice the tightening political control in recent years with discomfort and aversion.[11] With a much larger size and various alumni organizations, the social impact of this circle of China-educated Malaysians is considerably much stronger compared to the above-mentioned circle of China-educated Malays. Interactions between these two circles, however, appear to be limited. While both circles have opportunities to engage each other in Beijing, once they return to Malaysia, the interactions and engagements seem to slow down, with both circles primarily reverting to their respective communities. Nevertheless, there are signs of more engagement between the two circles.[12]

SHORT-TERM TRAINING COURSES IN CHINA

In addition to the formal multi-year higher education, various entities in China also encourage and provide funding and opportunities for Malaysians to undergo short-term training. These courses last from either a few weeks to a few months, in China's universities or other training institutions, and the subjects range from technical field and engineering to language training and even political governance.[13] Due to their diverse and decentralized nature, there is no known total tally for all these training programmes that Malaysians participate in.

As an example, a particular training programme is highlighted here. Before the pandemic, the Capital Normal University (CNU) hosted a Chinese language teaching training programme for Chinese school teachers in Malaysia. Since 2007, 290 teachers from Malaysia's Chinese primary and secondary schools have undergone this training programme, all fully funded by China. See Table 8.3.

In a focus group interview with several former course participants in this programme, all expressed overwhelmingly positive impressions of China.[14] Despite their relatively short time in China, they were deeply impressed by the convenience and technological progress they witnessed in Beijing. They also appreciated the pedagogical methodology and

TABLE 8.3
Short-Term Training Course at Capital Normal University, Beijing

	Year	Organizers	Traning Period	Number of Course Participants
1.	2007	China Embassy in Kuala Lumpur, Office of Chinese Language Council International (Hanban), and Ministry of Higher Education of Malaysia	16 May – 15 June 2007	34
2.	2011	Beijing Center for International Chinese Education (BCICE), Beijing Teachers Training Center for Higher Education (BTTCHE), Center for International Education, Capital Normal University (CIE), Institute of China Studies (ICS), UM	22 May– 18 June 2011	40
3.	2012	Hanban, Ministry of Higher Education of Malaysia, ICS	23–29 September 2012	51
4	2013	Beijing International Education Exchange Center (BIEE), Malaysian Chinese Research Centre, UM	5–24 August 2013	35
5.	2014	BIEE, BHSTTC, CIE, ICS	7–21 July 2014	22
6.	2015	BIEE, ICS	21 November – 2 December 2015	31
7.	2015	BIEE, ICS	14–24 December 2015	28
8.	2016	BIEE, CIE, ICS, Persatuan Kebajikan Guru-Guru Bahasa Cina Sekolah Menengah Selangor (Selangor Chinese Language Secondary School Teachers Association)	13–26 December 2016	29
9.	2019	BIEE, CIE, ICS, Persatuan Kebajikan Guru-Guru Bahasa Cina Sekolah Menengah Selangor	19–31 December 2019	20

Source: Dr Fan Pik Shy as she was directly involved in this programme.

techniques taught by the CNU faculty. These participants were already Chinese-language teachers trained within Malaysia's very own Chinese education (*huajiao*) system. However, their time in China exposed them to China's latest Chinese-language pedagogy and technology, which were backed by vast resources from both the state and society in China. They were also brought to visit certain successful teaching sites in China, while being allowed free time and even paid some small stipends to experience the city on their own. A former course participant described the experience as "broadening the horizon".[15]

Short-term training programmes like these prove to be very useful for China's soft power. Compared to the conventional academic scholarships that usually cover tuition fees and stipends that last for several years, sponsoring foreign course participants in short-term training programmes is less costly and China is able to organize these programmes more often. Mid-career individuals make up the majority of the course participants in these short-term programmes, as they are not able to undertake extended leaves to pursue conventional higher education in China. Therefore, sponsoring such short-term programmes allows China to extend its educational outreach beyond the university-age youth cohorts. The relatively short duration of these programmes enables participants to immerse themselves in China for an extended period that goes beyond a short tourist visit, yet long enough to form lasting and potentially positive impressions of the country, contributing to China's soft power efforts on an international level.

Confucius Institutes in Malaysia

The Confucius Institute (CI) is the most famous "soft power" project of China. The CIs are embedded within partnering universities of the host countries, together with the matching partnering universities from China. The placement of the CIs within hosting universities has raised a lot of objections from certain Western countries on the grounds of academic freedom. However, no such controversies have erupted in Malaysia. As of today, six CIs have been established in Malaysia (Table 8.4).

Among these CIs, the oldest and best-developed is the Kong Zi Institute at the University of Malaya (KZIUM). Established in 2009 with a first batch of 300 students enrolled in 2010, by 2021, the student body had grown to 14,221 (see Figure 8.1).

What is notable about KZIUM is that it has teaching sites all over Malaysia (see Table 8.5), essentially making itself an equivalent to several functional CIs. All these teaching sites are hosted within other public universities or, in some cases, secondary national schools, with the number of students in these sites ranging in the hundreds and sometimes thousands. Many of these teaching sites are also located in relatively rural or remote areas outside of the Kuala Lumpur metropolitan region, inside some public universities that otherwise have very little formal engagement with China's universities or bodies. The presence of KZIUM teaching sites in these

TABLE 8.4
Confucius Institutes in Malaysia

Confucius Institute	Year	Partnering Institution from China	Official Website/Social Media	Number of Students
Kong Zi Institute University of Malaya	2009	Beijing Foreign Studies University	http://www.kongzium.edu.my/; https://www.facebook.com/KZIUM/	In 2021, students totalled 14,221.
Confucius Institute SEGi University	2015	Hainan Normal University	https://university.segi.edu.my/?page_id=18172; https://www.facebook.com/Segiconfucius/	Each year: 250–630[a]
Confucius Institute Universiti Malaysia Pahang	2011/2018	Hebei University	https://ci.ump.edu.my/index.php/en/; https://www.facebook.com/Confucius-Institute-100623258174139/	Around 1,600 students annually registered in both credit and non-credit courses.[b]
Confucius Institute Universiti Malaysia Sabah (UMS)	2019	Changsha University of Technology	https://www.ums.edu.my/ci/; https://www.facebook.com/profile.php?id=100064972362454	Between 2020 and 2023, a total of 482 students enrolled in various programmes of the CI at UMS.[c]
Confucius Institute University College of Technology Sarawak	2020	North China University of Water Conservancy and Electric Power	https://confuciusinstitute.uts.edu.my/about-us/	N.A.
Confucius Institute at Shen Jai Education Group	2022	Xidian University	https://ci.shenjai.edu.my/newsite/?page_id=8	N.A.

Notes:
a. The website of the CI of SEGi University once provided the figure of 250 annually (http://cisegi.my.chinesecio.com/zh-hans/node/1688) but the particular webpage has since been removed. A former staff member of this Confucius Institute revealed to the authors that in 2022, about 630 students registered. Among them, about half were SEGi University students, and the rest came from the public. Interview with a former staff member of the CI of SEGi University, 29 December 2022.
b. A former PhD student under one of the authors' supervision who had done fieldwork at Universiti Malaysia Pahang (UMP) provided this number. Before 2018, UMP and Hebei University had already collaborated on a Chinese language teaching centre as the predecessor of the CI; the centre reportedly graduated over 12,000 students (Yang 2019).
c. Data supplied by the CI of UMS, 19 January 2024.

CHINA'S EDUCATIONAL SOFT POWER

FIGURE 8.1
Annual Numbers of Total Registered Students at Kong Zi Institutes

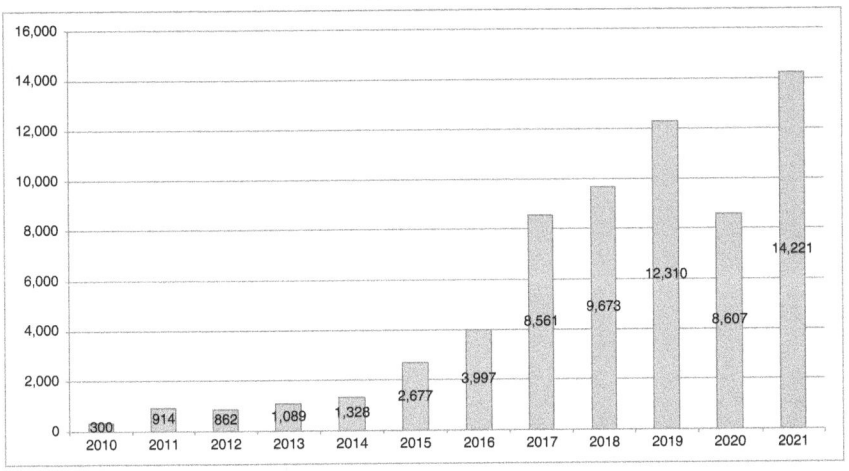

Source: *Annual Report of Kong Zi Institute 2018*, *Annual Report of Kong Zi Institute 2019* and through personal contacts with Kong Zi Institute.

remote places provided the opportunities for KZIUM to link up China's universities with the institutions hosting these teaching sites, therefore, in a way, increasing the connection, collaboration, and impacts of China's soft power in the more remote regions in Malaysia.[16]

Within KZIUM headquarters at the University of Malaya, another notable aspect was that it has been providing several specialized courses for Malaysian government bodies. As disclosed in the *Annual Report of Kong Zi Institute 2018* and *Annual Report of Kong Zi Institute 2019*, within these two years, the Kong Zi Institute provided Chinese language training to selected officials of the Ministry of Home Affairs, the Royal Malaysian Police, and the Immigration Department. These courses are designed in a different and specialized way to cater to the professional needs of these agencies and are different from the standard curricula that follow the *Hanyu Shuiping Kaoshi* (HSK) standard and the TCSOL teaching structure.

The vast majority of students at KZIUM, including both the headquarters and teaching sites, however, are university students who follow the standard HSK learning process. Most of them had only completed HSK1 or HSK2 levels (a basic requirement of entry into China's universities for foreign students is HSK5). As acknowledged by a former director of KZIUM, many students who underwent Chinese language training at KZIUM expressed a desire to continue learning about the Chinese language and culture.

TABLE 8.5
Various Programmes of Kong Zi Institute 2018–19

University/School/Teaching Site	Programmes	Level	Number of Students (2018)	Number of Students (2019)
Kuala Lumpur				
• Headquarters: Kong Zi Institute, University of Malaya	Comprehensive Course	HSK 1-6	254	245
	Faculty of Language and Linguistics, UM	HSK 1	119	—
	Faculty of Arts and Social Sciences, UM	HSK 1-2	20	6
	Specialized Course: Control and Enforcement Division, Ministry of Home Affairs	HSK 3-4	8	—
	Specialized Course: Shearn Delamore & Core	Legal Chinese	11	—
	Specialized Course: Royal Malaysian Police	Tailor-made	—	40
	Specialized Course: Immigration Department of Malaysia	Tailor-made	—	40
	Specialized Course: PETRONAS	Intensive Mandarin	—	5
Universiti Pertahanan Nasional Malaysia			326	361
Universiti Teknologi Mara (inclusive of Selangor, Pahang, Terengganu, Perak, Kedah, Kelantan, Melaka, Sabah and Perlis campuses)			4,308	6,191
Universiti Utara Malaysia			2,547	2,572
Kolej Universiti Islam Melaka			208	276

Universiti Tun Hussein Onn	300
Universiti Teknologi Malaysia	369
Universiti Sultan Zainal Abidin	204
Universiti Malaysia Kelantan	116
Universiti Malaysia Perlis	182
Politeknik Nilai	—
Sri Awaf Primary School	77
Matrix Global Schools	29
Kolej Yayasan Saad Melaka	480
Sekolah Menengah Imtiaz Ulul Albab	126
Total	9,673

	224
	334
	463
	276
	336
	80
	224
	—
	490
	147
	12,310

Source: *Annual Report of Kong Zi Institute 2018, Annual Report of Kong Zi Institute 2019.*

Nevertheless, in practice, after completing the programme, they encountered limited opportunities to continue practising the language. Consequently, very few students of KZIUM have chosen to continue to study in China, and those who have done so were mostly offered scholarships.[17]

In 2019, KZIUM organized a career fair in collaboration with China's enterprises investing in Malaysia. One of KZIUM's primary objectives is to engage more with the industry, to create a "Chinese language +" structure, where students can be readily hired by China's enterprises or enable employees of these enterprises to receive basic Chinese language training at KZIUM. In this regard, the CI at Universiti Malaysia Pahang has been particularly successful. Situated in Kuantan, where the Malaysia-China Kuantan Industrial Park and the East Coast Rail Link, both backed and invested by China, are located, the institute actively collaborates on various joint degree programmes, particularly those related to engineering, in partnership with Beijing Jiaotong University (Confucius Institute at Universiti Malaysia Pahang 2021). Similarly, the CI at Universiti Malaysia Sabah has a collaborative partnership with CCCC Dredging Group, a major construction state-owned enterprise from China, which has offered collaboration to train specialists in engineering with Universiti Malaysia Sabah (Kan 2023).

The CI at SEGi University is the second CI in Malaysia and the first one affiliated with a private institution. Subsequently, three more CIs have been announced since 2019, with locations in Sabah, Sarawak, and Perak, respectively. Among them, the most recent CI was established in collaboration with the private education foundation Shen Jai Foundation (深斋教育集团), rather than a university.

Xiamen University Malaysia

Malaysia also hosts the most ambitious international branch campus project undertaken by any Chinese university—Xiamen University Malaysia. Xiamen University Malaysia has a 150-acre campus in a town on the outskirts of Kuala Lumpur, with the capacity to accommodate up to 10,000 students. As of September 2023, the size of its student body numbered around 7,000 students, with Malaysian students amounting to 4,100, students from China around 2,200, and students from 40 different countries comprising the rest (*Sinchew* Daily, 14 November 2023). Xiamen University Malaysia offers a comprehensive range of academic programmes, encompassing disciplines ranging from the humanities and business studies to natural sciences and engineering, with most courses offered in the English language (Ngeow

TABLE 8.6
Number of Graduates of Xiamen University of Malaysia

Year	Malaysian Students	International Students (mostly from China)	Total
2019	242	129	371
2020 and 2021	1,043	726	1,769
2022	696	504	1,200
2023 (until September)	N.A.	N.A.	1,455

Source: *Sina News* 29 September 2019; *Sinchew Daily* 13 August 2022, 17 December 2022, and 24 September 2023.

2022, pp. 236–39). The teaching of the Chinese language is de-emphasized by Xiamen University Malaysia. However, the social and cultural milieu of the university otherwise very much resembles a typical university in China—the prevalent use of the Chinese (Mandarin) language in office buildings and signboards, the mostly non-halal food offered in the canteen, and the substantial student and faculty body comprising nationals from China. As aptly observed by a scholar, Xiamen University Malaysia can be seen as a "reterritorialized higher education enclave" of China within Malaysia (Koh 2022).[18]

Xiamen University Malaysia enrolled its first batch of students in 2016. As shown in Table 8.6, as of the end of 2022, 1,981 Malaysian students had graduated from the university, and as of September 2023, all together around 4,800 students had graduated from the university. In his convocation speech in August 2022, Professor Wang Ruifang, the president of Xiamen University Malaysia, proudly said that after graduation, many of its graduates have been able to join renowned private sector enterprises (some of which are Chinese companies such as Huawei or Bank of China) or to continue postgraduate studies in other renowned universities in the world such as Oxford, Columbia, London School of Economics or others (*Sinchew Daily*, 13 August 2022). As of now, it is clear that not many graduates of Xiamen University Malaysia have joined the public sector, an employment pattern similar to the ethnic Chinese students graduating from universities in China discussed above.

Conclusion

This chapter outlines and discusses the various groups of "China-educated Malaysians". There are at least four groups of China-educated Malaysians:

Malaysians experiencing university education in China; Malaysians experiencing short-term training courses in China; Malaysians learning Chinese language at Confucius Institutes within Malaysia; and Malaysians studying at Xiamen University Malaysia. Each group of China-educated Malaysians has its distinct characteristics and demography. A fifth group, the Malaysians who go through short-term training courses in technical and vocational areas provided by China's bodies or through the Chinese government initiative Luban Workshop, is not covered in this chapter.

Among the four groups, the largest group and the most transformative in terms of personal exposure to China is undoubtedly those who pursue higher education in China to obtain a university degree. There are also two different circles within this group: the non-Chinese-educated (mostly Malays) and the Chinese-educated (mostly ethnic Chinese). Each circle exhibits unique characteristics, demography, career track, and social impacts. The most influential China-educated Malaysians almost certainly are those from the Chinese-educated circle; this circle possesses a long history, has a larger community, and boasts an active alumni network vigorously engaged in community affairs and people-to-people ties between China and Malaysia. The most influential alumni organization is *Liu Hua*, which serves as an organizational platform to connect its members, articulate and magnify their voices and interests, mobilize resources, and liaise with other bodies and entities, including those from China.

From the perspective of China's soft power, all these categories of China-educated Malaysians generally (though not necessarily entirely) hold positive views about China. Those who have been to China are, in general, impressed by its rapid economic and technological development, the orderliness of its cities, and the dynamism of its people and society. However, some express concerns about the growing political restrictions within China and feel uncomfortable about this trend. For the Malaysians who experience China's education within Malaysia (through the Confucius Institutes and Xiamen University Malaysia), the exposure to China at a personal level is limited, but China is still largely perceived positively, albeit at a more superficial level.

Despite the increasing numbers, the China-educated Malaysians remain a minority group among the broader population of Malaysians receiving foreign education. Notably, so far there are currently no prominent political leaders, top civil servants, or think-tank analysts in Malaysia with a China education background. The current Minister of International Trade and Industry, Tengku Zafrul Aziz, who holds an Executive Master of Business Administration (EMBA) degree from Tsinghua University, is a rare exception. In contrast, a few well-known youth and ethnic Chinese leaders of the ruling Pakatan Harapan political coalition are educated in Taiwan. Outside of the ethnic Chinese community, no notable Malaysian businesspersons are known to have a China education background. Nonetheless, as China's universities continue to attract students from Malaysia, from both Malay and Chinese circles, it is likely that more and more important China-trained or -educated leaders may emerge in Malaysian society over time.

Notes

1. There is also a fifth category that is not covered in this chapter: Malaysians who receive short-term training within Malaysia provided by China's companies such as China Communication Construction Company or with Chinese government support (for examples, see *Sinchew Daily*, 14 November 2020; Bernama 2024).
2. Still, today many Chinese-educated Malaysians go to Taiwan for higher education despite the growing popularity of mainland Chinese universities.
3. Before 2019, it was called *hanyu guoji jiaoyu* (汉语国际教育). TCSOL is somewhat equivalent to the concept of TOEFL (Teaching of English as a Foreign Language) in English. In China, an entire academic discipline is built around TCSOL, with specialized academic bodies, certification and standards, journals and departments.
4. One of the most successful examples here is Arina Safwah (with a Chinese name Jian Lan 简兰). She did exceptionally well at BFSU and won an international debate competition in Chinese language (Siti Nur Mas Erah Amran 2018). She and her friends opened a Chinese language business venture called *Jom Mandarin* (https://kelasmandarin.com/).
5. Focus group interview, 23 September 2022.
6. Ibid.
7. Chinese-educated Malaysians usually graduate from two kinds of Chinese secondary schools. Graduates of the Chinese independent secondary schools (*duzhong*) are exempted. Graduates of the governmental schools with Chinese language teaching (*guozhong*) are still required to take the HSK test. However, this normally will not be difficult for graduates of *guozhong* also.
8. The establishment of *Liu Hua* back in 2005 was a somewhat contentious issue as its founders were graduates of universities in Taiwan, not mainland China. *Liu Hua* deems that any graduates from the universities from mainland China, Taiwan, Hong Kong and Macao are eligible to be members. The founding of *Liu Hua* drew rebuttal and protest from the major alumni organization of Taiwan, the Federation of Alumni Associations of Taiwan Universities, Malaysia (FAATUM) (Shi and Pan 2011). However, years later both organizations managed to resume friendly ties.
9. For a chronology and detailed description of the activities of *Liu Hua*, see Malaixiya Liuhua Tongxuehui (2015), pp. 26–60.

10. Interview with president of Peking University Alumni Association of Malaysia, 16 September 2022.
11. Interview with a PhD graduate of a Chinese university, 14 September 2022. The interviewee said that in her several years in China, daily life had become more and more convenient due to the adoption of technology, which was a good progress, but this convenience was contrasted to the more and more inconvenient access to information, which was a terrible regress.
12. In a high-profile event organized by the Peking University Alumni Association in early December 2022, one of the authors observed the invited attendance of several BFSU and BLCU ethnic Malay graduates.
13. Training in political governance often occurs under party-to-party interactions (see Ngeow 2017).
14. Focus group interview, 14 September 2022.
15. Ibid.
16. Interview with a former KZIUM director, 3 October 2022.
17. Ibid.
18. It should be noted, however, that many of the characteristics mentioned by Koh can also be found within the campus of other higher education institutions supported by the ethnic Chinese community in Malaysia, such as New Era University College, Southern University College, Han Chiang University College of Communication, Universiti Tunku Abdul Rahman and Tunku Abdul Rahman University of Management and Technology.

References

Bernama. 2024. "China Offering 1,000 More Scholarships to M'sian Post-TVET Students—DPM Zahid". 16 January 2024. https://www.bernama.com/en/news.php?id=2263003

China Daily. 2022. "Young Malaysians Get Careers on the Move with China-Backed Rail Project". 30 July 2022. https://global.chinadaily.com.cn/a/202207/30/WS62e487c9a310fd2b29e6f438.html

Confucius Institute at Universiti Malaysia Pahang. 2021. "MoA Signing Ceremony of Dual Degree Programme in Railway Engineering between UMP-BJTU". 24 May 2021. https://ci.ump.edu.my/index.php/en/65-activities-2021/866-moa-signing-ceremony-of-dual-degree-programme-in-railway-engineering-between-ump-bjtu

He, Lan, and Stephen Wilkin. 2019. "The Return of China's Soft Power in South East Asia: An Analysis of the International Branch Campuses Established by Three Chinese Universities". *Higher Education Policy* 32, no. 3: 321–37.

Kan, Yaw Chong. 2023. "Strengthening Collaboration via Confucius Institute at UMS." *Daily Express*, 21 July 2023. https://www.dailyexpress.com.my/news/216642/strengthening-collaboration-via-confucius-institute-at-ums/

Koh, Sin Yee. 2022. "The Inversion of Majority/Minority at the De/Reterritorialised Urban Higher Education Enclave: Xiamen University Malaysia". *Urban Studies* 59, no. 16: 3347–64.

Kong Zi Institute, University of Malaya. 2019. *Annual Report of Kong Zi Institute 2018*. Kuala Lumpur: Kong Zi Institute, University of Malaya.

———. 2020. *Annual Report of Kong Zi Institute 2019*. Kuala Lumpur: Kong Zi Institute, University of Malaya.

Malaixiya Liuhua Tongxuehui 马来西亚留华同学会 (Liu Hua). 2015. *Liufang Mazhong, Huaye shengkai: Malaxiya liuhua tongxuehui chuanghui shizhounian jinian tekan, 2005–2015* 留芳马中，华叶盛开：马来西亚留华同学会创会十周年纪念特刊 2005–2015 [A Special Commemorative Volume of Ten Years of Associations of Graduates from Universities and Colleges in China, Malaysia, 2005–2015]. Kuala Lumpur: Liu Hua.

Ngeow, Chow Bing. 2017. "Barisan Nasional and the Chinese Communist Party: A Case Study in China's Party-Based Diplomacy". *China Review* 17, no. 1: 53–82.

———. 2022. "China's Universities Go to Southeast Asia: Transnational Knowledge Transfer, Soft Power, Sharp Power". *China Review* 22, no. 1: 221–48.

Shi, Cangjin 石沧金, and Pan Lang 潘浪. 2011. "Jianxi Malaixiya Liuhua Tongxuehui 简析马来西亚留华同学会" [A Brief Analysis of the Association of Graduates from Universities and Colleges in China, Malaysia]. *Dongnanya Yanjiu* 东南亚研究 [*Southeast Asian Studies*], no. 5: 86–91.

Sinchew Daily 星洲日报. 2020. "Shuchu xianjin zhuangpeideng jishu fuwu, Liaoning Xin Yijiyuan chuang Luban Gongfang 输出先进装配等技术服务，辽宁新纪元创鲁班工坊" [Export of Advanced Equipment and Other Technical Services, Liaoning and New Era to Co-Establish Luban Workshop]. 14 November 2020. https://www.sinchew.com.my/20201114/%E8%BE%93%E5%87%BA%E5%85%88%E8%BF%9B%E8%A3%85%E9%85%8D%E7%AD%89%E6%8A%80%E6%9C%AF%E6%9C%8D%E5%8A%A1-%C2%B7-%E8%BE%BD%E5%AE%81-%E6%96%B0%E7%BA%AA%E5%85%83%E5%88%9B%E9%B2%81%E7%8F%AD%E5%B7%A5%E5%9D%8A/

———. 2022a. "Ouyang Yujing: zizhu Dama youyisheng, Xiada fenxiao xushe dashi jiangxuejin 欧阳玉靖：资助大马优异生，厦大分校续设大使奖学金" [Ouyang Yujiing: Financial Supporting Excellent Malaysian Students, Continuation of Ambassador Scholarship at Xiamen University Malaysia]. 13 August 2022. https://www.sinchew.com.my/20220813/%E6%AC%A7%E9%98%B3%E7%8E%89%E9%9D%96%EF%BC%9A%E8%B5%84%E5%8A%A9%E5%A4%A7%E9%A9%AC%E4%BC%98%E5%BC%82%E7%94%9F-%E5%8E%A6%E5%A4%A7%E5%88%86%E6%A0%A1%E7%BB%AD%E8%AE%BE%E5%A4%A7%E4%BD%BF%E5%A5%96%E5%AD%A6%E9%87%91/

———. 2022b. "*Maxiada biyesheng 3000 ren, Ong Ka Ting: zai yejie xueshujie baochi jingzhengli* 马厦大毕业生3000人，黄家定：在业界学术界保持竞争力 [Xiamen University Malaysia Graduated 3000 Students, Ong Ka Ting: Maintaining Competitiveness in Industry and Academia]. 17 December 2022. https://metro.sinchew.com.my/20221217/%E5%8E%A6%E9%97%A8%E5%A4%A7%E5%AD%A6%E5%A4%A7%E9%A9%AC%E5%88%86%E6%A0%A1%E6%AF%95%E4%B8%9A%E7%94%9F%EF%BC%9A%E9%BB%84%E5%AE%B6%E5%AE%9A/

———. 2023. "Xiada Mafenxiao di-san chang biye dianli 厦大马分校第三场毕业典礼" [The Third Graduation Ceremony at Xiamen University Malaysia]. 24 September 2023. https://www.sinchew.com.my/news/20230924/nation/5007230

Sina News 新浪新闻. 2019. "Malaixiya fenxiao shoujie biye dianli juxing 马来西亚分校首届毕业典礼举行" [The First Convocation of an Overseas Branch in Malaysia]. 29 September 2019. https://news.sina.cn/2019-09-29/detail-iicezueu9069566.d.html

Siti Nur Mas Erah Amran. 2018. "Penuntut Malaysia Juara Debat Bahasa Mandarin" [Malaysian students champions of Mandarin language debate contest]". *Berita Harian*, 21 June 2018. https://www.bharian.com.my/berita/pendidikan/2018/06/439923/penuntut-malaysia-juara-debat-bahasa-mandarin

Wang, Ruikun 王瑞坤. 2022. "Malaixiya Hanyu shizi xiangmu benke liuxuesheng biye lunwen xuanti yanjiu 马来西亚汉语师资项目本科留学生毕业论文选题研究" Research on the Thesis Topics of the Undergraduate Students from Malaysia on Chinese Teacher Training Programme. Master's thesis, Beijing Foreign Studies University.

Wojciuk, Anna, Maciej Michalek, and Marta Stormowska. 2015. "Education as a Source and Tool of Soft Power in International Relations". *European Political Science* 14, no. 3: 298–317.

Yang, Jiayi 杨嘉怡. 2019. "9 nian 1 wan 2000 xueyuan, Hanyu zhongxin jinsheng Kongzi Xueyuan 9年1万2000学员，汉语中心晋升孔子学院" [12,000 students in 9 years, Mandarin Language Center Upgraded to Confucius Institute]. *China Press*, 7 November 2019. https://eastcoast.chinapress.com.my/20191107/9%E5%B9%B41%E4%B8%872000%E5%AD%A6%E5%91%98%E6%B1%89%E8%AF%AD%E4%B8%AD%E5%BF%83%E6%99%8B%E5%8D%87%E5%AD%94%E5%AD%90%E5%AD%A6%E9%99%A2

9

SEEK KNOWLEDGE AS FAR AS CHINA
Santris' Educational Mobility to China and Its Meanings for China's Soft Power Projection in Indonesia

Ardhitya Eduard Yeremia

INTRODUCTION

The rise of China in the twenty-first century has had far-reaching implications on international student mobility. In 2019, China became the world's largest source of international students, with more than 700,000 Chinese nationals studying overseas (Ministry of Education China 2020). Most of them flocked to traditional world-leading study destinations, like the United States, the United Kingdom, and Australia. Since 2014, China has emerged as a popular destination for inbound international students, making it the only Asian country to rank among the top three lists of preferred destinations (Institute of International Education 2016, 2019). This development is remarkable, considering China did not even make the top-ten list in the early 2000s. In 2018, 492,185 international students from 196 countries or regions pursued their studies in China (Institute of International Education 2020). With this achievement, Beijing was on track to achieve its goal of attracting half a million international students by 2020, were it not for the disruption caused by the COVID-19 pandemic (Chen 2010).

For Beijing, internationalizing China's higher education system is intrinsically linked to its foreign policy objectives. Seeking to counteract the prevailing 'China threat theory' propagated within the US-led international order, the Chinese government seeks to improve global understanding of China by attracting young people to gain first-hand experience living in China and interact with the Chinese people (Liu and Lin 2016). This agenda received an extra boost following the introduction of President Xi Jinping's ambitious foreign policy initiative: the Belt and Road Initiative (BRI). The Chinese government is determined to expand both the quantity and quality of international students' education, recognizing that promoting international student mobility would enhance the interactions between China and countries along the Belt and Road (Chan and Wu 2020). China further intends to cultivate individuals proficient in Mandarin and sympathetic to China's perspectives, to help the country promote its positive image (Kuroda 2014).

China's continued success in attracting international students has proven to be a valuable medium to project soft power. Previous studies have shed light on the appeal of China's economic development to prospective international students (Jiani 2017; Yu, Cheng, and Xu 2021). China's economic growth gives international students access to many job and business opportunities (Wu et al. 2021; Ahmad and Shah 2018; Liu and Lin 2016). In addition, the distinctiveness of the Chinese language and China's abundant historical and cultural resources also strongly attract students to do their higher education in mainland China (Ding 2016; Yue, Gong, and Ma 2021).

The aforementioned factors also contributed to the expanding number of Indonesians who chose to study in China. In 2018, Indonesia was China's seventh largest source of international students, with a total of 15,050 students (Ministry of Education China 2019). This number marks a significant surge from ten years earlier when only 2,700 Indonesians studied in China (Theo 2018). In recent years, China has also become Indonesians' most popular study-abroad destination, replacing Australia, the United States, and Malaysia. In 2017, while around 14,700 Indonesians studied in China, there were less than 9,000 Indonesian students in Australia and the United States respectively and less than 6,000 in Malaysia (Kasih 2022; Theo 2018).

Theo's (2018) analysis of the Indonesia-China student mobility corridor following the fall of Suharto's authoritarian regime reveals some critical findings. Firstly, Chinese Indonesians account for the vast majority of Indonesian international students in China, most of whom are self-funded students. Secondly, cultural, political, and economic motives have driven Indonesian students' voluntary mobility to China. Thirdly, this mobility practice takes place under the context surrounding narratives of China's future economic prospects, Indonesia's expanding bilateral relations and economic exchanges with China, China's rich historical and cultural heritage, and China as the ancestral land for Chinese Indonesians.

However, this article investigates the marginal but expanding group of non-Chinese Muslim students who are pursuing education mobility from Indonesia to China. This group of students primarily consists of the *santri* (the students or graduates of Islamic boarding schools called *pesantren*) from East and Central Java. Over the past decade, their numbers in Chinese universities have significantly increased. Initially, most of them pursued their first degree in the Chinese language, however recently their interests have expanded to non-Chinese language majors, including pursuing second and even third degrees.

The education mobility of this group to China raises two puzzling aspects. Firstly, their choice of China markedly contrasts with the traditional, if not stereotypical, association of *pesantren* and Islamic universities in Muslim countries. *Santri*, considered religiously oriented individuals, are commonly perceived as having more interest in deepening their understanding of Islam, leading to their preference for Muslim countries as their study-abroad destinations. Secondly, Islam, China and Communism are traditionally perceived as incompatible and even antagonistic in Indonesia (see Yeremia and Raditio 2023). This perception stems from the historical rivalry between Islamic political forces and communists during the proto-nationalist phase in the early twentieth century (Shiraishi 1990). Following the alleged communist coup of 1965, Suharto's regime further propagated negative sentiments against China, the communists, and the ethnic Chinese by portraying them as threats to Indonesia's very existence as a country throughout his thirty-two-year reign. Recent studies have highlighted the persistence of general suspicion and fear of this "Triangular Threat" among the Indonesian public (Sukma 1999).

Other scholars have predominantly approached this phenomenon from the Chinese perspective, suggesting that the educational mobility of *santris* to China is primarily a result of deliberate design and successful Chinese strategies. Rakhmat, for example, frames these *santris*' educational mobility as an "important part of China's Muslim diplomacy in Indonesia" (Rakhmat 2002, p. 248). In this regard, the provision of scholarships is understood as China's instrument to court these *santris* and to ensure that they see the country's policies and images solely from the Chinese standpoint. The active involvement of these *santris* in promoting narratives that favour China evidences the effectiveness of China's Muslim diplomacy in Indonesia (ibid., p. 249). Similarly, Suryadinata (2022) notes that these *santris*, compared to their Western-educated Indonesian counterparts, often express views on China that differ from or even oppose mainstream narratives. This phenomenon, in his view, further indicates how China's efforts to garner support from Indonesian Muslims since the early twenty-first century have seemingly outperformed those of the United States.

While existing literature has mainly examined this issue from the perspective of China, this article aims to explore how non-Chinese Muslim Indonesian students pursue higher education in China and actively shape public discourse about China in Indonesia. This paper primarily draws on fieldwork conducted in Indonesia and China in 2019. During the five-day fieldwork in the regency of Probolinggo, East Java, the author visited Pondok Pesantren Nurul Jadid (Ponpes NJ), a *pesantren* from which hundreds of *santris* have pursued higher education in mainland Chinese universities since 2010. Interviews were conducted with the *pesantren*'s leaders, teachers, and prominent *santris* who had graduated or were still studying in China. Additional interviews took place in Jakarta, Beijing, and Wuhan involving some notable *santris* with Chinese educational backgrounds.

This chapter finds that Indonesia's internal changes following the fall of Suharto's authoritarian regime and the involvement of various actors at both national and local levels have contributed to the educational mobility of these *santris* to China. Indonesians should not solely be regarded as targets of China's soft power projection; they have also been adept at maximizing the opportunities that have emerged from their interactions with China. As a result, they have partially shaped the outcomes of China's public diplomacy rather than serving as instruments to advance Chinese interests. Within this context, these *santris*' educational mobility to China and their active role in bridging Indonesia and China by promoting favourable narratives about the country cannot be solely credited to China. It takes two to tango. China is far from being the sole determinant of the outcomes it achieves through its soft power projection and public diplomacy efforts in Indonesia.

This chapter is divided into four sections. Following this introductory section, the second section outlines the contextual factors contributing to the educational mobility of hundreds of *santris* from Ponpes NJ to China. The third section explores how the transnational identity of these *santris* enables them to bridge the gap between the Indonesians, particularly the Muslim community, with the mainland Chinese. Finally, the conclusion discusses the implications of the findings from the previous sections for China's soft power projection and public diplomacy in Indonesia.

Santris' Educational Mobility to China: Contexts and Actors

It is common among Indonesian Muslims pursuing higher education in China to quote a *hadith*: "Seek knowledge as far as China". Many of them feel accomplished in fulfilling the teaching of Prophet Muhammad. Nevertheless, the Indonesian Muslim community's responses to the *hadith* are varied, with some individuals displaying a positive attitude towards it while others ignore it. Furthermore, even among those enthusiastic about the *hadith*, few choose China as their study-abroad destination. This variation suggests that the *hadith* alone has a rather limited impact on the educational mobility of hundreds of *santri* to China. In light of this, this section looks into the situational contexts in both China and Indonesia that contribute to shaping the mobility of these *santri* to pursue higher education in mainland Chinese universities.

As China's economic capacity and geopolitical prominence have steadily expanded since the beginning of the twenty-first century, it is natural for the country to become one of the world's largest hubs for international student mobility (Chen and Barnett 2000). However, China's appeal as a study destination for international students cannot be solely attributed to its future prospect as a global economic superpower. It is imperative to acknowledge the deliberate efforts made by the Chinese government to facilitate the continuous influx of international students to China. For example, in 1989, the Chinese government allowed universities to independently determine how they could benefit from the global education market. As Chan and Wu (2020) noted, this policy of marketization and internationalization of China's higher education resulted in the massive inflow of self-funded international students to China during the 1990s. Subsequently, the Chinese state took additional measures to open up its higher education sector, including increasing the number of scholarships, standardizing the management of international students' education, expanding the number of English-medium degree programmes, promoting international educational collaboration and exchange, and establishing connections with international alumni.

In response to the growing interest in China and its future development prospects, the Chinese government established Confucius Institutes (CIs) worldwide. CIs serve as platforms for promoting the Chinese language and culture in their host countries (Liu 2019). CIs seek to expand and enhance the teaching of the Chinese language, thereby fostering educational and cultural exchanges between China and the world.[1] The first CI was established in Seoul in 2004, and by December 2019, 550 CIs and 1,172 Confucius Classrooms were reportedly operational in 162 countries (*Chinaqw.com* 2019).

On the Indonesian side, internal socio-political changes in the early 2000s are central in shaping Indonesians' responses to the opportunities a rising China presents. Indonesia's first democratically elected president, Abdurrahman Wahid, played a crucial role in this regard. By choosing China as his first destination for a state visit, he signalled Indonesia's readiness to engage with China to both domestic and international audiences. (Sukma 2002). This change marked a stark contrast to the predominant discourse throughout Suharto's authoritarian rule, which portrayed China, the ethnic Chinese, and the Communists as threats to Indonesia's very existence (Sukma 1999). President Wahid also lifted the ban on the display and use of Chinese culture and language in public and attempted, albeit unsuccessfully, to lift the 1966 ban on Communism, Marxism, and Leninism (Hoon 2008; Tjhin 2011). These changes paved the way for the unprecedented enthusiasm for learning Mandarin among Indonesians, commonly known as the "Mandarin Fever" (Hoon and Kuntjara 2019; Sutami 2007).

President Wahid's successors continued the policy trajectory of improving Indonesia-China relations (Wibowo and Hadi 2009; Sukma 2009; Tjhin 2012; Yeremia and Raditio 2020). Under Yudhoyono's presidency, Indonesia and China signed the 2005 Strategic Partnership and the 2013 Comprehensive Strategic Partnership. These two significant bilateral agreements set the wheels in motion for more robust and broader ties between Jakarta and Beijing. President Jokowi further expanded bilateral economic exchanges beyond two-way trade, making China one of Indonesia's key economic partners. Consequently, Indonesia and China have cultivated closer political and economic relations, increasing people-to-people interactions, particularly in travel, tourism, and international student exchanges (Yuniarto and Thung 2021).

Pondok Pesantren Nurul Jadid as the Epicentre of Santris' Educational Mobility to China

Against the backdrop of these developments and changes in Indonesia and China, Ponpes NJ has witnessed a notable increase in the number of its *santri* pursuing higher education in Chinese universities. The first group of NJ *santri* departed for China in 2010. The subsequent three years saw four, seven, and eleven *santris* followed suit in consecutive years. In 2017, no less than 112 *santris* from Ponpes NJ embarked on their journey to China for higher education.

This phenomenon can be traced back to the implementation of the 2004 *Kurikulum Berbasis Kompetensi* (Competency-Based Curriculum) by the Indonesian Ministry of National Education. The new curriculum included Mandarin as an extracurricular subject alongside English, offering primary and secondary school students the opportunity to learn Mandarin. Responding to this official inclusion of Mandarin in the formal education system, Ponpes NJ introduced the subject in its high school. In 2005, Mandarin became one of the elective subjects for students enrolled in the language program at the school.

Practical considerations primarily drove the selection of Mandarin. Arabic, widely used in Islamic educational institutions like NJ, was not viable. Resources for teaching German, French or Japanese were only accessed from Surabaya, the capital of East Java province, located approximately 150 km away. The only resource available was an English teacher who had studied Mandarin as his minor during college. NJ also instructed another English teacher to learn Mandarin from a Chinese Indonesian, who taught Mandarin at a Chinese temple located 37 km west of Ponpes NJ. These teachers became the first two Mandarin instructors at NJ, stimulating the students' passion for the language.

Moreover, volunteer teachers from China played a crucial role in developing Mandarin learning at the high school. China had reportedly sent these volunteer teachers to Indonesia as early as 2001 (*Tempo.co* 2008). In 2004, the Indonesian Ministry of National Education signed an agreement with *Hanban* to ensure a continuous flow of these volunteer teachers (Hu 2021; Kompas 2004). Sources estimate that around 1,200 volunteer teachers have been dispatched to Indonesia, providing Mandarin lessons across twenty provinces (Jalal 2021). From 2007 to 2019, NJ's high school received seven volunteer Chinese language teachers.

Support from the Chinese Indonesians should also not be overlooked. In post-Suharto Indonesia, Chinese Indonesians established organizations like *Badan Koordinasi Pendidikan Bahasa Mandarin* (BKPBM, Coordinating Board for Mandarin Education)—also known as *Lembaga Koordinasi Pendidikan Bahasa Tionghoa* (LKPBT, Coordinating Agency for Chinese Language Education)—to promote the Chinese language. From 2010 to 2017, these organizations provided scholarships to half of the *santris* who went to China. They also organized Chinese language competitions at national and local levels, in which many NJ *santris* participated to enhance their language skills.

Additionally, the Surabaya-based Indonesia Tionghoa Cultural Centre (ITCC), established by Dahlan Iskan in 2001,[2] served as another significant source of scholarship for NJ *santris*. Dahlan, a representative from outside the Chinese Indonesian community known for expressing sympathetic views about China and the Chinese, founded the organization. Besides providing scholarships, ITCC has been active in promoting Mandarin learning and organizing study tours to China, offering various opportunities for high school graduates to continue their studies in Mainland China and Taiwan.

Support and facilitation also come from within. As a *pesantren* affiliated with Nahdlatul Ulama (NU), Indonesia's most prominent moderate Muslim organization, NJ provides a fertile ground for the development of Mandarin learning. In *pesantren*/NU culture, the *kiai* (religious scholar or leader) holds significant influence. Notably, President Wahid, a *kiai* and member of NU's nobility, had cordial relations with NJ leaders,[3] influencing their thinking and attitudes (*Nuruljadid.net* 2022). His sympathetic attitudes towards China and Chinese Indonesians have been held up as an authoritative example for NU members to follow.[4] This relationship helped to lower the barrier to introducing Mandarin into Islamic educational institutions—an unimaginable situation during Suharto's era when China and the ethnic Chinese were predominantly perceived as threats, and the use of the Chinese language was banned.

NJ is also recognized for its open and receptive attitudes. It stands among the first major *pesantren* in East Java that allow their *santris* to explore non-religious subjects.[5] NJ embraces Muhammad Al-Fayyadl, an Indonesian Muslim intellectual promoting *Islam Progressive* (Progressive Islam), despite his activism attempting to reconcile Islam and Marxism—an ideology still officially banned by the state (French 2020; Al-Fayyadl 2015). NJ also celebrates Lailatul Fitriyah,[6] one of its *santris*, who actively promotes the compatibility of feminism and Islam on Indonesian social media (*Nuruljadid.net* 2020). Due to NJ's progressiveness, its enthusiasm for further developing Mandarin learning within *pesantren* should not come as a surprise.

Moreover, Mandarin learning at NJ serves as a competitive advantage in attracting new *santris* and sustaining the *pesantren's* existence. Mandarin learning has set NJ apart from the other *pesantrens*, making it a desirable gateway to China. Many *santris* perceive NJ as an opportunity to obtain scholarships for studying in China. Since 2017, NJ has been designated as the official centre for the Chinese Proficiency Test (*Hanyu Shuiping Kaoshi*), making it the only *pesantren* in Indonesia with this distinction. NJ's success has prompted other *pesantrens* in East Jawa and public schools in the regency to seek assistance from NJ in developing Mandarin learning within their own institutions. With its achievements and recognition, Mandarin learning in NJ has truly become the *nurul jadid* (the new light) for the *pesantren*.

Considering the phenomena described in China and Indonesia, the example of Novi Basuki, the first NJ *santri* to pursue further studies in China in 2010, illustrates how educational mobility among Indonesian *santri* to China came to be. After enrolling at an NJ high school in 2007, Novi got acquainted with Mandarin through the school's language programme. Two volunteer teachers from mainland China subsequently assisted him in advancing his Chinese language skills. Novi gained attention from several Chinese Indonesians through articles published in a Surabaya-based Chinese-language newspaper. As a non-Chinese Indonesian teenager, his accomplishments, including winning the first and the fourth prizes at national and international Chinese proficiency competitions in Jakarta and Beijing respectively, further intrigued these Chinese Indonesians and prompted them to visit NJ to observe the development of Mandarin learning in the *pesantren*—a non-mainstream environment to learn Mandarin. Some Chinese Indonesians, leveraging their networks in mainland China, provided the necessary funding for Basuki to study in China. Novi's example has thus inspired hundreds of other *santris* to follow in his footsteps to pursue their higher education in China.

This section has demonstrated that the educational mobility of Novi and numerous other NJ *santris* cannot be attributed solely to their individual endeavours. While the *santris*' enthusiasm and dedication to learning Mandarin are essential, they alone are insufficient to explain the unprecedented educational mobility of non-Chinese Muslim Indonesians in the Indonesia-China corridor. Their mobility is enabled by various interconnected phenomena at the international, national, and local levels. China's liberalization of its higher education market and soft power projection align with Indonesia's post-Suharto domestic changes, creating an environment that fosters the expansion of Mandarin learning. NJ acts as the gateway for introducing the Chinese language into Islamic educational institutions due to its open and moderate nature. Novi's pioneering educational journey in China, supported by Chinese volunteer teachers and scholarships from Chinese Indonesians, inspires other *santris* and propels their aspirations to pursue Mandarin learning and study abroad in China.

Santris and Their Activism: Bridging Roles Between Indonesia and China

Indonesian students in China engage in activities that extend beyond knowledge acquisition (Theo 2018). They play a crucial role in bridging the gap between Chinese and Indonesian societies, which has resulted from limited two-way exchanges during the twenty-three-year suspension of diplomatic relations. They also foster connections among Indonesian students through the Indonesian Student Association in China (*Perkumpulan Pelajar Indonesia Tiongkok*, PPI Tiongkok) and other student-based religious organizations. Additionally, their transnational identity as Indonesian students in China allows them to act as intermediaries. They link various actors and agencies from both sides, contributing to the expansion of economic and people-to-people exchanges between Indonesia and China. This section focuses on the active role of *santris* in connecting places, peoples, and societies, both during their stay in China and after graduating from Mainland Chinese universities.

These *santris* have undertaken activities that help narrow the knowledge gap between Indonesian and Chinese societies. For instance, during the summer break, *santris* who return home voluntarily organize seminars on studying in China. These forums promote the opportunities for pursuing higher education in mainland Chinese universities and even conduct workshops on applying for Chinese government scholarships. They also share their experiences as Muslims in China, often addressing topics that the audience is inquisitive about, such as religious freedom in China, mainland Chinese attitudes towards Muslims, Chinese Muslim society, and the practice of religious obligation in China.[7]

Others have initiated the establishment of a special branch of NU called *Pengurus Cabang Istimewa Nahdlatul Ulama* (PCINU) in China, connecting *santris* while they study abroad. This organization has also contributed to filling the knowledge gap between Indonesian and Chinese societies. For example, it organized a series of online talk shows tracing the historical development of Islam in China. PCINU even published a book titled *Islam, Indonesia, dan China: Pergumulan Santri Indonesia di Tiongkok* (Islam, Indonesia, and China: The Striving of Indonesian Santri in China), which documents the lives of *santris* pursuing higher education in China. Acting as intermediaries, PCINU further promotes the notion of *diplomasi santri* (*santri* diplomacy) to highlight the unique position of these *santris* in promoting transnational *ukhuwah* (brotherhood/sisterhood) between Indonesia and China.

Moreover, PCINU has actively contested representations of China in Indonesia. In April 2018, PCINU protested the Muslim national broadsheet newspaper *Republika*'s false coverage of China. *Republika*'s online news portal had reported under the title "*Di Cina, Pelajar Indonesia Dapat Pelajaran Ideologi Komunis*" (In China, Indonesian Students [Have To] Take Courses on Communism). PCINU believed that such a portrayal did not align with the experiences of its members as foreign students in China. *Republika* eventually met PCINU's demands by issuing an apology and providing the necessary space for the right to reply.

In many cases, completing studies in China does not deter *santris* from continuing to bridge and narrow the knowledge gap between the two nations. Novi, for example, is worth mentioning for his ongoing activities. In 2019, he published *Ada Apa Dengan China?* (What's Up with China?), a collection of his essays on China's dynamics of religion and politics. Two years later, the book publishing unit of *KOMPAS*, Indonesia's largest national newspaper, published his other book, *Islam di China: Dulu dan Kini* (Islam in China: Then and Now). In this book, he traces the historical development of Islam in China and chronicles the challenges faced by the Chinese Muslim community. He has also published numerous writings to *Mojok.co*, an online media platform, discussing Chinese culture, politics, philosophy, Muslim life in China, and Islam's position within the Sino-U.S. rivalry.

Promoting "Alternative" Narratives about China
Indonesia's vibrant social media have provided a space for *santris* who have graduated from China to establish connections between Indonesians and developments in China. Among these individuals, Novi stands out due to his notable activities. Together with other Indonesian Muslim graduates from China, Novi initiated a YouTube show called *Chaguan* (茶馆, teahouse).[8] As of May 2022, the show has published sixteen videos addressing various China-related issues, including China's socio-political and economic situation. Four videos discuss themes related to China's foreign relations, while another three use China as a point of reference to discuss the socio-political situation in Indonesia. Given their Islamic background, Novi and the other hosts naturally explore China's interaction with the Muslim world in their videos.

The hosts employ multiple approaches to establish credibility as reliable sources on China and Islam. Firstly, they emphasize their experience of living in China, allowing them to observe and engage with Chinese society directly. Secondly, Novi highlights his identity as a *pesantren*-educated

Muslim. He does so via his choice of clothing, where he wears a *peci*, a cap that is commonly worn by male *santri*. Thirdly, Novi and the other hosts demonstrate their proficiency in Mandarin and occasionally speak in Arabic when quoting *hadiths* or verses from the Quran. By accentuating their dual identities, the hosts of *Chaguan* distinguish themselves from other sources and simultaneously undermine other content creators without their bilingual ability or bicultural insights. These approaches also enable the hosts to differentiate themselves from their viewers. The hosts generally portray their viewers as having a deep suspicion of China due to their lack of exposure to the country. Therefore, the hosts ascribe the China-scepticism of their viewers as a manifestation of an Indonesian proverb: "*katak dalam tempurung*" (frog under a coconut shell), an analogy to describe laziness in seeking knowledge resulting in limited perspectives.

On the other hand, the *Chaguan* videos portray China in a sympathetic light as a source of opportunities for Indonesia. For example, one video describes the BRI as China's business expansion beyond its borders. Indonesians are invited to benefit from the initiative by expanding economic cooperation with China. The *Chaguan* also favourably presents the Jakarta-Bandung Highspeed railway, the BRI's landmark project in Indonesia. The video underscores China's commitment to technology transfer and emphasizes the project's potential to generate multiplier effects within Indonesia's economy, framing these facets as beneficial to Indonesia. By highlighting the numerous opportunities that China presents, the hosts consider the reluctance to engage with China perplexing. A video delving into Afghanistan's relationship with China encapsulates this sentiment, revealing that despite the resurgence of the Taliban, Afghanistan continues to establish stronger ties with China. Therefore, the *Chaguan* hosts argue that Indonesia should likewise foster closer relations with China.

In addition, the *Chaguan* hosts portray China as far from being hostile towards Islam. This portrayal stands in stark contrast to the prevailing narratives in Indonesia, which allege that the Chinese Communists hold antagonistic views towards Islam and other religions. In a video, Novi asserts that the CCP regime has "*taubat nasuha*" (repented and lamented) in the post-Mao era. This transformation is further evinced by the regime's non-opposition to the expansion of Islam in China, evident from the pronounced increase in the number of Chinese Muslims. *Chaguan* also stresses China's unwavering support for Palestinian independence. Concerning Xinjiang issues, the CCP regime is depicted as combating violent extremism rather than targeting Islam. In fact, a *Chaguan* even contends that the Communist regime in China incorporates Islamic principles in practice, suggesting that China could be regarded as a centre of the Islamic Caliphate.

However, it is important to note that the videos discussed in the paragraph above overlook certain dimensions of the issues, either giving them insufficient attention or completely sidelining them. For instance, *Chaguan* primarily focuses on the geopolitical dimension of the allegations of human rights abuses in Xinjiang. While the show elaborates on the US's involvement in these allegations, it fails to provide any insight into the actual situation in Xinjiang, let alone address the state's use of repressive measures in the name of countering violent extremism. *Chaguan* also reproduces the CCP regime's rhetoric on its commitment to uphold freedom of religion in China without providing critical insight into how these principles are implemented in practice. Additionally, *Chaguan* does not offer any commentary on the financial, social and environmental problems that have emerged from the implementation of projects related to the BRI. Consequently, the "alternative" narratives of China promoted by *Chaguan* only present a partial understanding of the country.

The description above demonstrates how the transnational identity of the *santris* pursuing education in mainland Chinese universities enables them to bridge the gap between the peoples and societies of Indonesia and China. Playing such a role is common among Indonesians seeking higher education in China. Nevertheless, the Islamic credentials of the *santris*, allow them to establish connections with Indonesian Muslim communities in ways that other groups of Indonesian students, such as Chinese Indonesians, may not be able to. This role is significant in the context of Indonesia, where Islamic identity has traditionally been among the factors that could give rise to anti-China/Chinese sentiment, thus complicating the country's relations with China.

Conclusion

This study has shown how the complexities of interactions between Indonesian and Chinese agencies facilitate the mobility of *santris* pursuing higher education in China. It has also demonstrated the active role played by these *santris* in bridging Indonesian Muslim communities with China and shaping public discourse about China through mainstream and social media.

What these findings mean to China's soft power or public diplomacy in Indonesia is twofold. Firstly, China's soft power in Indonesia has resonated beyond the Chinese Indonesian community. This development is neither new nor unique in the interaction between the two nations. Regardless, this is an encouraging phenomenon considering the traditional perception of incompatibility between Islam and China in Indonesia. Increased exchanges between China and non-Chinese communities in Indonesia can contribute positively not only to Indonesia-China relations but also to intergroup relations in Indonesia.

Secondly, China alone does not determine the overall outcome of its soft power projection in Indonesia. Power asymmetry between Indonesia and China does not imply that China always holds the dominant position in their interaction. The case study highlights how various Indonesian agencies have also undertaken initiatives to engage with China, contributing to the educational international mobility of NJ's first *santri* to China and hundreds of others who followed. Indonesians are not merely passive targets for China's public diplomacy but active participants who define their own objectives in their interactions with China.

Moreover, complex motivations drive the decision of Indonesians to engage with China beyond mere attraction. They have the agency to determine what they seek to obtain from their interaction with China. For example, NJ's interest in maintaining its competitiveness vis-à-vis other *pesantren* has influenced its continued engagement with various Chinese agencies and Mandarin learning. The *santris'* activism in promoting China and studying opportunities also benefits their upward social mobility. Their promotional activities enable them to project their status as foreign-educated individuals, accumulating social capital from their educational mobility to China. However, in the context of Indonesia, being a China graduate can also be more of a liability than an asset when associated with Communism. Therefore, their efforts to counter false narratives about China and lingering suspicions of Chinese communist ideological indoctrination in Chinese higher learning institutes are rational. Their activism regarding China should be understood as serving their own interests rather than being solely driven by China or part of its public diplomacy strategy. Thus, the roles of Chinese agencies in facilitating *santris'* educational mobility to China and their activism in bridging between the two nations should not be overstated.

This study further demonstrates the limitations of the *santris'* activism in bridging the Indonesian Muslim community and China. For example, despite *Chaguan* consistently highlighting the favourable aspects of China, it has not received overwhelmingly positive responses from its viewers. Critics have questioned the credibility of the videos, and the *Chaguan* even faced accusations that they were merely a mouthpiece for the Chinese regime. Therefore, it is important not to overestimate the extent to which China, through its public diplomacy, gains from the *santris'* activism in shaping the public discourse about the country in Indonesia.

It is worth noting that the *santris*, in their bridging role, face dilemmas. Having lived in China, they are aware that not everything about the country is positive. On the other hand, those residing in Indonesia are also mindful of the abundance of negative coverage about China, which could easily fuel anti-China/Chinese sentiments that may ultimately harm the Chinese Indonesian community. As a result, they deliberately promote a narrative that is favourable to China, seeking to prevent the potential negative effects resulting from their efforts to bridge the knowledge gap. This indicates that these *santris* are driven by complex motivations and should not be reduced to mere instruments of China's soft power projection. Taking their agency into consideration prevents one from unfairly labelling their activism as a mere example of China's successful public diplomacy towards the Muslims in Indonesia, but rather acknowledging their multifaceted engagement.

Notes

1. As scholars have argued, nevertheless, that through the medium of language and culture, the Chinese might also have projected its soft power, and thus, channelled their economic interests to the host countries as well as balanced the Americans' dominant cultural influence (Hartig 2016; Wang, Uzodinma, and Niu 2021).
2. Dahlan is a former journalist and ex-CEO of a Surabaya-based national newspaper, *Jawa Pos*, who reached the pinnacle of his national career becoming the Minister for State-Owned Enterprises in the second period of Yudhyono's presidency. During his years as a journalist, he is widely known for his massive coverage about China as well as its development progress, thanks to his frequent visit to China since the late 1980s. The author would like to thank Saiful Hakam for highlighting this.
3. President Wahid is also a *kiai* and the chairman of the NU's executive council from 1984 to 1999. His father and grandfather were the ex-chairman and even the founder of the organization, respectively.
4. Interview with a Mandarin teacher at Pondok Pesantren Nurul Jadid.
5. Interview with Amin Mudzakir from LIPI-BRIN.
6. You may find out more about her at her X (formerly Twitter) handle: @MahameruLee
7. According to an interview with one of the *santri*s at Wuhan.
8. This show is hosted by Asumsi, a multi-platform media-tech company. Asumsi specifically targets the younger demographic, presenting them with coverage on current affairs and pop culture. Asumsi's YouTube channel also claims to cover

stories in a critical angle and tell stories from the unheard, believing that media should be used for political education.

References

Ahmad, Ahmad Bayiz, dan Mahsood Shah. 2018. "International Students' Choice to Study in China: An Exploratory Study". *Tertiary Education and Management* 24, no. 4: 325–37. https://doi.org/10.1080/13583883.2018.1458247 (accessed 23 January 2023).

Al-Fayyadl, Muhammad. 2015. "Apa Itu Islam Progresif?". *Indoprogress.com*, 27 July 2015. https://indoprogress.com/2015/07/apa-itu-islam-progresif/ (accessed 15 January 2023).

Chan, Wing-kit, and Xuan Wu. 2020. "Promoting Governance Model Through International Higher Education: Examining International Student Mobility in China between 2003 and 2016". *High Education Policy* 33: 511–30. https://doi.org/10.1057/s41307-019-00158-w (accessed 24 January 2023).

Chen, Jia. 2010. "China Looks to Attract More Foreign Students". *China Daily*, 28 September 2010. https://www.chinadaily.com.cn/china/2010-09/28/content_11355912.htm (accessed 25 January 2023).

Chen, Tse-Mei, and George A. Barnett. 2000. "Research on International Student Flows from a Macro Perspective: A Network Analysis of 1985, 1989 and 1995". *Higher Education* 39, no. 4: 435–53. http://www.jstor.org/stable/3447941 (accessed 19 January 2023).

Chinaqw.com. 2019. "8个国家首次设立孔子学院 全球孔院数目达550所". *Chinaqw.com*, 11 December 2019. https://baijiahao.baidu.com/s?id=1652580064427730759&wfr=spider&for=pc (accessed 18 January 2023).

Ding, Xiaojiong. 2016. "Exploring the Experiences of International Students in China". *Journal of Studies in International Education* 20, no. 4: 319–38. https://doi.org/10.1177/1028315316647164 (accessed 22 January 2023).

French, Sawyer Martin. 2020. "A Place for Marxism in Traditionalist Fiqh: Engaging the Indonesian Thinker Muhammad Al-Fayyadl". *Themaydan.com*, 19 May 2020. https://themaydan.com/2020/05/a-place-for-marxism-in-traditionalist-fiqh-engaging-the-indonesian-thinker-muhammad-al-fayyadl/ (accessed 15 January 2023).

Hartig, Falk. 2016. *Chinese Public Diplomacy: The Rise of the Confucius Institute*. London and New York: Routledge.

Hoon, Chang-Yau. 2008. *Chinese Identity in Post-Suharto Indonesia: Culture, Politics, and Media*. Portland, Oregon: Sussex Academic Press.

———, and Esther Kuntjara. 2019. "The Politics of Mandarin Fever in Contemporary Indonesia: Resinicization, Economic Impetus, and China's Soft Power". *Asian Survey* 59, no. 3: 573–94. https://doi.org/10.1525/as.2019.59.3.573 (accessed 17 January 2023).

Hu, Anqi. 2021. "Persahabatan Tiongkok dan Indonesia: Bantuan di Bidang Pembelajaran Bahasa Mandarin". In *Ragam dan Prospek Hubungan Antarwarga*

Indonesia-Tiongkok, edited by Paulus Rudolf Yuniarto and Thung Ju-lan. Surabaya: Airlangga University Press.

Institute of International Education. 2016. "Project Atlas Infographic 2016". https://iie.widen.net/s/j65wlbmcs7/project-atlas-infographics-2016 (accessed 26 January 2023).

———. 2019. "Project Atlas Infographic 2019". https://iie.widen.net/s/frqlvhdjfb/project-atlas-infographics-2019 (accessed 26 January 2023).

———. 2020. "Project Atlas Infographic 2020". https://iie.widen.net/s/g2bqxwkwqv/project-atlas-infographics-2020 (accessed 26 January 2023).

Jalal, Fasli. 2021. "Peran Bahasa Mandarin Menjembatani Hubungan China-Indonesia". *Kompas.com*, 2 February 2021. https://nasional.kompas.com/read/2021/02/02/14180091/peran-bahasa-mandarin-menjembatani-hubungan-china-indonesia- (accessed 16 January 2023).

Jiani, M.A. 2017. "Why and How International Students Choose Mainland China as A Higher Education Study Abroad Destination". *High Education* 74: 563–79. https://doi.org/10.1007/s10734-016-0066-0 (accessed 24 January 2023).

Kasih, Ayunda Pininta. 2022. "15 Negara Ini Jadi Favorit Siswa Indonesia Lanjutkan Kuliah". *Kompas.com*, 19 January 2022. https://www.kompas.com/edu/read/2022/01/19/133336971/15-negara-ini-jadi-favorit-siswa-indonesia-lanjutkan-kuliah?page=all (accessed 20 January 2023).

Kompas. 2004. "Bantuan Guru Bahasa Mandarin dari China". *KOMPAS*, p. 9.

Kuroda, Chiharu. 2014. "The New Sphere of International Student Education in Chinese Higher Education: A Focus on English-Medium Degree Programs". *Journal of Studies in International Education* 18, no. 5: 445–62. https://doi.org/10.1177/1028315313519824 (accessed 24 January 2023).

Liu, Wei, and Xiaobing Lin. 2016. "Meeting the Needs of Chinese International Students: Is There Anything We Can Learn from Their Home System?". *Journal of Studies in International Education* 20, no. 4: 357–70. https://doi.org/10.1177/1028315316656456 (accessed 24 January 2023).

Liu, Xin. 2019. "China's Cultural Diplomacy: A Great Leap Outward with Chinese Characteristics? Multiple Comparative Case Studies of the Confucius Institutes". *Journal of Contemporary China* 28, no. 118: 646–61. https://doi.org/10.1080/10670564.2018.1557951 (accessed 18 January 2023).

Ministry of Education, China. 2019. "Statistical Report on International Students in China for 2018". 18 April 2019. http://en.moe.gov.cn/documents/reports/201904/t20190418_378692.html (accessed 21 January 2023).

———. 2020. "Statistics on Chinese Learners Studying Overseas in 2019". 16 December 2020. http://en.moe.gov.cn/news/press_releases/202012/t20201224_507474.html (accessed 27 January 2023).

Nuruljadid.net. 2020. "FKO Nurul Jadid Gelar Talkshow Pemuda Inspiratif". 18 February 2020. https://www.nuruljadid.net/9370/fko-nurul-jadid-gelar-talkshow-nasional-pemuda-inspiratif. (accessed 14 January 2023).

———. 2022. "Gus Yahya: Satu Abad NU, Nurul Jadid Tuan Rumah Muktamar

Internasional Fiqh Peradaban". 20 May 2022. https://www.nuruljadid.net/12924/gus-yahya-satu-abad-nu-nurul-jadid-tuan-rumah-muktamar-internasional-fiqh-peradaban (accessed 15 January 2023).

Rakhmat, Muhammad Zulfikar. 2022. "Getting Nods from the Muslims: China's Muslim Diplomacy in Indonesia". *International Journal of China Studies* 13, no. 2: 237–64.

Shiraishi, Takashi. 1990. *An Age in Motion: Popular Radicalism in Java, 1912–1926*. Ithaca: Cornell University Press.

Sukma, Rizal. 1999. *Indonesia and China: The Politics of a Troubled Relationship*. London: Routledge.

———. 2002. "Indonesia's Perceptions of China: The Domestic Bases of Persistent Ambiguity". In *The China Threat: Perceptions, Myths and Reality*, edited by Herbert S. Yee and Ian Storey. New York: Routledge Curzon.

———. 2009. "Indonesia-China Relations: The Politics of Re-engagement". *Asian Survey* 49, no. 4: 591–608.

Suryadinata, Leo. 2022. "China's Islamic Diplomacy in Indonesia Is Seeing Results". *Thinkchina.sg*, 9 February 2022. https://www.thinkchina.sg/chinas-islamic-diplomacy-indonesia-seeing-results. (accessed 19 January 2023).

Sutami, Hermina. 2007. "Kekhasan Pengajaran Bahasa Mandarin di Indonesia". *Wacana* 9, no. 2: 222–37.

Tempo.co. 2008. "Cina Kirim 76 Guru Bahasa Mandarin". 29 January 2008. https://nasional.tempo.co/read/116462/cina-kirim-76-guru-bahasa-mandarin (accessed 17 January 2023).

Theo, Rika. 2018. "Unravelling Indonesian Student Mobility to China: Politics, Identities, and Trajectories". PhD dissertation, Utrecht University, Netherlands.

Tjhin, Christine Susanna. 2011. "Indonesia's Perception of the 'China Threat': From 'Yellow Threat from the North' to 'Strategic Partner'". In *China's Rise: Threat or Opportunity?* edited by Herbert S. Yee. London and New York: Routledge.

———. 2012. "Indonesia's Relations with China: Productive and Pragmatic, but Not Yet a Strategic Partnership". *China Report* 48, no. 3: 303–15.

Wang, Yanwei, Uzodinma, Chinenye Gerlof, and Caoyuan Niu. 2021. "The Path, Value and Limits of The Confucius Institute in Carrying Out Public Diplomacy". *Economic and Political Studies* 9, no. 2: 217–29. https://doi.org/10.1080/20954816.2021.1914416 (accessed 18 January 2023).

Wibowo, I., and Syamsul Hadi, eds. 2009. *Merangkul Cina: Hubungan Indonesia-Cina Pasca Suharto*. Jakarta: Gramedia Pustaka Utama.

Wu, Mao-Ying, Zhai, Junqing, Wall, Geoffrey, and Qiu-Cheng Li. 2021. "Understanding International Students' Motivations to Pursue Higher Education in Mainland China". *Educational Review* 73, no. 5: 580–96. https://doi.org/10.1080/00131911.2019.1662772 (accessed 23 January 2023).

Yeremia, Ardhitya Eduard, and Klaus H. Raditio. 2020. *Minding the Grassroots: Celebrating 70 Years of Sino-Indonesia Relations amid the Coronavirus Pandemic*. Trends in Southeast Asia, no. 16/2020. Singapore: ISEAS – Yusof Ishak Institute.

———, and Klaus Heinrich Raditio. "Getting Our Piece of the 'National Cake': The

Islamists' Attitude toward Yudhoyono's and Jokowi's China Policies". *International Journal of Asian Studies* (2023): 1–21. https://doi.org/10.1017/S1479591423000232

Yu, Yun, Cheng, Ming, and Xu Yuwei. 2022. "Understanding International Postgraduate Students' Educational Mobility to China: An Ecological Systematic Perspective". *Higher Education Research & Development* 41, no. 6: 2137–53. https://doi.org/10.1080/07294360.2021.1973383 (accessed 24 January 2023).

Yue, Yun, Lei, Gong, and Yin Ma. 2021. "Factors Influencing International Student Inward Mobility in China: A Comparison between Students from BRI and non-BRI Countries". *Educational Studies.* https://doi.org/10.1080/03055698.2021.1978939 (accessed 22 January 2023).

Yuniarto, Rudolf, Paulus, and Thung Ju-lan, eds. 2021. *Ragam dan Prospek Hubungan Antarwarga Indonesia-Tiongkok*. Surabaya: Airlangga University Press.

10

ASSESSMENT OF CHINA'S SOFT POWER AMONG CHINA-EDUCATED FILIPINOS
Impact on the Philippines

Jane Yugioksing

Overview of the Chinese Education in the Philippines

As immigrants in the Philippines, the Chinese desired to pass down the Chinese language and culture to the next generation by establishing Chinese schools with the support of Chinese chambers and associations. However, the political divide between the Kuomintang (KMT) and the Chinese Communist Party (CCP) created a rift among the Chinese and prompted the Philippines to sign the Treaty of Amity with the Republic of China from 1949 to 1975. This treaty granted the Republic of China jurisdiction over all Chinese schools in the Philippines. KMT members within the Chinese Chamber of Commerce and some Chinese associations instituted curricula based on Dr Sun Yat Sen's Three People's Principles, focusing on Chinese geography, politics, literature and philosophy. According to Blaker (1970), the KMT gained significant power and control, turning Chinese schools into a vehicle for spreading nationalist ideas and encouraging Chinese involvement in Chinese political affairs.

In 1955, a report known as the "Un-Filipino Activities" alleged the communist infiltration of Chinese schools resulted in the Chinese community isolating themselves from the mainstream community out of pride and political loyalty, rejecting assimilation with Filipino society. Simultaneously, rumours of a "fifth column" operating under the guise of Chinese schools resulted in the issuance of Presidential Decree 176 by

President Marcos in April 1973. This decree mandated the Filipinization of curricula, ownership and board members of Chinese schools. It also stated that only Filipino citizens could administer educational institutions in the Philippines. Furthermore, it prohibited the establishment or exclusive operation of educational institutions for aliens and by aliens, and no group of aliens could make up more than one-third of the enrolment of any school. President Marcos emphasized that the purpose of Presidential Decree 176 was to "prevent Chinese schools from becoming vehicles to propagate a foreign ideology and to inculcate patriotism, loyalty and a true spirit of citizenship among aliens residing in the country". This decree significantly limited, if not eliminated, the opportunity for the younger generation to learn about the Chinese language and culture.

In the 1990s, the declining quality of Chinese language education in the Philippines prompted Chinese philanthropists and alumni associations to establish the Philippine Chinese Education and Research Center (PCERC). This centre spearheaded efforts to promote Chinese as a second language and introduced a pedagogy based on China's educational practices. The revival of Chinese education coincided with China's thriving economy, offering job opportunities for Mandarin speakers. The rising attractiveness of Mandarin piqued the interest of both ethnic Chinese and native Filipinos. While both mainland China and Taiwan provided free language training, exchange programmes, and scholarship grants, more people were enticed by China's scholarships due to higher stipends. In addition, China's use of *pinyin* (Beijing Romanized phonetic alphabet) and simplified Chinese characters provides more appeal for Mandarin learners compared to Taiwan's use of *guoyin* (Taiwan phonetics) and traditional Chinese characters. In addition, China began reaching out to both ethnic Chinese and mainstream Philippine society by donating Chinese books, audio and learning materials. China also sponsored teachers to teach Chinese in different parts of the Philippines, with most sponsorships coming from *Hanban*.

Generating Soft Power

The transformation of China's image and influence has long been associated with its effective use of soft power. Coined by Harvard University professor Joseph Nye, the term "soft power" refers to a state's ability to attract others through persuasion rather than coercion. It involves gaining desired outcomes by making others want what you want and admiring your ideas. This concept has greatly influenced many Chinese academics and was first introduced by Wang Huning, head of China Central Policy Research Office and professor of Fudan University, in his 1993 article titled "Culture as National Power: Soft Power" (Wang 1993).

The concept received further attention when journalists, commentators, and political leaders began to reference soft power in their discourse. As early as 4 January 2006, during a meeting of the Central Foreign Affairs Leadership group, President Hu Jintao noted the importance of using not only hard power such as economic and defence capabilities, but also soft power, particularly through cultural means. He highlighted the need to enhance China's cultural soft power to address domestic and international challenges, publicly announcing this during the 17th Party Congress in October 2007.[1] Culture is often regarded as the bedrock of soft power, and China has made it the core of its soft power strategy.

China's attempts to project a peaceful and harmonious image have been showcased through the Confucius Institute (CI) and the China Scholarship Council, enabling international scholarship recipients to experience the beauty of Chinese culture first-hand. The effectiveness of China's soft power strategy, which utilizes education programmes and exchanges as a strategic foreign policy, has garnered both positive and negative remarks. This paper aims to assess the success of China's educational strategy in achieving its national interests by examining how Filipino students perceive China before and after their educational experience in China. Did their study and life experience in China result in a better image of China, and was soft power effective in exhibiting real behavioural outcomes in the form of better support for China and its discourse? To do this, I will explore three areas: (Pre-China) the decision-making process for choosing to study in China; (In China) experiences during their study in China; (Post-China) impacts in terms of perception and attitudes towards China. This article begins with a brief overview of Chinese educational institutions in the Philippines that offer scholarship opportunities to study in China. It is followed by a discussion of theoretical arguments, collection of data and findings, and lastly, the conclusion.

CHINA'S CHANNEL OF SCHOLARSHIP IN THE PHILIPPINES

An affiliate of the Ministry of Education of China, the CI is a non-profit organization that promotes the Chinese language and culture, similar to Alliance Française of France or Goethe Institute of Germany. However, the design of the CI differs from the other language-promoting institutions in other countries. Each CI follows specific criteria, one of which is partnering with a Chinese university. In the Philippines, there are four recipients of the Confucius Institute Start-Up Grant. The first CI in the country was established in 2006 between Ateneo de Manila University and Sun Yat-Sen University. A year after, *Hanban* and Bulacan State University signed an agreement, and on 28 February 2009, Northwest University in Xi'an was formally launched as its Chinese university partner. The third CI, approved by *Hanban*, was formed through a partnership between the Angeles University Foundation and Fujian Normal University on 10 January 2010. The fourth and latest CI in the Philippines was established on 13 October 2015, between the University of the Philippines and Xiamen University.

Each CI operates on a three-party system, consisting of the CI Headquarters, a Chinese university, and the host university in the Philippines. Operations are jointly funded by CI Headquarters and the host university on a 1:1 ratio, with additional support from China for teaching resources such as textbooks to teachers. On the other hand, the host university is responsible for providing a venue and administrative staff, and shouldering necessary expenses. This form of partnership enables each CI to introduce courses and activities to local students, expanding its influence in the local community. Additionally, the CI organizes lectures, cultural and festival shows, teacher seminars and film screenings, which are open to mainstream Filipinos and are provided for free.

One of the notable features of the CI is the *Hanban* scholarship programme, now known as the International Chinese Language Teachers Scholarship programme. This scholarship supports prospective scholars pursuing a career in teaching Chinese. It offers scholarships for degrees ranging from bachelor's to doctorate in Teaching Chinese to Speakers of Other Languages (BTCSOL and MTCSOL). Non-degree scholarship programmes for learning Chinese culture, language and history are also available for durations of one month, six months, or one academic year. The *Hanban* scholarship and the China Scholarship Programme grant Filipino scholars the opportunity to pursue a degree of their choice at no cost. In 2019, eighty Filipinos received the Chinese Government Scholarship, which covered tuition fees, accommodation, health insurance, and a stipend allowance. Recipients of the scholarship range from undergraduate to doctorate degrees with majors from International Relations to Clinical Medicine from universities like Peking University, Tsinghua University, Jinan University, and many other universities in China that are partnered with CSC.

A unique sending institution in the Philippines that provides a scholarship for China is the Philippine Chinese Education Research Center (PCERC). This non-profit educational institution aims to develop Chinese language education among the Chinese-Filipino community by aiding Chinese language teachers and being a liaison agency between and among Chinese language teachers in the country. In so doing, one of their projects is to sponsor future Chinese teachers to obtain their Teaching Chinese degree in China. This project is co-sponsored by the Overseas Chinese Affair Office of China in partnership with Jinan University. As recipients of the sponsored scholarships, scholars have the opportunity to study in China with a minimal monthly allowance while gaining first-hand experience of the country.

Over the past decade, a significant number of Filipinos have benefited from these scholarship opportunities provided by various institutions, including the International Chinese Language Teachers Scholarship, the PCERC scholarship, and the China Scholarship Council Scholarship, with over 1,000 recipients in total.

Participants Profile and Data Collection Method

This qualitative study involved twenty-two participants who were selected based on specific criteria related to their study experience in China, whether long-term or short-term. Only four of the participants were self-supporting and all the rest were scholarship holders (Table 10.1). Twelve of the participants were of Filipino descent, while the other ten participants had Chinese Filipino background or Chinese heritage. None of the participants held positions affiliated with China-sponsored institutions prior to their study in China, although two participants later assumed positions in the China-sponsored CI. Notably, five participants became prominent political analysts of the country sought after for their perspectives on Philippine-China-related topics. See Table 10.1 for the full demographics of the scholars.

A semi-structured interview was conducted with each participant, ranging from live interviews to online interviews lasting between 30 minutes to an hour. A few participants opted to respond via email exchanges, while others opted for phone interviews. Pseudonyms are used in the data analysis to protect the identity of the participants, in accordance with the waiver of the Data Privacy Act.

TABLE 10.1
Demographics of China-Educated Filipino Scholars in the Survey

Gender	
Female	8
Male	14
Degree of Studies	
Bachelor's Degree	4
Masteral Degree	5
PhD Degree	4
Diploma & Certificate	8
Careers/Professions	
Political analyst	5
Professors/Chinese Language Teacher	11
Businessman/self-employed	2
Non-Government Organization	2
Government work/diplomats	2
Chinese University with Filipino Scholars	
Peking University	4
Central China Normal University	1
Fudan University	1
Huaqiao University	1
Jinan University	3
Jilin University	1
Renmin University	1
Xiamen University	2
Zhejiang University	1
Xi'an University	1
Fuzhou University	4
Sun Yat-Sen University	2

The interview process focused on capturing the academic, social, cultural, and political experiences of Filipino scholars who had studied in China. The interviews were structured into three phases: the pre-China story, the actual China experience, and the post-China worldview. The pre-China story explored the scholars' decision-making process, expectations, and perceptions of why they chose to study in China. The actual China experience encompassed the scholars' perceptions and experiences during their time studying in China. The post-China worldview examined any changes in values or perceptions resulting from their study experience.

The pre-trip stories constitute an important link in understanding the scholars' initial impressions and comparing them with their actual experiences in the host country. This helped identify any shifts in perceptions that occurred during their time in China. The actual China experience played a crucial role in shaping their cultural, social, academic and political experiences, which in turn contributed to the assessment of potential gains in soft power. Finally, the post-China worldview seeks to identify any changes in the scholars' positional outlook or value system after their China experience. According to Kondakçı (2011), soft power influence comes into effect within a two-time framework, the pre-departure period and the post-departure period. The pre-departure soft power influence relates to the student's perceptions in choosing the destination country. The post-departure soft power influence focuses on whether their experiences in China translate into a favourable image of the host country, and if these China-educated scholars tend to align with the host country's foreign policy goals.

Soft power is evident in the pre-China story as the scholars' attraction to China reflects the behavioural outcome of soft power influence. Likewise, soft power is also at work when scholars develop a positive perception of China during their time there, which is also translated into behavioural outcomes that are evaluated by assessing their perception.

Data Results and Analysis

A qualitative approach is employed in this study, as it deals with data that is not easily quantifiable and has not been extensively researched (Corbin and Strauss 2008). Specifically, this study will be using the lens of interpretative phenomenology. In the realm of qualitative research, the term "phenomenology" refers to the study of phenomena, where a phenomenon is anything that appears to someone in their conscious experience. Phenomenology also takes into account the various interpretations of the same phenomenon as described and experienced by different individuals. The goal is to uncover the essence of the phenomenon by focusing on shared aspects across multiple individuals' experiences. Interpretative Phenomenological Analysis is concerned with the detailed examination of individual lived experience and how individuals make sense of that experience (Eatough and Smith 2008). Moustakas (1994) notes that analysing individual experiences entails descriptions rather than explanations, as lived experiences are perceived through the context and history of the individual.

In addition to using the interpretative phenomenological approach, the researcher also employed the use of descriptive coding, emotion coding, values coding, and magnitude coding to analyse the impact of soft power as conveyed through the participants' narratives. Saldaña (2021) describes "[a]ffective coding as means of investigating subjective qualities of human experience (e.g., emotions, values, conflicts, judgments) by directly acknowledging and naming those experiences". Emotions, on the other hand, are a universal human expression that can provide insights into participants' perspectives, worldviews, living conditions, and their intrapersonal and interpersonal experiences and actions. According to Corbin and Strauss (2008), emotion and action are interconnected, constituting a continuous flow of events, one leading into the other. In condensing participants' responses, descriptive and emotional codes were utilized, which were further categorized into favourable, unfavourable, and neutral applying magnitude coding. Saldaña (2021) explained that magnitude coding adds supplemental substance to codes, and "sometimes words say it best; sometimes numbers do, and sometimes both can work in concert to compose a richer answer and corroborate each other". The added layer of quantifiable measures can help evaluate soft power outcomes.

For participants' post-China narratives, the researcher used values coding to explore the participants' integrated values, attitudes, and beliefs that shape their worldview. This approach allows the researcher to examine whether China's soft power has produced any discernible results. The variables were then summarized and presented in combination with direct quotations from participants who were labelled as PM-1 (Participant Male-1), and PF-1 (Participant Female-1). From this approach, the researcher can observe any changes (if any) in the participants' pre-China, in-China, and post-China experiences to evaluate the effects of soft power.

Pre-China Education: Decision-Making Process, Convenience, Impulse and Benefit

Studying abroad is often influenced by both push and pull factors. Push factors can stem from limited domestic opportunities or perceived low education quality, while pull factors can include proximity, reputation, or incentives. Ahmad and Buchanan (2016) pointed out several push factors, such as poor economic prospects and employment opportunities in China, social-political conditions, the low quality of education, and limited access to accommodation and funding. On the other hand, Bodycott (2009) identified pull factors that attract students to specific destinations, including the reputation and knowledge about the country and its institutions, safety, immigration policies, employment prospects, and existing social or professional links in the host country.

This part of the research revealed that most of the participants did not initially choose China as a point of destination for further study or exchange programmes. Instead, their decision was driven by convenience, the benefits offered to them, and, in some cases, impulse. The category of "convenience, impulse, and benefit" emerged from the final cycle of coding analysis. The codes "scholarship, recommendations and flexible admissions" were initially extracted from narratives provided by the participants on how they ended up studying in China. Common reasons provided by the participants included receiving a Chinese scholarship, the opportunity to go abroad and study, free tuition and accommodation, and receiving a stipend. Another reason mentioned was the lack of authentic Chinese language schools in the Philippines. However, there were a couple of respondents who personally chose to study in China for reasons provided below, as exemplified by the following responses:

> Many of my colleagues have been educated in the US and other Western-oriented universities in Asia and Australia. I hope that my China-based education will provide a different perspective on politics as a discipline.[2]

> China is the world's most populous nation, poised to become the world's largest economy, stepping up to become a technology power and developing a strong military Managing relations with China requires intimate knowledge of the drivers of Chinese security and foreign policy. Hence, studying China is imperative.[3]

Below are some sample narratives from five participants where the themes of convenience, impulse, and benefits can be inferred.

> I selected all universities in the south of China during the application process since it is nearer to the Philippines, and that can allow me cheaper fares when I return home during school breaks. However, in my acceptance letter, the university suggested to me is far up in the north. It took quite some time to decide to go for it, but at the last minute, I went for it since I realize (*sic*) that the scholarship opportunity might be once in a lifetime.[4]

I applied to several leading universities in and out of China that can provide scholarships with good stipends. The American university I applied to didn't accept me. I was accepted into a university in Korea, however, I need to study one year of language before going to a degree course and I feel it is a waste of time. I considered going to China because I have a working knowledge of Chinese, and I just need to take the language exam. That would lessen one year of staying in a foreign country.[5]

I heard from my friend about this college course on Teaching Chinese as Foreign Language that offers free tuition fees and an opportunity to go to China. I feel that this is my chance to help with the family's financial

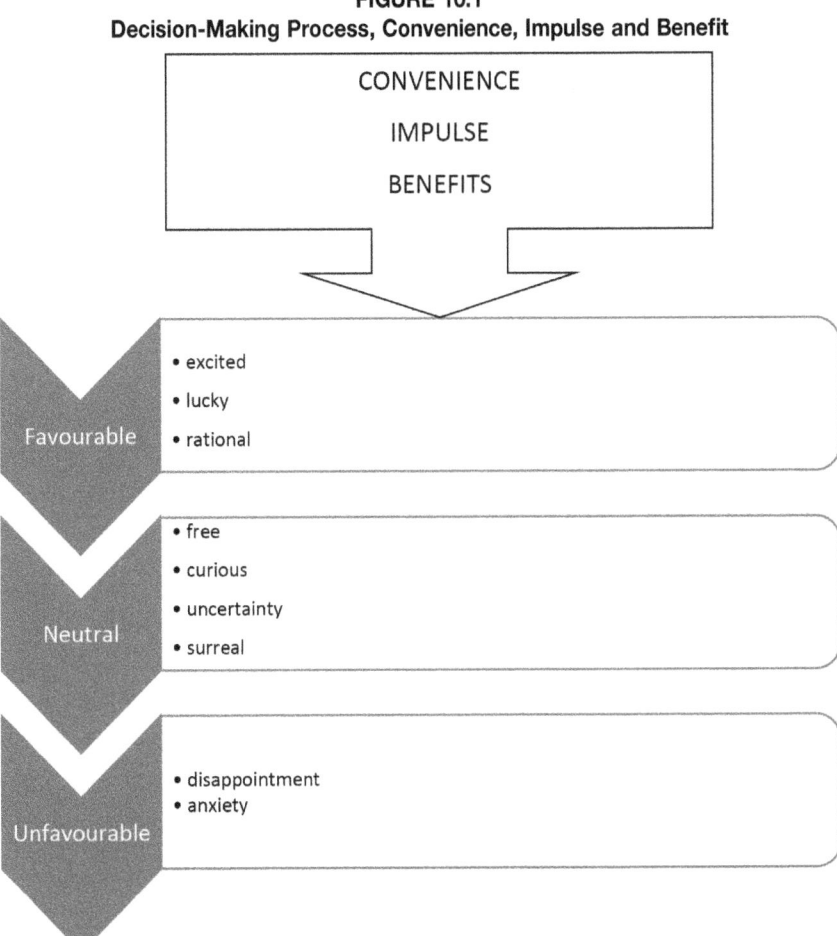

FIGURE 10.1
Decision-Making Process, Convenience, Impulse and Benefit

situation, and even though I am pure Filipino, my parents were very supportive that I may become a Chinese teacher in the future.[6]

I was employed in the government when they announced a special scholarship programme for our unit, I saw the stipend was high (higher than my salary) I tried to apply and luckily I got into the special scholarship programme to go to Beijing.[7]

Back then in college, I joined the Chinese Bridge contest and I won, one of the prizes is a full scholarship of your choice, and since I have plans to pursue graduate studies, I just grab (sic) hold of this good opportunity.[8]

In China Education: Living Experience: Support, Security and Immersion

The merit of positive social interaction and a shared sense of belonging is an important aspect in pursuing gains for soft power. As China's universities accept more foreign students, there now exists a diverse mix in the pool of the student body. This adds to the diverse experience of a foreign student. Besides being exposed to the Chinese system, environment and culture, foreign students get a glimpse of other cultures as they interact with classmates from different countries. In capturing an individual's interpretation of their new socio-cultural experience, the researcher refers to Giddens's (1991) reflexive project of the self "that allows exploration of extrinsic, intrinsic, cultural, social, and psychological factors" which play a role in shaping one's experience". By employing this approach, the researcher infers the complexity of students' experiences in China using descriptive emotion codes categorized under a common theme.

This part of the research revealed that most of the respondents were fairly satisfied with their China experience with minimal complaints or negative experiences. Even now, they still connect with people they met during their time of study in China, and some of them became all-time friends. The interview also revealed that while it cannot be considered a negative experience, one participant expressed that he had more foreign friends while studying in China because he feels that it is harder to connect with his local Chinese classmates and he finds it easier to get along with people who came from Southeast Asian countries.[9] Initial and secondary coding after the interview revealed three general themes: Immersion, Security, and Support. More than half of the participants expressed that they agreed to go to China to experience things for themselves, and to verify the accuracy of how the media portrays China. According to PM-17, his time of study in China made him realize that China is nowhere as "bad" as the mainstream media portrays the country to be, although his immersion made him realize whether he could survive the system if the Philippines tried to take the path China took. As students continue to involve themselves with society, they begin to develop a deeper understanding of China. This is exhibited in the response of PF-7 when she narrates that her experience taught her how to get along with Chinese people on a day-to-day basis and that it is part of life's learning experience that no book can teach. She also added that "at the end of the day, you understand your host country better, and you grow."

Being foreign students abroad, many express the need to step out of their comfort zone and that there is the need to connect and to find connection since the whole environment sometimes makes one feel "naïve or stupid". Finding a support system is crucial to survival. Most of the participants expressed getting the help and support they need whereas school life is a concern. They are grateful that the university's international office employs good English-speaking staff who help with foreign students' needs. According to PM-4, he felt that his China study experience made him realize that Chinese education is more culturally sensitive and conscious of the students' needs compared to his Western education experience where he finds that it is too individualistic and impersonal.[10] Although several responses expressed that they found it easier to form connections with other foreign students, most participants expressed that they appreciated how their Chinese classmates were very polite and helpful, assisting them with requirements they could not understand. One respondent added, "I had to bother our class president and class secretary almost always on what is happening in the class and the requirements that we need to submit, and they always help me. I appreciate how everyone helps each other in China, and how they assist foreign students like me."[11]

In most of the participant's narratives, the theme of security emerged frequently, although it was expressed in different ways. In the same situation, some participants found it a positive experience, while some saw it as a negative one. For instance, two participants shared their experiences of dorm life wherein there is a curfew at midnight, and the main door of their dorm is locked by the on-duty staff. One participant viewed this policy favourably because it made her feel safe while sleeping, knowing that no one could enter the dorm beyond midnight. On the other hand, the other participant felt that this curtailed their freedom. Another participant also expressed annoyance with the requirement to "sign in" or go through fingerprint identification every time they wanted to leave the university premises. Additionally, they needed permission from their adviser to go on tours or explore China. Three other participants corroborated this account, but they saw it in a positive light. They believed that the monitoring system in China was efficient and resulted in lower crime rates, giving them a sense of security to walk alone, even at night.

However, one participant expressed an alternative perspective on security. He felt uncomfortable with the pervasive presence of CCTV cameras and the feeling of being constantly watched. He also mentioned how not accessing the Internet through a VPN provided a sense of peace, albeit at the cost of being less aware of the reality outside.[12]

FIGURE 10.2
Living Experience: Support, Security and Immersion

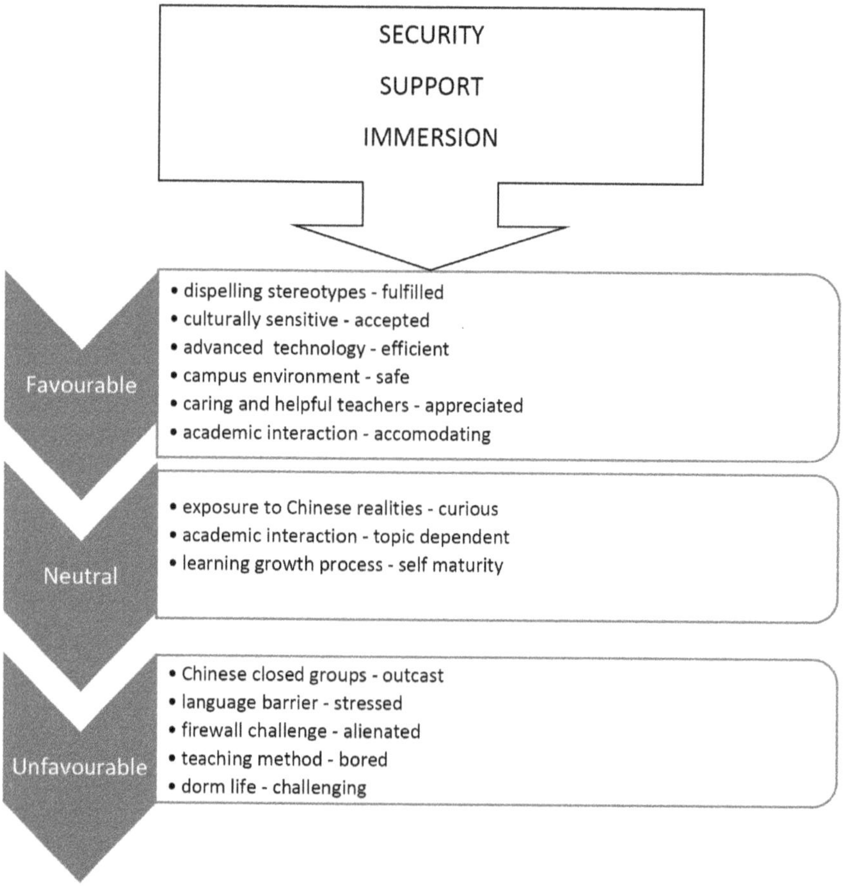

SECURITY

SUPPORT

IMMERSION

Favourable
- dispelling stereotypes - fulfilled
- culturally sensitive - accepted
- advanced technology - efficient
- campus environment - safe
- caring and helpful teachers - appreciated
- academic interaction - accomodating

Neutral
- exposure to Chinese realities - curious
- academic interaction - topic dependent
- learning growth process - self maturity

Unfavourable
- Chinese closed groups - outcast
- language barrier - stressed
- firewall challenge - alienated
- teaching method - bored
- dorm life - challenging

Post-China Education

To examine the influence of soft power on China-educated Filipinos, it is important to explore potential changes in their worldview. These changes are best exhibited by a shift in values (V), attitudes (A), and beliefs(B)—hereafter referred to as VAB—among the participants after their study time abroad. Values (V) pertain to what is important after a period of judgement while Attitudes (A) are related to the way how a participant thinks or feels about a certain matter. Beliefs (B) are based on the participants' acceptance of something to be true based on personal experience or opinions. The interplay of these three VAB constructs manifests itself in thoughts and feelings in responses made by the participants. To capture VAB, the following questions were asked of the participants: How has your experience in China impacted your relationship with your home country? How has your China education helped you in your future plans? Through the first question, I hoped to see whether the participants of the interview were at least aware of the implications of their China educational experience as unique constituents in fostering Philippine-China relations. For the second question, I wanted to see the impact of Chinese education on their choice of career paths.

In dissecting the responses of the participants, consistent with the argument of Dwyer (2004) that study abroad has a significant impact on students in terms of their career choices and personal development. Several of the participants demonstrated a positive shift in outlook based on previous knowledge about China. They expressed that having knowledge of the Chinese language is a real deal-breaker because it not only helped them manoeuvre themselves in the environment but also gave them more confidence in finding future work since China is the second emerging superpower and has had consistent economic growth for the past eight years.[13]

The first-hand experience of living in China also helped dispel negative impressions caused by a lack of understanding of China's culture and society. The positive impressions continue to exhibit their impact even after their period of study. Several of the participants continue to express their admiration for China's advanced infrastructure and technology. From their initial impression of a laid-back old-fashioned society as portrayed in many Western media movies of China, they expressed being incredibly surprised at how advanced the society is. The majority of the participants compared China's modern city with the Philippines and expressed that they were impressed at the technological advancement China has made. Some

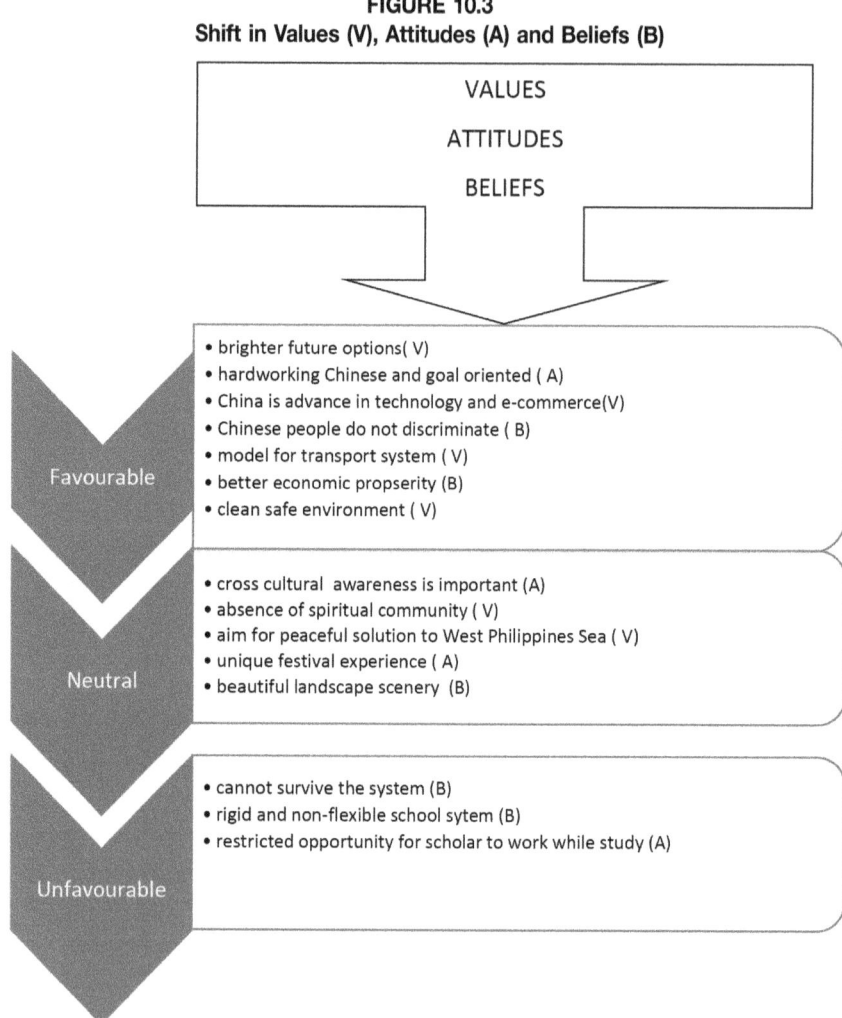

FIGURE 10.3
Shift in Values (V), Attitudes (A) and Beliefs (B)

participants expressed a more neutral outlook as to how they enjoyed the scenery of China, the festivals, and the food.[14]

The same study conducted by Dwyer (2004) reveals that studying abroad will cultivate friendships with people of the host country stands true with some of the people interviewed in this study. A participant expressed that he felt at home in China because people do not discriminate and the longer he stayed, he expressed to have understood and appreciated Chinese people better as to why they work hard and always plan ahead. He also added that he felt safer in China rather than in the Philippines. He also added that it should be the priority of the Philippine government to give a safe environment to their citizens.[15]

The last key point to process from the interview is the rationale that studying in China will likely influence the political outlook of participants. It can be inferred that the period of study among some participants does change their political views since some participants were indeed very receptive to China's foreign policies.[16] However, some participants whose political opinions remain unclear whether it was formed before their initial decision to study in China or during their stay in China created the shift in their value system.[17]

Beyond China Education

To summarize the interviews coded, it becomes apparent that participants' decision to study in China during the pre-China phase was often "accidental, non-targeted and by default". However, the majority of the coded responses fall under the "Neutral" category, indicating that they approached their study abroad experience in China with neither a positive nor negative impression - essentially as blank slates.

Upon arrival in China, which marked the beginning of their "In-China" experience, participants' responses exhibited a mixture of negative and positive sentiments. Opinions varied, ranging from approval to disapproval of China's education system to China's political system. However, it can be inferred from many participants that they developed a positive image of China despite encountering academic or social difficulties or disappointments. Participants commonly expressed admiration for China's infrastructural development and enjoyed experiences such as the transportation system and e-commerce, especially when compared with the Philippines. They also narrated enjoying China's different festivals and regional foods together with exploring different well-known tourist spots. These positive encounters contributed to China's soft power by attracting students to appreciate its culture and society. Indeed, from the initial decision to study in China to their overall experience, it is evident that Filipino students cultivated an intercultural understanding that can be a source of transformative experience. Nye says that soft power consists of the "ability to shape the preferences of others" (Nye 2004). Therefore to gauge the true effectiveness of soft power, it becomes essential to observe changes in values, beliefs, and attitudes among China-educated scholars, especially after they are back in the Philippines.

In the post-China phase, the survey findings coded under Values, Attitude and Beliefs (VAB) represented more favourable responses towards China. Participants' views shifted from a neutral stance in the pre-China phase to a positive impression during their time in China, culminating in an improved post-China perception. Broadly speaking, a common comment from participants is their desire to work in China due to the higher remuneration and perception of a more advanced life. Another common response reflects participants being "ambassadors" or "gap fillers", feeling that their first-hand experiences in China provided them with a deeper understanding of the country compared to those who have not been to China or solely rely on media reports. Taking into account Nye's definition of soft power encompassing political ideas, it can be concluded that many of the participants, who come from a Western-influenced liberal background, expressed knowledge, understanding and respect for China's single-party system, which they believe hastened China's economic development and uplifted the lives of its citizens. Therefore, when considering the broad definition of soft power as the power of attraction, it is evident that China-educated scholars can be seen as a source of soft power. Their transformative experiences and changed perceptions of China contribute to the country's ability to shape the preferences of others, thereby enhancing its soft power influence.

Limitations of the Study

While conducting the initial study for this research, it was expected that the study would include a minimum of fifty to eighty participants. However, due to various constraints, the researcher was only able to gather twenty-two participants who responded to the interview invite. One of the factors contributing to the smaller sample size is the time constraint during data collection. The process of arranging and conducting one-on-one interviews proved to be challenging, as some participants had busy schedules that made it difficult to accommodate the interviews. Therefore, due to the classification and limited sample size of this study, the findings cannot fully represent the entire population of China-educated scholars in the Philippines.

Conclusion and Implications

Soft power dynamics can be very complex and highly debatable, and China's soft power influence through education shows different levels of acceptance. However, in this study, with the help of indicators, the author found the academic experiences and personal exposure of these scholars have led to a changed perception of China before and after their time in the country. Regardless of the duration of their studies, first-hand experience plays an important role in increasing appreciation and understanding of China, its people, and its society.

The different institutional agencies by which China promoted its scholarship in the Philippines are crucial instruments in shaping China's image. The opportunities provided through these scholarship opportunities have contributed to a more positive outlook on China among Filipino scholars. Despite controversial issues such as the West Philippine Sea dispute, participants expressed a belief that China has never conquered any country by force and that bilateral talks remain the best approach. This view is also often promoted by three of the well-known China-educated political analysts in the country.

The interview data also showed that the economic growth of China has influenced many scholars to pursue Mandarin language learning and degrees that will benefit their future career plans. Many scholars are impressed by the economic progress of China, and their experiences in China affirmed their beliefs. In addition, despite China's different political system from the Philippines, many scholars express that they experience a sense of security with the system and witness China's productive economic development. These factors play a substantial role in China's soft power among China-educated Filipino scholars such that they share their good experiences of China with others. Therefore, studying in China and experiencing the country first-hand has proven to be an effective tool for China to "fraternalize" its values and ideas among Filipino scholars, setting its soft power into action. However, due to the relatively small number of China-educated recipients, the impact of China's soft power is not widely felt in mainstream Philippine society.

Notes

1. University of Southern California. China Institute, "Report to the Seventeenth National Congress of the Communist Party of China on Oct. 15, 2007", https://china.usc.edu/hu-jintao-17th-party-congress-report-2007 (accessed 2 September 2022).
2. Interview with PF-16, 11 May 2022, Quezon City, Philippines.
3. Interview with PM-11, 19 May 2022, Taguig City, Philippines.
4. Interview with PF-21, 12 May 2022, Binondo Manila, Philippines.
5. Inteview with PF-13, 11 May 2022, Quezon City, Philippines.
6. Interview with PF-14, 12 May 2022, Binondo Manila, Philippines.

7. Interview with PM-3, 12 April 2022, Makati, Philippines.
8. Interview with PM-12, 20 April 2022, via Zoom online.
9. Interview with PM-5, 27 April 2022, Makati City, Philippines.
10. Ibid.
11. Ibid.
12. Interview from PM-19, 29 April 2022, Quezon City, Philippines. Excerpt from his response: "my life is the Internet so when I get to China, I was aware of the firewall, so I had a lot of VPNs ready. But I guess technology has a way of catching up, after staying more than a year in China, you realized that you were behind reality although your one year was a peaceful haven."
13. Summarized response from interviews with PF-14, 12 May 2022, and PM-20, 12 June 2022, Ortigas City Philippines.
14. Summarized response from Interviews with PF-19, 29 April 2022, Quezon City, and PF-21,12 May Binondo, Philippines.
15. Interview with a male participant who took his bachelor's degree at Fuzhou University and is currently a Mandarin teacher.
16. Interview with a male participant who is a PhD graduate from Fudan University and is currently a professor.
17. Interview with a male participant who took his Master's degree from Jinan University and is currently working with the Philippine government.

References

Ahmad, Syed Zamberi, and Frederick Robert Buchanan. 2016. "Choices of Destination for Transnational Higher Education: 'Pull' Factors in an Asia Pacific Market". *Educational Studies* 42, no. 2: 163–80.

Blaker, James Roland. 1970. *The Chinese in the Philippines: A Study of Power and Change*. Columbus, OH: Ohio State University.

Bodycott, Peter. 2009. "Choosing a Higher Education Study Abroad Destination: What Mainland Chinese Parents and Students Rate as Important". *Journal of Research in International Education 8*, no. 3: 349–73.

Clarke, Victoria, and Virginia Braun. 2013. *Successful Qualitative Research: A Practical Guide for Beginners*. New York: Sage.

Corbin, Juliet, and Anselm Strauss. 2008. "Strategies for Qualitative Data Analysis." In *Basics of Qualitative Research: Techniques and Procedures for Developing Grounded Theory*, 3rd ed., pp. 67–85. USA: Sage Publications. https://doi.org/10.4135/9781452230153

Dwyer, Mary. 2004. "More Is Better: The Impact of Study Abroad Program Duration". *Frontiers: Interdisciplinary Journal of Study Abroad* 10: 151–63.

Giddens, Anthony. 1991. *Modernity and Self-Identity: Self and Society in the Late-Modern Age*, pp. 70–242. Cambridge, England: Polity Press.

Kondakci, Yasar. 2011. "Student Mobility Reviewed: Attraction and Satisfaction of International Students in Turkey". *Higher Education* 62: 573-92.

Kurlantzick, Josh, 2006. "China's Charm: Implications of Chinese Soft Power". *Policy Commons,* 1 June 2006. https://policycommons.net/artifacts/977248/chinas-charm/1706374/ (accessed 24 July 2022).

Moustakas, Clark. 1994. *Phenomenological Research Methods,* pp. 120–55. USA: Sage Publications.

Nye, Joseph S. 2021. "Soft Power: The Evolution of a Concept". *Journal of Political Power* 14, no. 1: 196–208.

Saldaña, Johnny. 2021. *The Coding Manual for Qualitative Researchers,* pp. 1–440. USA: Sage Publications.

Wang, Hu Ning. 1993. "Culture as National Power: Soft Power". *Journal of Fudan University* 3.

11

CHINESE LANGUAGE EDUCATION IN BRUNEI DARUSSALAM
An Instrument of China's Soft Power?

Hannah Ming Yit Ho and Chang-Yau Hoon

INTRODUCTION

Language serves as a cultural tool for identity affirmation and plays a significant role in shaping social interactions and communal spheres (Cummins 2013; Riley 2007). It contributes to the construction of identity and fosters a sense of belonging within communities. Within Southeast Asia, language has played an important role in influencing cultural identity that may induce a sense of conflict along bifurcated national and global lines (Ho and Ho 2019). Moreover, language transmission is integral to preserving linguistic heritage. In view of the surge in Mandarin language learning across the globe, it appears that China's rise as a global power has been a significant factor in the uptick in Chinese language lessons observed within Southeast Asian nations. The Belt and Road Initiative (BRI) spearheaded by China attests to its effective investments in building a transnational infrastructure along both land and maritime routes (Dollar 2015; Dellios 2005). As mainland Chinese forge multilateral cooperation across various Southeast Asian nations, Mandarin has taken on a growing relevance in a world where China has a long reach.

The "Mandarin fever" (Hoon and Kuntjara 2019) is not serendipitous but a direct consequence of China's proactive public diplomacy (Chan and Hoon 2022, p. 85). Education plays a pivotal role in China's soft power strategy (Suryadinata 2017; Chan and Hoon 2022, pp. 85–87). In addition to increasing its resources to expand its domestic population of international students, China's international outreach is evident in the global rise of the Chinese language and culture through the promotion of Mandarin language learning by Confucius Institutes (CIs) around the world. Enrolment in Chinese language schools has increased due to this surge in Chinese language education.

This study examines the motivations behind Chinese language learning in Chinese schools in Brunei Darussalam. Through interviews conducted with thirty-six parents from five Chinese schools from 2017 to 2022, who either send their children to these schools or are alumni, two research questions are addressed:

(1) What factors influence parents' decisions to enrol their children in Chinese language education?
(2) To what extent is Mandarin language learning regarded as an instrument of China's soft power?

These questions are based on the premise that the motivations for Mandarin language learning in Chinese schools in Brunei have not been adequately explored. Understanding these motivations is crucial as parents are paying patrons of Chinese schools and are key stakeholders in their children's future. Secondly, investigating the implications of China's soft power in language education in Brunei Darussalam provides insights into its impact on parents, children and the nation. Beyond national social spheres, the uptake of Chinese language education can also serve as an indicator of transnational ties and multilateral relations.

The findings demonstrate that parents are aware of the benefits of an additional language of Mandarin taught in Chinese schools as part of a cultural dissemination tied to China's global reach. While cognizant of China's soft power, this is not the topmost reason for parents to send their children to study in Chinese schools in Brunei. Instead, their interview responses showed that Mandarin classes offered additional subject knowledge and multicultural and multilingual perspectives to prepare children for global or cosmopolitan citizenship. Multiple tokens of "knowledge" and "perspective" appeared more frequently on the interview transcripts contrasted with "language" ability. Except for a few parents, most interview participants gloss over or do not factor the rise of China as a global power as the key reason for enrolling their children in Chinese language lessons in these schools. Instead, parents would cite other academic, financial, and communicative advantages. These factors include the academic reputation of the Chinese schools, high levels of discipline, securing job prospects in local and regional companies owned and run by the ethnic Chinese, and practical communication with the Chinese diaspora who are located in and beyond Southeast Asia.

Brunei Darussalam: Social, Political and Historical Contexts

Brunei Darussalam (hereafter, Brunei) is located on the northeastern tip of Borneo island. It is flanked by the Malaysian states of Sarawak and Sabah as well as the Indonesian province of Kalimantan (Deterding and Ho 2021). After gaining its independence on 1 January 1984, *Melayu Islam Beraja* (MIB, Malay Islamic Monarchy) was declared as the national ideology. With a population of 445,400 residents, Brunei is a Malay-dominant nation with the Malays as the majority and Malay as the official language. Unlike Malaysia, the Malays are not necessarily Muslims, although the conflated Malay/Muslim label has been commonly assumed in Brunei as it is in Malaysia. According to the Constitution, the "Malays" comprise seven indigenous groups subsuming the Brunei Malay, Bisaya, Kedayan, Murut, Dusun, Tutong and Belait (Ho 2019). Localization has been on the agenda in national development plans (H. Ho 2021b), which aim to promote Malay cultural identity and local capacity building to secure jobs for citizens and permanent residents within the nation.

The ethnic Chinese in Brunei make up 9.6 per cent of the total population (Department of Economic Planning and Statistics 2022) and are the largest ethnic minority group. Through their ethnicity, they are precluded from the Malay national ideology (H. Ho 2021a). The Chinese are a heterogeneous community who speak several vernacular languages or dialects, such as Hokkien, Cantonese, Hakka and Hainanese (D. Ho 2021). The local Chinese community tend to differentiate themselves from mainland Chinese who have recently arrived in the country to work temporarily on infrastructures, such as the petrochemical plant on Pulau Muara Besar, managed by Hengyi Industries, which deals with oil refining (Zhao and Hoon 2023). This joint venture between the Brunei government and a private company in China is part of the BRI, which benefits Brunei via foreign direct investment from China. The Bruneian government's bid for economic diversification from hydrocarbon dependence has seen a boost through this initiative spearheaded by China since its economic outreach extends to Southeast Asia.

According to a study by Koh, Hoon and Noor Azam (2020), there is little to no evidence of Mandarin fever in Brunei. While other countries may exhibit a demand for Mandarin classes that have become popular over recent years, Brunei's response has been comparatively lukewarm. The study concludes that "the rise of China has had limited impact on Chinese language-learning among Chinese students and their parents in Brunei"

(Koh, Hoon and Noor Azam 2020, p. 325). Considering that China's global and transnational dynamics have not been a major stimulus for Chinese language learning in Brunei, this present study then asks: What are the motivations of sending students to receive a Chinese language education? This is linked to the first research question that seeks to investigate the factors that influence parental decisions to send their children to Chinese schools.

THE HISTORY OF CHINESE SCHOOLS IN BRUNEI

Chinese schools were originally set up to preserve the Chinese language and identity by Chinese entrepreneurs who invested in heritage schools for their children. There are eight Chinese schools in Brunei Darussalam, with three offering K-12 education and the rest offering kindergarten and primary education. Yik Chye School (育才学校) was the first Chinese school established in Brunei in 1916; it was renamed Chung Hwa School in 1922 and was further renamed Ching Hwa Middle School (CHMS BSB) in 1955 when it started offering secondary education. Following on from its predecessor, Chung Hua School in Kuala Belait was established in 1931 and renamed Chung Hua Middle School Kuala Belait (CHMS KB) in 1949. Not long after, Chung Ching School in Seria was also established in 1938, and was renamed Chung Ching Middle School when it began to offer secondary education in 1954. Chung Hwa Tutong and Chung Hwa Kiudang are among the Chinese primary schools. All Chinese schools are run as private academic institutions approved by the Brunei Ministry of Education.

The Chinese schools in Brunei adhere to the educational system set by the Ministry of Education. Under the post-independent *dwibahasa* (bilingualism) education system, English and Malay were taught as compulsory subjects in schools. From 2009 onwards, the National Education System for the twenty-first century (SPN21) took effect (Noor Azam, McLellan and Jones 2019). SPN21 has been analysed as a "language-in-education policy" with its "emphasis placed on English over the official language, Bahasa Melayu, with English being introduced much earlier in the curriculum, i.e., as the medium of instruction for Mathematics and Science from Year 1 onwards" (Salbrina and Jainatul 2019). In Chinese schools, Mandarin is the third compulsory language that every student studies. Contrasted with other state, private and international schools in Brunei, Mandarin is a requisite subject that has been integrated into the core curriculum in these Chinese schools. Mandarin lessons are, therefore, a fundamental part of the educational system offered in Chinese schools. The integration of Mandarin into the school curriculum has resulted in students being trilingual.

Mandarin used to be the language of instruction in Chinese schools in Brunei before the bilingual education policy was introduced in 1984. After the policy was implemented, private schools, including Chinese schools, were given a grace period until 1992 to adopt English as the main medium of teaching and Mandarin has since been offered as a stand-alone subject. Mandarin was taught in assigned Chinese language periods from kindergarten level onwards. The schools stock several reading materials in Chinese in their libraries for the use of their students. Apart from a few local ethnic Chinese, most Mandarin teachers in Chinese schools in Brunei come from Malaysia, China and Taiwan. Before 1970, Mandarin teaching materials were sourced from Taiwan to prepare students for the Taiwan national exams. Today, however, Chinese schools in Brunei adopt teaching materials from Singapore and China, and teachers often have to construct their own materials because the imported materials may not reflect the local context (Ho 2008, p. 11).

Apart from the three Chinese middle schools in Bandar Seri Begawan, Kuala Belait and Seria that have maintained a high student enrolment, most Chinese primary schools, especially those in rural towns, struggle to attract students. This is likely due to several factors, which include the outward migration of stateless ethnic Chinese, relocation of Chinese to urban towns and the capital city, and limitations experienced by these schools in raising funds and building school facilities. To ensure continuity and survival, these schools have increasingly welcomed non-Chinese students.

Methodology

Interview data were collected from parents across five schools, namely Chung Hwa Middle School Bandar Seri Begawan (CHMS BSB), Chung Hua Middle School Kuala Belait (CHMS KB), Chung Ching Middle School (CCMS), Chung Hwa Tutong and Chung Hwa Kiudang from 2017 to 2022. The first three schools listed here offer both primary and secondary level education. Parents of children attending these schools were approached to participate in semi-structured interviews to investigate their reasons for sending their children to receive a Chinese school education. A proportion of these parents are also alumni of the Chinese schools. The snowball method was applied to acquire the thirty-six interview participants involved in this project.

The language medium that was used in these interviews was mixed as they consisted of the official language of Malay, the widely spoken English language, and Mandarin. Parents were permitted to choose the communicative language that allowed them to feel most comfortable during the interview. In cases when parents spoke in Mandarin and Bahasa Melayu, these interviews were translated and transcribed into English to facilitate systematic coding across all the interviews. Having resided in Brunei, several parents were bilingual after studying under Brunei's educational system of *dwibahasa*—a system that was introduced in the post-independent period until the early twenty-first century, which promoted the official Malay language and recognized English as an international language. Parents who were educated in Chinese schools were also literate in Mandarin.

A Muted Awareness of China's Soft Power among Bruneians

Bruneians are generally apolitical and possess a limited awareness of international and regional affairs. Political education is absent at all levels of education in Brunei. As a welfare state driven by hydrocarbon revenues, most Bruneians lead complacent lives that shelter them from taking an interest in global politics. However, the process of globalization as a cultural process also runs the risk of local cultural demise and fragmentation (Ullah and Ho 2020). Often, the state and monarch will call for Bruneians to reject external influences that oppose the national ideology of a Malay Islamic Monarchy (*Borneo Bulletin*, 2 March 2023). Hence, it is not surprising that the parents interviewed in this study expressed minimal concerns about China's rise as a global power.

A parent highlighted that "if China was [sic] to become a global superpower",[1] their children, who are learning Mandarin in Chinese schools, would be well-prepared to face that reality. The parent points out that it is necessary to "prepare themselves in case [of] the global switch to China", citing the popularity of Chinese search engines like Baidu and the prevalence of the Chinese language: "Chinese is everywhere. They [Chinese people] are everywhere. It's as if Chinese [Mandarin] is the number one language nowadays in comparison to English".[2] With the rise of China and the fact that ethnic Chinese constitute the largest diaspora in the world (Wang 1993), Mandarin is on track to become a global language like English (Gil 2020). However, China as a single destination for Bruneian children was not considered a significant factor. As one parent explains, "It's mostly based on the individuals themselves.... So, even with that rise of China, so far it has no influence on our kids. Unless they have their own interest to be in that particular [country or position] [*sic*]".[3] Likewise, another parent opines that,

> [E]ven if China is known to conquer half of the world, it does not really matter. It depends on where you want to go and which area of expertise you want to venture into. So, if your area of expertise leans more towards Chinese culture, it is advantageous to learn Chinese.[4]

The soft power of China that is held through the popular appeal of the Chinese language is also rather subdued for one Bruneian parent, who carries the perspective that Anglophone cultures exert a stronger influence on children in Brunei than Chinese culture. Citing the widespread use of English among her children, she shares the view:

> Even though you said China now has a lot of power and those kinds of things, the kids here, they are more into American, British. Even the teachers sometimes get mad at the Chinese students right, [because] they don't speak Chinese to each other. They speak in English. The [Chinese] teachers sometimes get mad. "Do you not appreciate your own language?[5]

Here, affective responses to language choices are alluded to in the Chinese language teacher's irritation with the children's use of English rather than Mandarin in classes. The rhetorical question aims to instil an appreciation for the Chinese language by getting the children to reflect on their lack of Mandarin usage during their Mandarin lessons. Furthermore, this enquiry evokes the connection between language and identity, as explored in Ien Ang's (2001) book, *On Not Speaking Chinese*. The students' default language of communication is Anglophone rather than Sinophone. By suggesting that language use is synonymous with a self-approval of Chinese identity, the teacher implies that her Chinese students have failed to uphold their Chinese identities as they have chosen to converse in another language instead of their mother tongue.

Academic Knowledge, Teaching Standards and Co-Curricular Activities

According to several parents, Mandarin offers an "added advantage" in terms of building a linguistic knowledge base that is used by millions, if not billions, of people around the world. However, the benefits of Mandarin are manifold and extend to the aims of cultural preservation for Chinese parents and students, as well as communicative advantages for the Chinese and non-Chinese in local and transnational spaces. On one hand, the Mandarin mother tongue is seen as a valuable commodity that Chinese parents want to transmit to their children. As a Chinese parent confesses, "I don't want to lose our mother tongue. So that's the reason."[6] Another parent sends her children to receive a Chinese language education because "it would be a shame if [my children] can't speak Chinese"[7] since they are from a half-Chinese family. The same parent talks about her "hope [that] my kids are able to learn Chinese, if maybe, their future spouse will be Chinese. So, it's not a waste [to send your kids to Chinese schools]."[8] Here, Chinese linguistic continuity within the family is emphasized.

For non-Chinese parents who were interviewed, they see value in their children learning Mandarin: "With the population growing, more non-Chinese are interested in sending their kids to Chinese schools".[9] Often, the academic goals of Chinese educational institutions are cited as a strong reason for sending their non-Chinese children to learn Mandarin in Chinese schools. Referring to Chinese schools as "top schools" with "structure and also transparency" in terms of expectations and goals, one parent praises the academic standards of these schools.[10] The parent also mentions the "[high] outputs" and "excellent results amongst private schools".[11] Alongside awards and incentives for high-performing students, parents value the "strong support system"[12] offered by teachers and the parent-teacher association to maintain students' motivational levels. One parent also blatantly states that "Chung Hwa BSB's [academic] reputation out there is good".[13] Chung Hwa Middle School students consistently achieve high scores in the Primary School Examinations (PSR) and Cambridge GCE "O" Level examinations (RSSing 2018). The three top-performing GCE "O" Level candidates in the country in 2022 were from CHMS BSB (Kon 2023).

Other parents comment on the teaching quality in Chinese schools. They hold the view that "any private schools tend to give their best. Teachers tend to give their best education to the students."[14] The best education, here, entails the caring attitudes of the teachers whom they have encountered. In Chinese private schools, teachers are also seen to "love giving encouragement"[15] to their students. One parent highlights the teaching styles of Chinese language teachers, who engage with students interactively to help them excel academically. Another set of parents have commented that their son's academic achievements had improved since moving to study at a Chinese school: "He likes activities and [likes to have] encouraging teachers. If the teachers are [passionate] and caring, students would be more enthusiastic to work harder. That is what we see here. So far, his grades have improved."¹⁶ Likewise, other parents comment about outstanding student development under these teachers, noting the increased focus on interactions with other students and teachers, as well as the resources allocated to organize such activities aimed at exposing students to these interactions. These learning activities introduced by committed teachers contribute to the school's teaching quality and academic performance.

Furthermore, parents praise the value added to Mandarin language learning in Chinese schools through extra-curricular cultural activities and language activities beyond the classroom. Speaking about the high standards maintained by Chinese schools, one parent lists two key areas of satisfaction: "Firstly, I [have high] expectations in terms of language. Secondly, their involvement [in school]. Because CCA and ECA offered in Chung Hwa are way more than [other] school[s] now."¹⁷ Co-curricular and extra-curricular activities serve to supplement students' language learning. These include cultural funfairs, language quizzes and school speeches organized by teachers who set up language projects for their students to complete. Another parent comments that her child enjoys an array of performing arts like dance and the Chinese martial art form of *taichi,* which is conducted every morning at school. Additional values offered through Mandarin language learning in Chinese schools, such as socialization and prospects in the job market, will be discussed in the next section.

COMMUNICATIVE MEANS AND JOB-READY ECONOMIC GOALS

Beyond the urgency of preserving the Chinese language as an integral part of their familial identity, some subscribe to Mandarin lessons for practical communication purposes when interacting with Chinese business owners in Brunei and Malaysia. As a non-Chinese parent admits, Mandarin is "super helpful" or "useful in interacting" to avail themselves of discounts—"For example, when you dealt with cars, if you go to the workshop and you are able to speak in Chinese, you will be entitled to discounts."¹⁸ Another example involves crossing the border to the neighbouring Malaysian town of Miri, where a parent talks about being able to read Chinese marketing posters and advertisements to take advantage of special discounts in shops located there. He explains, "So if you shop for example, gold jewellery in Miri, Malaysia, can see such signboards [in Chinese] notifying of the promo[tion]".¹⁹ Another parent shares that his brother, who studied in a Chinese school in Brunei, has made several Chinese friends due to his

Mandarin proficiency. Hence, the ability to speak, read and write Mandarin facilitates participation, inclusion and expansion of social circles. It also aids in accessing promotional discounts offered by Chinese business owners within the region.

Apart from the communicative advantages provided by Mandarin proficiency, parents also cite financial prospects in potential job opportunities that arise from learning Mandarin in Chinese schools compared to government schools. While socialization with Chinese peers features highly on the list of reasons, parents are primarily concerned with the financial gains of prospective jobs that Mandarin proficiency can offer. As a parent iterates, "in Brunei, if people have the ability to speak Mandarin, it opens up their opportunities to get better jobs".[20] Local and national efforts to diversify away from a heavily reliant government job sector have led to the rise of private sector jobs. Coupled with the view that the demand for the Chinese language is high both locally and globally, a parent states that Mandarin serves as "an extra point when looking for jobs".[21]

Citing the trend of local graduates from the national university struggling to secure employment, one Bruneian parent believes that language skills are essential for their children's future, particularly in an era of great uncertainty when earning a stable income is increasingly challenging. As this parent explains:

> I hope that it'll be easy for them [my children] to get jobs in the future. If not here, then abroad. It's part of the preparation. They have [Islamic] religious studies, and they know Chinese, English and Malay; that is the entire package. If they don't have that, it'll be difficult.[22]

It is evident here that this parent views Chinese language lessons as part of a broader preparation that complements Islamic, Arabic, Malay and English language studies. For future-ready youths, Bruneian parents are keen to equip their children with the knowledge that aligns with the two pillars of "Malay" and "Islam" within the national ideology of *Melayu Islam Beraja*. Moreover, they actively expose their children to English and Chinese language learning with the hope that it will facilitate their future job prospects beyond Brunei.

GLOBAL CITIZENSHIP: A MULTICULTURAL PERSPECTIVE AND TRANSNATIONAL PARTICIPATION

While Mandarin language teaching plays a significant role in transmitting Chinese culture and heritage, parents also reveal that they enrol their children in Chinese language education with the wider objective of fostering global citizenship. Even as China's power continues to grow, parents express their aspirations for their children to become "global citizens" themselves. The concept of global citizenship encompasses a cosmopolitan sense of identity that embodies "an attitude of open-mindedness and impartiality" (Kleingeld and Brown 2006, p. 7). In terms of relationships, global citizenship encourages relations with different races and their religious beliefs within a community that can transcend the insularity of nationalism. Contemporary notions of cultural cosmopolitanism influence the global citizen striving to embrace cultural diversity while protecting the "rights to culture", including minority cultures that are at risk of being marginalized (ibid., p. 12).

This multicultural perspective, which is fostered in Chinese schools that offer Chinese language learning, is espoused by parents who send their children to study there. As a parent plainly states, "I don't want them [my children] to have prejudice or be racist like not wanting to make friends with Indians or Chinese."[23] Another parent emphasizes the importance of their children acknowledging the existence of different races. Comparing Chinese private schools to state schools, another parent remarks, "If you go to normal schools, referring to government schools, they are mostly Malays."[24] In contrast to Chinese schools, "you get to know more of the races from other families. This means your friends, are not only Malays, but in Chinese schools you have Indian friends, you have Chinese friends. You even have other indigenous friends."[25] Parents express their desire for their children to have friends from diverse backgrounds, not just Malays. In terms of a multi-faith school community, parents applaud the respect accorded to observing religious holidays, which are taught informally to their children in these schools:

> If they [my children] have Muslim friends who celebrate Raya [Eid], or Indian friends who celebrate Deepavali, they would question as to why these friends did not attend school during certain times of the year. So, I would explain to them that it's currently Deepavali, for example.[26]

A diverse ethnic community is present in these schools, comprising not just the Chinese diaspora, but also the Indian diaspora. While all students study Mandarin, they collectively offer a rich knowledge of multicultural identities and distinctive religious celebrations that inform their transnational perspectives. Through socializing with peers from different ethnicities and religions, children gain awareness of diverse cultural practices and develop a sense of transnational participation through their interaction with the various diasporas.

Conclusion: Learning Chinese Beyond China's Soft Power

As discussed in this chapter, although the informants in this study demonstrate a cognizance of China's soft power, they are largely unfazed by it. Their decision to send their children to learn Chinese did not solely stem from China's rising global power. The findings of this study indicate that parents do not view Chinese language education as an instrument of China's soft power. On the contrary, their responses showed that China is not the primary destination for their children in terms of its geography and culture. In their study of Chinese Bruneians, Ho and Ho (2021) contend that the Southeast Asian Chinese are distinct from mainland Chinese even when sharing similar traditional Chinese values that include celebrating cultural festivals, observing Chinese rituals, and observing familial obligations. Across the disparate groups of the Chinese, the ethnic Chinese in Southeast Asia, comprising the Chinese overseas or diasporic community, maintain an interest in "local customs, values and systems of their adopted 'homes'" (Ho and Ho 2021, p.155). This explains the recognition and local efforts to integrate various linguistic cultures of Malay, English, Arabic and the Islamic religious culture for Muslim converts. Beyond learning the Mandarin language, both local Chinese and non-Chinese parents in Brunei Darussalam display an open-minded attitude towards diverse cultures.

Even though parents are aware of China's rising global power, the findings of this present study corroborate with Koh, Hoon, and Noor Azam's (2020) study, which suggests that Brunei is not significantly impacted by the global phenomenon of Mandarin fever. Parents choose Chinese schools not predominantly for Mandarin language learning alone. Instead, while communicative Mandarin proficiency is useful for future jobs and economic gains, parents send their children to Chinese schools for the broader objective of fostering global citizenship in an evolving and multicultural world. While Chinese parents may view Chinese language learning as part of their identity or cultural heritage, they also emphasize academic performance and extra-curricular programmes offered in conjunction with Chinese language lessons. The pursuit of academic excellence and job preparedness within both national and transnational social spheres are definitive aims of Chinese language education in Chinese schools.

Considering that Chineseness is a contested marker of identity (Hoon and Chan 2021; Ang 2022), this study provides evidence that the Southeast Asian Chinese view their links to China in an increasingly attenuated way. Drawing from immediate social interactions, parents who sign up their children for Mandarin language learning are more interested in benefiting from discounts when shopping at Chinese-owned businesses in Brunei Darussalam and neighbouring Malaysia. When discussing future employment prospects, they do not commonly cite China as a potential destination. Instead, parents focus on the regional presence of Chinese nationals, recognizing that Chinese-speaking people are increasingly found "everywhere".[27] Hence, Mandarin language learning is catered to increase participation, opportunities, and relevance within the context of Brunei and the Southeast Asian region.

Notes

1. Interview with participant 21 conducted on 2 July 2022. All interviewees who participated in this project have chosen to remain anonymous.
2. Interview with participant 29 conducted on 6 October 2022.
3. Interview with participant 25 conducted on 27 July 2022.
4. Interview with participant 24 conducted on 23 July 2022.
5. Interview with participant 25 conducted on 27 July 2022.
6. Interview with participant 22 conducted on 3 July 2022.
7. Interview with participant 23 conducted on 27 July 2022.
8. Ibid.
9. Ibid.
10. Interview with participant 20 conducted on 29 June 2022.
11. Ibid.
12. Interview with participant 18 conducted on 10 May 2022.
13. Interview with participant 24 conducted on 23 July 2022.
14. Interview with participant 20 conducted on 29 June 2022.
15. Interview with participant 24 conducted on 23 July 2022.
16. Ibid.
17. Interview with participant 20 conducted on 29 June 2022.
18. Interview with participant 18 conducted on 10 May 2022.
19. Interview with participant 21 conducted on 2 July 2022.
20. Interview with participant 24 conducted on 23 July 2022.
21. Interview with participant 31 conducted on 12 November 2022.
22. Interview with participant 24 conducted on 23 July 2022.
23. Interview with participant 34 conducted on 23 November 2022.
24. Interview with participant 20 conducted on 29 June 2022.
25. Ibid.
26. Interview with participant 34 conducted on 23 November 2022.
27. Interview with participant 29 conducted on 6 October 2022.

References

Ang, Ien. 2001. *On Not Speaking Chinese: Living Between Asia and the West*. London: Routledge.

Ang, Sylvia. 2022. *Contesting Chineseness: Nationality, Class, Gender and New Chinese Migrants*. Amsterdam: Amsterdam University Press.

Borneo Bulletin. 2023. "Be Open-minded and Free from Outside Influence". 2 March 2023. https://borneobulletin.com.bn/be-open-minded-and-free-from-outside-influence/ (accessed 9 June 2023).

Chan, Ying-Kit, and Chang-Yau Hoon. 2022. *Southeast Asia in China: Historical Entanglements and Contemporary Engagements*. Washington: Rowman and Littlefield.

Cummins, Jim. 2013. "Language and Identity in Multilingual Schools: Constructing Evidence-Based Instructional Policies". In *Managing Diversity in Education: Languages, Policies Pedagogies*, edited by David Little, Constant Leug, and Piet Van Avermaet, pp. 3–26. Bristol: Multilingual Matters.

Dellios, Rosita. 2005. "The Rise of China as a Global Power". *Culture Mandala: The Bulletin of the Centre for East-West Cultural and Economic Studies* 6, no. 2: Article 3. http://epublications.bond.edu.au/cm/vol6/iss2/3

Department of Economic Planning and Statistics. 2022. "Population". Ministry of Finance and Economy, Bandar Seri Begawan, Brunei Darussalam.

Deterding, David, and Hannah Ming Yit Ho. 2021. "An Overview of the Language, Literature and Culture of Brunei Darussalam". In *Engaging Modern Brunei: Research on Language, Literature and Culture*, edited by Hannah Ming Yit Ho and David Deterding, pp. 1–17. Singapore: Springer.

Dollar, David. 2015. "China's Rise as a Regional and Global Power". *Horizons* 4: 162–72.

Gil, Jeffrey, 2020. "Will a Character-Based Writing System Stop Chinese Becoming a Global Language? A Review and Reconsideration of the Debate". *Global Chinese* 6, no. 1: 25.

Ho, Debbie Guan Eng. 2008. "Mandarin as Mother Tongue School Language in Brunei Darussalam: A Case Study". Report presented at SEAMEO Workshop, 19–21 February 2008, Bangkok, Thailand. http://www.seameo.org/SEAMEOWeb2/images/stories/Projects/2008_MotherTongueBridgeLang/CaseStudy/papers_and_pdf/Brunei_MotherTongue_CaseStudy20jan08.pdf

———. 2021. "Chinese Dialects in Brunei: Shift, Maintenance or Loss?". In *Engaging Modern Brunei: Research on Language, Literature and Culture*, edited by Hannah Ming Yit Ho and David Deterding, pp. 67–93. Singapore: Springer.

———, and Hannah Ming Yit Ho. 2021. "Ethnic Identity and the Southeast Asian Chinese: Voices from Brunei". In *Contesting Chineseness: Ethnicity, Identity and Nation in China and Southeast Asia*, edited by Chang-Yau Hoon and Ying-Kit Chan, pp. 149–66. Singapore: Springer.

Ho, Hannah Ming Yit. 2019. "Women Doing Malayness in Brunei Darussalam". *Southeast Asian Review for English* 56, no. 2: 149–65.

———. 2021a. "Chinese Bruneian Identity: Negotiating Individual, Familial and Transnational Selves in Anglophone Bruneian Literature". *Wenshan Review of Literature and Culture* 14, no. 2: 1–34.

———. 2021b. "Localisation of Malay Muslim Identity: A Modern Nation's Economic and Cultural Goals". In *Engaging Modern Brunei: Research on Language, Literature and Culture*, edited by Hannah Ming Yit Ho and David Deterding, pp. 127–43. Singapore: Springer.

———, and Debbie Guan Eng Ho. 2019. "Identity in Flux: The Sarong Party Girl's Pursuit of a Good Life". *Asiatic: Journal of Language and Literature* 13, no. 2: 146–66.

Hoon, Chang-Yau, and Esther Kuntjara, 2019. "The Politics of Mandarin Fever in Contemporary Indonesia Resinicization, Economic Impetus, and China's Soft Power". *Asian Survey* 59, no. 3: 573–94.

———, and Ying-Kit Chan, eds. 2021. *Contesting Chineseness: Ethnicity, Identity and Nation in China and Southeast Asia*. Singapore: Springer.

Kleingeld, Pauline, and Eric Brown. 2006. "Cosmopolitanism". *Stanford Encyclopedia of Philosophy*, pp. 1–24. Stanford: Stanford University Press.

Kon, James. 2023. "The Road to Success". *Borneo Bulletin*, 12 February 2023. https://borneobulletin.com.bn/the-road-to-success/ (accessed 9 June 2023).

Koh, Sin Yee, Chang-Yau Hoon, and Noor Azam Haji-Othman. 2020. "'Mandarin Fever' and Chinese Language-Learning in Brunei's Middle Schools: Discrepant Discourses, Multifaceted Realities and Institutional Barriers". *Asian Studies Review* 45, no. 2: 325–44.

Noor Azam, Haji-Othman, James McLellan, and Gary M. Jones. 2019. "Language Policy and Practice in Brunei Darussalam". In *Routledge Handbook of Language Policy and Practice in Asia*, edited by Andy Kirkpatrick and A. Liddicoat, pp. 314–25. London: Routledge.

Riley, Philip. 2007. *Language, Culture and Identity: An Ethnolinguistic Perspective*. London: A&C Black.

RSSing. 2018. "Top CHMS BSB Students Receive Awards". 11 July 2018. https://borneo363.rssing.com/chan-61976226/article6371.html (accessed 9 June 2023).

Salbrina, Sharbawi, and Jainatul Halida Jaidin. 2019. "Brunei's SPN21 English Language-in-Education Policy: A Macro-to-Micro Evaluation". *Current Issues in Language Planning* 21, no. 2: 175–201.

Suryadinata, Leo. 2017. *The Rise of China and the Chinese Overseas: A Study of Beijing's Changing Policy in Southeast Asia and Beyond*. Singapore: ISEAS Publishing.

Ullah, A.K.M.A., and Hannah Ming Yit Ho. 2020. "Globalisation and Cultures in Southeast Asia: Demise, Fragmentation, Transformation". *Global Society* 35, no. 2: 191–206.

Wang, Gungwu. 1993. "Greater China and the Chinese Overseas". *China Quarterly* 136: 926–48.

Zhao, Kaili, and Chang-Yau Hoon. 2023. "Navigating the Brunei-China Economic Connectivity under the Belt and Road Initiative: Achievements and Challenges". *Malaysian Journal of Chinese Studies* 12, no. 1: 95–116.

Part IV
CHINA'S SOFT POWER AND POPULAR CULTURE

12

THE POWER OF FANTASY
Southeast Asians' Obsession with Chinese *Xianxia* Dramas

Gwendolyn Yap

Introduction

On 21 September 2019, a 9,000-strong crowd eagerly watched the stage of IMPACT Arena, Bangkok, Thailand (*naewna.com* 2019). They were not there for K-pop stars or Japanese celebrities. Instead, they were awaiting the leading cast of *The Untamed* (陈情令), a Chinese *xianxia* (仙侠) drama. Earlier in 2019, this fifty-episode *xianxia* was released on the Chinese online streaming site, Tencent Video. It swept domestic and regional markets, ranking first in popularity among 631 web dramas from 2019 to 2020 at the 8th China Internet Audio and Video Convention.[1] *The Untamed* is a drama adaptation of the web novel *Grandmasters of Demonic Cultivation* (魔道祖师),[2] written by Mo Xiang Tong Xiu (墨香铜臭) on the Chinese web novel site, Jinjiang Literature City (晋江文学城). Briefly, it chronicles the resurrection of an ostracized demonic cultivator Wei Wuxian (魏无羡) who—across the course of the series—eventually redeems himself through investigating a string of mysterious events tied to his initial death, including soul-eating ghosts and demons. Throughout the journey, he is accompanied by his soulmate, Lan Wangji (蓝忘机).

The wildfire of *The Untamed* did not leave Southeast Asia unscathed, having garnered 106 million views in the region (Li 2019). Due to its popularity in Southeast Asia, a world tour for the cast of *The Untamed* was announced, with Bangkok being the first stop followed by Vietnam, Singapore and Malaysia. Unfortunately, this was derailed due to the pandemic (Hudson 2020). By 2021, two years after its initial release, *The Untamed* had acquired 9.8 billion views on Tencent Video.[3] The success of *The Untamed* heralded a new wave of Chinese *xianxia* dramas, with the genre producing thirteen new dramas in the second half of 2022, and sixteen drama releases projected for release in 2023 (*SoHu* 2022). These new dramas have been made available on regional streaming sites such as Netflix, Disney+, WeTV and iQiYi, to feed the demand.[4] To illustrate the types of *xianxia*s that are garnering regional interest, Table 12.1 showcases the top releases from 2018 to 2023 as well as the main international distributors of these *xianxia*s.

Like the Korean wave of the 2000s that has now translated into a tool of soft power for the Korean government (Shim 2017, p. 36), this surge in *xianxia*'s popularity represents a potential source of soft power for China. Soft power is defined by Joseph Nye as the attractiveness of a country's culture and values that may eventually develop into political advantages for the primary country. These sources of soft power include culture, political values and foreign policies and can be harnessed by institutions—state or otherwise—to achieve the desired outcomes (Nye 2004). Case in point, *xianxia* dramas were born out of China's push to globalize its entertainment industry, following in the footsteps of Korea's success (Shim 2017, p. 39). However, with the Chinese state moving to regulate *xianxia*'s production domestically, complications regarding the spread of Chinese soft power have arisen. The state's restriction on *xianxia*s suggests that there are times when institutional-driven soft power actions do not necessarily translate into the desired outcomes sought after by the primary country. Due to societal preferences, the 'undesired' might proliferate instead. Thus, *xianxia*'s popularity in Southeast Asia raises two important questions: First, how and why did *xianxia* reach this level of popularity in Southeast Asia? Second, what does this sudden popularity bode for China's regional soft power?

What Exactly is *Xianxia*?

Xianxia derives its name from two words, *shenxian* (神仙) and *xia* (侠). *Shenxian* broadly refers to gods, demons and immortals in the Chinese mythological realm, while *xia* refers to tales of *wuxia* (武侠), the hero-warrior figure. *Xianxia* merges the characteristics of these two terms in its literature, positioning the immortal as the hero-warrior who overcomes difficulties to save the world. However, the titular character of *xianxia* does not need to be a god or an immortal. Many *xianxia*s feature humans who go on to attain god-like spiritual powers—and even immortality—through "cultivation" (修炼 *xiulian*). For instance, in *The Untamed*, Wei Wuxian is a human "cultivator" who dabbled in the demonic arts, eventually becoming

TABLE 12.1
Top 10 *Xianxia* Releases from 2018 to 2023*

Title	Original Author	Year Released	Originally Released On	Main International Distributors
Ashes of Love 香蜜沉沉烬如霜	Dian Xian 电线	2018	Jiangsu TV	Netflix/iQiyi /Viki
Legend of Fuyao 扶摇	Tian Xia Gui Yuan 天下归元	2018	Tencent Video	Amazon/ Viki
The Untamed 陈情令	Mo Xiang Tong Xiu 墨香铜臭	2019	Tencent Video	WeTV/Netflix /Amazon/ AppleTV
Love and Redemption 琉璃	Shi Si Lang 十四郎	2020	Youku	WeTV/Viki
Eternal Love (The Pillow Book) 三生三世枕上书	Tang Qi Gong Zi 唐七公子	2020	Tencent Video	WeTV/ Viki
Love Between Fairy and Devil 苍兰诀	Jiu Lu Fei Xiang 九鹭非香	2022	iQiyi	Netflix/WeTV/Viki/ iQiyi
Who Rules the World 且试天下	Qing Ling Yue 倾泠月	2022	Tencent	Netflix/WeTV/iFlix
Immortal Samsara (Part 1) 沉香如屑	Su Mo 苏莫	2022	Youku	Netflix/Viki
The Starry Love 星落凝成糖	Yi Du Jun Hua 一度君华	2023	Youku	Viki
Till the End of the Moon 长月烬明	Teng Luo Wei Zhi 藤萝为枝	2023	Youku	Netflix/Viki

Note: This list is non-exhaustive.
Source: Collated from various online ranking sites including MyDramaList, IMDb and Medium.

a demonic cultivator named the Yiling Patriarch (夷陵老祖). While he grew up within the strict hierarchal structure of cultivator clans, his resistance to conformity eventually led him to practice demonic arts such as necromancy. These god-like powers eventually ostracized him from the clans and forced him into an untimely death. Even after his death, these powers were exploited when he is resurrected into another person's body sixteen years later, playing into the trope of immortality as not merely a continuation of life within a singular physical entity, i.e., his original body, but also through multiple entities.

Sharing the root concept of a hero-warrior triumphing over evil, *xianxia* and *wuxia* are often conflated on drama ranking pages, making it difficult to distinguish between them.[5] This conflation of the two is understandable when the core of the two genres is considered. Stephen Teo's *Chinese Martial Arts Cinema: The Wuxia Tradition* notes that the "emphasis of the wuxia [...] is the pursuit of righteousness" (Teo 2009, p. 4). Similarly, *xianxias* often feature the lead character undergoing trials and tribulations to follow what is morally justified, even if it goes against the laws of the system they are governed under. However, even while there are similarities in essence, *xianxias* carry distinctive differences from *wuxias* and should be viewed as a separate phenomenon of its own (see Table 12.2).

To expand on the general differences between *xianxia* and *wuxia* listed in Table 12.2, *The Untamed* will be used as the basis of analysis against the general themes of *wuxia*. It is worth noting, however, that the *xianxia* genre spans a wide range of interpretations within the boundaries of these characteristics and is not merely confined to the ones illustrated through *The Untamed*.

TABLE 12.2
Differences between Xianxia and Wuxia*

Characteristics	Wuxia	Xianxia
Focus	Physical action	Magic and fantasy action
Characters	Working-class descent	Noble/deity descent
Dramatization	Historical realism	Historical aestheticism
Thematic Concerns	Brotherhood and Loyalty	Love and Romance
		Beauty
Authors	Dominated by men	Dominated by women

Notes: * Characteristics of *wuxia* were gleaned from Teo's exposition on the *wuxia* genre in his book *Chinese Martial Arts Cinema: The Wuxia Tradition* (2009). The comparisons to *xianxia* were derived from personal observations of popular *xianxia* dramas.

Magic and Fantasy Action

In the *wuxia* tradition, the emphasis is placed on the kung fu (功夫) skills that the character achieves through "training and practice". There is also the element of "flight", which depicts these martial art masters flying through the air using *qigong* (气功 or inner energy) that they cultivated (ibid., p. 4). These are both elements found within *xianxia* as well, with physical action scenes such as sword fighting, and the use of *qi* in cultivating their swordsmanship. However, more emphasis is placed on the combative magical powers that the heroes possess. For instance, Wei Wuxian carries a flute that when played, conjures black spirits that look like smoke. These black spirits can infiltrate and penetrate the minds of other characters, turning them into puppets. Lan Wangji, his partner, plays a *guqin* (古琴) that can confer with spirits when played correctly. More focus is also placed on how characters can manipulate talismans and spiritual objects to their benefit than on characters training to achieve higher levels of physical mastery.

Noble/Deity Descent

Wuxia often depicted members of the working-class population, dressed "commonly" and having humble origins (Teo 2009, p. 18). However, *xianxia* characters are associated with nobility and not with plebians. In *The Untamed*, most of the main characters are heirs to the five main clans that govern the region. They are dressed according to their clans' colours and are rarely shown in rags or common clothes.

This concern with nobility permeates the political structure found within *xianxia*. *Wuxia* often features outlaws who challenge the system externally, resorting to "violence to ensure justice and defend the common people against tyrants and warlords" (ibid., p. 19). In *xianxia*, the noble lineage of the characters meant that the politics that they engage in are often within the clan system itself. While there is the presence of violence, this violence is committed internally and does not affect the "common people". For instance, in *The Untamed*, the large interclan conflict takes place within the palace grounds and does not affect the general populace, who are portrayed as bustling and thriving despite the chaos.

Significantly, in *xianxia*, the dominant system is neither affected nor changed after the disruption to its order. Instead, it reverts to its original functioning state. When Wei Wuxian was ostracized by the dominant clans, the only way he could negotiate and defend his purpose was to re-enter the system. To clear his name, he has to rely on Lan Wangji—highly respected amongst the clans—to infiltrate and get other nobility to listen to his cause.

Once cleared of his name, he is allowed back into the system he was once ostracized from, with little to no change in its governing structure. In the drama adaptation, Lan Wangji even assumes the governing role of "Chief Cultivator" (仙督) at the end, reinforcing the functions of the dominant structure.

Historical Aestheticism
Some critics argue that *wuxia* is synonymous with period films due to the emphasis it places on the era it is written about (ibid., p. 6). However, in *xianxia*, it is impossible to pinpoint the specific historical era in which it takes place. This could be attributed to the *xian* (仙) nature of the genre, where immortals live on a different time scale compared to humans, thus allowing for flexibility in including traditional elements across different periods in Chinese historicity. This flexibility is illustrated through the art and aesthetics found within *xianxia*. The set of *The Untamed* is intricately decorated with many references to traditional Chinese architecture and art. However, there is no clearly established indicator of historicity from which these traditional arts emerge from. In short, all things aesthetic about Chinese traditional culture are concentrated and condensed within *xianxia*s for audience appreciation.

Beauty
Beauty is the key defining feature of *xianxia*, setting it apart from *wuxia*. It is not only limited to the aesthetic settings found within *xianxia* but also extends to the main characters' looks. Most, if not all, of the main characters in *Xianxia* are good-looking. There is a great emphasis on the beauty of the characters, with clean clothes and flawless makeup maintained even after a violent fighting scene. *Xianxia* characters may not possess a good character, but they must always have a good face. Directors of *xianxia* dramas even acknowledge that good looks are of priority over the skillset of the actors when it comes to casting.[6]

Love and Romance
Romance takes centre stage in *xianxia* narratives, as seen in *The Untamed*. Lan Wangji's love for Wei Wuxian drives the entire story, even beyond his initial death, as he searches for him for sixteen long years. Once reunited, Lan Wangji's continual affection and protectiveness are what allow Wuxian the freedom to investigate and uncover the culprit behind his evil reputation. It is worth noting that in the original novel, Lan Wangji and Wei Wuxian are depicted as lovers who eventually marry. However, due to censorship

laws in China regarding homosexuality, the drama portrays their close relationship as that of soulmates instead. The emphasis on romance as the dominant theme is carried through to other *xianxia*s, reflected in their promotional posters (see Figure 12.1).

This emphasis on romance differs from *wuxia*, where brotherhood and loyalty are the focus of the story. For comparison, Figure 12.2 shows the promotional posters of *wuxia*.

Dominated by Women Authors

The *wuxia* genre is dominated by men including Jin Yong (金庸), Gu Long (古龙) and Liang Yusheng (梁羽生). However, the *xianxia* genre is mostly dominated by women. Mo Xiang Tong Xiu (墨香铜臭), Jiu Lu Fei Xiang (九鹭非香) and Tang Qi Gong Zi (唐七公子)—while all anonymous names—are all women.[7] There are, however, *xianxia* authors who are men who have achieved fame with their works, such as Wo Chi Xi Hong Shi (我吃西红柿). Wo Chi Xi Hong Shi is the author of *Snow Eagle Lord* (雪鹰领主), which has been adapted into an animation, drama series, and even a movie (Nam 2023).

It is significant that despite their success, many *xianxia* authors decide to remain anonymous. Some do reveal their real names—for instance, Jiu Lu Fei Xiang whose real name is Hong Wan Ling 洪婉玲, and Wo Chi Xi Hong Shi whose real name is Zhu Hong Zhi 朱洪志. However, most do not. This anonymity could be attributed to a few possibilities.

The most straightforward possibility is the culture of web novels where authors not only rely on their titles but also their humorous monikers to capture their audiences' attention. As these monikers leave lasting impressions on the reader, it will be difficult for the reader to associate the work with the author's real name afterward. Hence, publishing or production companies might not be keen to utilize the author's real name while promoting their work, instead relying on their moniker's initial popularity. The second possibility is the need for privacy. With the accessibility of social media and the aggressiveness of online fandom culture, popular authors always face the possibility of being harassed by their fans—especially if they are women or if they publish works that are contrary to the dominant discourse, such as LGBTQ+. Both of which are present in the *xianxia* genre. Therefore, authors may choose to remain anonymous for their own safety. The last possibility is that the authors wish for their lives to be kept separate from their works to prevent judgement from those around them. Due to the pressures of maintaining "face" or respectability (面子) in Chinese culture, being known for such novels may be perceived as disgraceful or

FIGURE 12.1
Other Promotional Posters of Xianxias Such as *Love Between Fairy and Devil* (2022) and *Eternal Love* (2017) Heavily Feature the Romance Between the Lead Characters

Source: Google Images.

THE POWER OF FANTASY 225

FIGURE 12.2
Promotion Posters of Wuxias Such as Nirvana in Fire (2015) and Side Story of Fox Volant (2022) Where the Characters Are Seen in Combative Stances and There Is No Clear Relationship Drawn between Them

Source: Google Images.

humiliating, leading the author to "lose face" (丢脸). This humiliation may lead to undesirable consequences in the author's life. Thus, remaining anonymous will protect the author from such judgment.

From the characteristics detailed above, one could say that *xianxia* represents not a continuation, but an extension of *wuxia*. Indeed, its predecessor, *wuxia*, has been highly popular in Southeast Asian markets since the 1930s, boasting a long and rich tradition that cannot be easily subsumed under the more recent phenomenon of *xianxia* (Teo 2009). Nevertheless, the interchangeable labelling of the two genres has led to criticism that *xianxia* is unable to live up to the legacy of *wuxia*. Critics declare the *jianghu* (江湖)—the alternate realm that *wuxia* novels are set in—dead, regarding *xianxia*s not inadequate to continue the complex world-building that the *wuxia* classics embarked upon (Cai 2023). Others bemoan the superficiality of *xianxia*, either in its overly romantic storytelling or its hyper-focus on good-looking actors.[8] Despite these criticisms, the explosive popularity of *xianxia* reflects an appeal that cannot be taken lightly. The next section will look at the possible reasons for the regional attractiveness of *xianxia*.

THE RISE OF *XIANXIA* IN SOUTHEAST ASIA

The popularity of *xianxia* in Southeast Asia can be attributed to two factors. First, *xianxia* is a hybrid cultural product that appeals to regional audiences. Secondly, the recent foray of Chinese streaming services into Southeast Asia coincided with the heightened attention paid to the *xianxia* phenomenon.

As mentioned, *xianxia* is a product of "cultural mixing", and this cements its appeal to Southeast Asian audiences. "Cultural mixing" is a term used to denote how different cultures merge through the processes of production and adaptation to generate new products that transcend national borders (Iwabuchi 2017, p. 28). In *xianxia*'s case, it originated through a blend of Japanese and Chinese cultural influences to be later translated onscreen through Korean-influenced production processes.

In the previous section, it was mentioned that *xianxia* originated from web novels. These web novels are published on online literature websites such as *Jinjiang* (now partially owned by Tencent) and JJWXC. These websites often featured fan fiction written in the *danmei* (耽美) style that originated in Japan as *yaoi* (Boys' Love). Featuring homoerotic relationships between men, the genre spilled over into China from Japan as early as the 2000s (Jin 2009, p. 2). *Danmei*, meaning "indulgence in beauty", features the leads as aesthetically beautiful and desirable (ibid., p. 5), and displaying traits contrary to traditional expectations of gender. The web novels reinterpreted Chinese classics and *wuxia*s into *danmei* novels for a dominantly female readership. Over time, it was this combination of influences that gave birth to the aesthetic-focused hybrid, *xianxia*.

Xianxia combines the elements of aesthetic beauty sought by *danmei* writers and the tales about loyalty, the triumph of good over evil, and justice as modelled by *wuxia*. As mentioned in the previous section, *The Untamed* is one such homoerotic *xianxia* adapted from the online web novel, *Grandmaster of Demonic Cultivation* (魔道祖师). In contrast to its origins, however, *xianxia* is not exclusively confined to homosexual relationships and often features heterosexual couples in storytelling. TV adaptations of *xianxia* web novels featuring heterosexual couples include *Love Between Fairy and Devil* (苍兰诀) and *Eternal Love of Dream* (三生三世十里上书) (2020).⁹ Briefly, *Love Between Fairy and Devil* tells the story of how a lowly fairy accidentally released a sealed demon lord. As their relationship blossoms, the series chronicles the redemption of the demon lord and the revelation of the lowly fairy as a Goddess. *Eternal Love of Dream*, the sequel to the drama *Eternal Love* (三生三世十里桃花) (2017), elucidates the romance between a fox spirit and the Heavenly Emperor that spans three lifetimes. As the story progresses, they navigate and overcome various events that threaten their relationship. Both series have garnered high viewership domestically and regionally. *Love Between Fairy and Devil* reached first place globally within four hours of its release on the international iQIYI app (*Global Times*, 30 August 2022). *Eternal Love of Dream* reached 5 billion views on Tencent upon its conclusion, achieving first in online view rankings in Thailand (She 2020).

If the *xianxia* web novel is a mixing of Chinese *wuxia* and Japanese *danmei*, then the drama adaptation is a product formed through the addition of Korean production aesthetics. Following the success of the Korean drama *My Love from the Stars* (2013) in China, the Chinese media industry sent delegates to Korea to learn from the "'success story' of the Korean Wave", sparking a tide of collaboration between Korea and China on production know-how (Shim 2017, p. 41). This led to the globalization of drama production in China, aimed at attracting external audiences and bolstering Chinese soft power. Through these collaborations, many Chinese studios began not only to adapt dramas from Korea for their local audiences but also to produce original stories for global consumption. The *xianxia*s are a result of this. Indeed, the separation between dramas for domestic and global consumption is not lost on critics, who observed that shows directed towards a domestic audience remain mostly propagandist, while shows made for an international audience deal with more universal themes (Yau 2021).

Indeed, the ability of *xianxia* to introduce traditional Chinese culture and mythology to a global audience aligns with the ambition of the state to increase the reach of its soft power (Tiong 2023). *Love Between Fairy and Devil* had thirty-two intangible cultural heritage traditional crafts presented, and twenty-seven intangible cultural heritage craftsmen working on the show (*Wang Yi Shou Ye* 2021). As noted in the earlier section, these heritage crafts are not constrained by the historical era they belong to. Instead, they are chosen where they can aesthetically promote Chinese culture the most. This phenomenon is noted by Appadurai in his book *Modernity at Large* where he observes how the past is "a synchronic warehouse of cultural scenarios, a kind of temporal central casting, to which recourse can be taken as appropriate" (Appadurai 1996, p. 30). Like how *Love Between Fairy and Devil* selects the type of Chinese cultural heritage to "cast" in their series, time can be transcended and consolidated into a single medium to be experienced by the public as an immersive cultural experience.

The effectiveness of this selective aestheticism is reflected on social media, with online communities sharing short-form videos of influencers donning traditional Chinese costumes (汉服 *hanfu*) and promoting traditional Chinese aesthetics (see Figure 12.3).

Thus, through cultural mixing, *xianxia* not only makes itself palatable to Southeast Asian audiences but provides enough uniqueness to set it apart from dramas produced by Japan and Korea.

Secondly, the accessibility and affordability of Chinese streaming services in the region contribute to the popularity of *xianxia*. From 2019 to 2020, Tencent—one of China's biggest tech companies—rolled out WeTV in Southeast Asia. WeTV is the international streaming arm of Tencent Video, the service responsible for releasing *The Untamed* to critical success. It is therefore unsurprising that *The Untamed* saw a surge in popularity in Southeast Asia in the same period, reportedly achieving 250 per cent growth for Tencent after the drama was made accessible through WeTV (*Blognone* 2019).

During its initial entry into the Thai market, WeTV only offered original Chinese content with Thai dubbing (Patpicha 2019). After acquiring iFlix, the second biggest regional streaming service next to Netflix (Kishimoto and Suzuki 2019; Goodfellow 2020), Tencent expanded to include Thai, Vietnamese and Indonesian subtitles to cater to regional audiences (Ngo 2021). This expansion indicates that the reach of the Chinese streaming

FIGURE 12.3
Search '#hanfu' on TikTok (Left) and Instagram (Right). There Are Over 288k Posts on Instagram Regarding This Hashtag

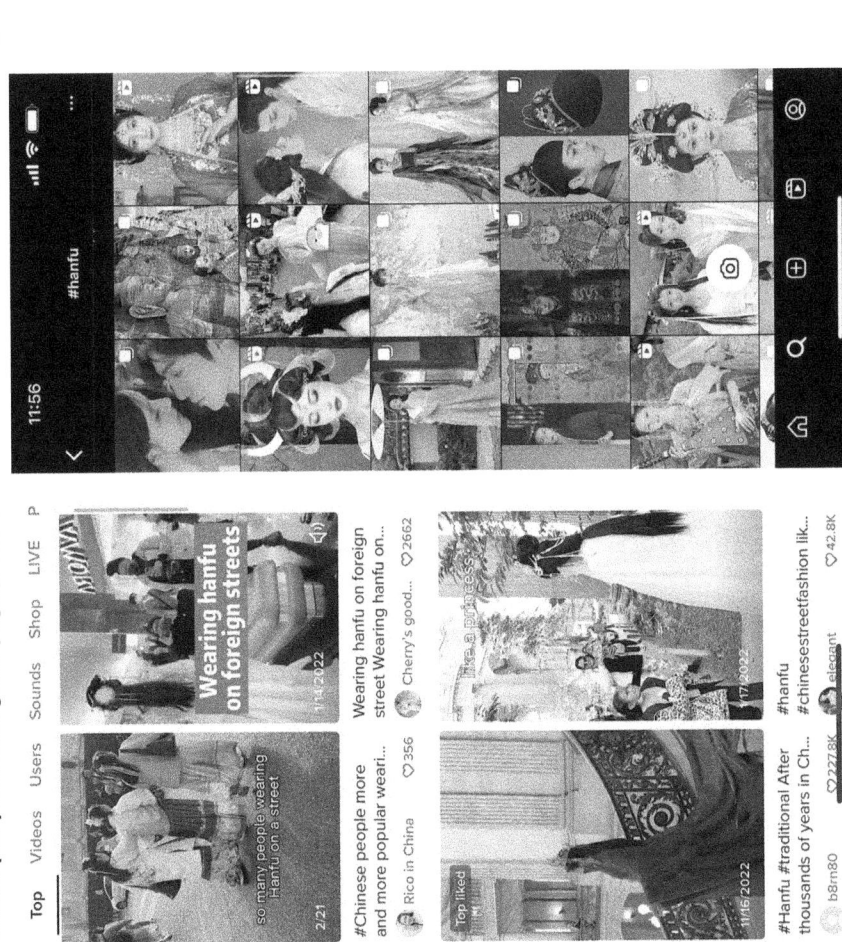

market has gone beyond that of the ethnic Chinese community to non-Chinese audiences in Southeast Asia.

To date, WeTV is one of the top three over-the-top (OTT) service providers in Southeast Asia (*Yahoo* 2022), taking up 10 per cent of viewership regionally and coming in third to competitors Disney+ and Netflix (*Media Partners Asia* 2022). Other Chinese streaming sites have also entered the regional market, including iQIYI and Bilibili. On regional streaming services, 13 per cent of content across all platforms is Chinese. It is worth noting, however, that Netflix—the largest viewing site regionally—has also contracted popular Chinese *xianxia*s for viewing (refer to Table 12.1), hence reducing the incentive for audiences to cross streaming platforms to view Chinese dramas.

Obstacles to the Popularity of *Xianxia*

While the Chinese state has largely encouraged the export of Chinese dramas to Southeast Asia, the *xianxia* genre has suffered domestic restrictions that threaten its status as a viable cultural product regionally. The sanctions slapped against it include crackdowns on online literature websites—from which many *xianxia*s were adapted—and tighter regulations in 2021 on how men should be portrayed on-screen.

The online literature websites from which *xianxia* dramas are drawn are highly popular in China, and in 2020 registered altogether over 460 million readers (Deng and Qu 2021). In 2019, tightening online regulation by the Chinese government called for these websites to remove obscene literature from their platforms. Obscene literature refers to materials with sexual or LGBTQ content (Kawakami 2019). This meant that many *xianxia* stories built around homoerotic relationships were now inaccessible through these websites. While it can be argued that many *xianxia* novels remain permissible because they depict heterosexual relationships, the ban effectively limits the pool of inspiration that *xianxia* dramas are adapted from. The irony is not lost on commentators who have observed that queer content is proven successful money-makers for streaming giants. However, its heavy reliance on the capital provided through adaptation means that these contents are now often swept under the rug as state regulations kick in (Wang 2023).

The second obstacle to *xianxia*'s popularity is the portrayal of men on-screen. In 2021, China's National Radio and TV Administration released a series of guidelines targeting the entertainment industry. The third clause states that artists are not allowed to be "sissy" (娘炮), and have to adhere to a "proper beauty standard" (正确审美导向).[10] While the terms remain vague, the statement suggests that effeminate portrayals of men are discouraged. These include having men with delicate or graceful mannerisms or acting in any manner not regarded as stereotypically masculine (Law 2021). This further limits the production ability of *xianxia* dramas, which now have to factor in the effeminateness of their costumes, actors and mannerisms. This poses a problem as *xianxia*'s main draw are good-looking, delicate-featured actors preferred by the dominantly female audience. As women are the highest-paying consumers of these "pretty boys", there have been sentiments that these crackdowns are indirectly discriminating against them (Chen 2021). With the increasing number of Chinese women choosing to pursue economic independence over traditional milestones such as marriage and children, the restriction of these entertainments can be regarded as a backlash against their new-founded independence.

While there are foreseeable effects on the domestic audience, the extent of these restrictions on *xianxia* production for a global audience remains uncertain. As Chinese streaming companies host differing applications for their domestic and international audience—for instance, Tencent Video caters to Chinese audiences while WeTV is internationally directed—what may impact the domestic market may not affect the international market. Nonetheless, as China's cultural image heavily relies on its portrayal through international channels, this image cannot stray too far from what is presented domestically, making the future of *xianxia*s uncertain. These sanctions might also deter Southeast Asians from visiting China as the aspects that initially attracted them to Chinese culture are perceived as "discouraged" by the state—potentially limiting economic opportunities in cultural tourism for China.

The Show Goes On

While domestic restrictions remain a central concern for *xianxia* adaptations, exported *xianxia* dramas have recorded a spike in production in the past and upcoming years. This indicates that the continued demand for *xianxia* outweighs the problems brought on by domestic censorship, reinforcing the notion that soft power is often societally driven and not state-motivated. As Nye observes, "[the] attraction to shared values and [...] duty of contributing to the achievement of those values" drives soft power (Nye 2004, p. 7). While Nye's statement is originally intended for geopolitical relationships, it can also reflect how the shared values and interests of regional audiences dominantly drive the production of *xianxia*s—not the state.

Indeed, *xianxia* dramas have opened doors for China-Southeast Asia collaboration in entertainment. After WeTV's success in establishing itself in the region using *xianxia*, it has moved to draft partnerships with production companies in Thailand, Indonesia and the Philippines to produce local content under WeTV Originals. These WeTV Originals include the Thai series *The Wife* (2023) and *609 Bedtime Story* (2023) and the Indonesian series *Mozachiko* (2023). It has also begun to open doors for regional advertisers on their streaming app (*Telecom Review* 2022).

iQIYI, a rival Chinese streaming service, inked a collaboration with Singaporean company G.H.Y Culture to produce a short drama series for Singaporean viewers (*G.H.Y Culture Media* 2022) and signed with Astro Malaysia to stream Chinese dramas for Malaysian viewers. These collaborations might allow production companies to sidestep Chinese restrictions and offer certain content—such as those relating to LGBTQ+ and other sensitive issues—for a global audience. With the increasing number of collaborations between regional production companies and their Chinese counterparts, it will not be surprising if examples of Southeast Asian *xianxia* appear in the near future.

The genre's popularity is also not lost on other East Asian countries, and Korea has released its own *xianxia*-esque drama on Netflix, titled *Alchemy of Souls* (환혼). Similar to Chinese *xianxia*s, this fantasy drama features humans who go through "cultivation" to achieve immortality. The main character, Jang Uk (장욱), struggles to be a worthy heir to his family name with his sealed magical powers. He meets Naksu (낙수), an assassin whose soul was mysteriously transferred to a lowly servant named Mudeok (무덕이). Through their budding romance, Mudeok (as Naksu) becomes his teacher and guides him in unsealing his magic and earning his rightful place. They eventually clash with other sorcerers who crave Jang Uk's newly unsealed powers that will allow them to achieve immortality. True to *xianxia* fashion, this Korean *xianxia* also heavily features Korean traditional culture and mythology. Though it represents a relatively new genre for Korea, it has been very well-received by Korean and Southeast Asian audiences, ranking top ten on Netflix for an average of twenty-five consecutive weeks across Southeast Asian countries.[11] This suggests that Chinese production companies face competition from their better-established East Asian counterparts, and should not take their recent popularity for granted.

While *xianxia*s gain more attention in the region, how it will benefit China and Chinese policymakers remains unclear. However, from the continued growth of Chinese TV shows in the region and the increased demand for new *xianxia*s, it appears that China's rise in popular entertainment in the region will only continue.

Notes

1. 微博电视剧. (@微博电视剧). #陈情令网络剧热度第一##第八届网络视听大会#【18个月上线631部网剧 《陈情令》成"剧王"】据《中国网络视听发展研究报告》显示，从2019年-2020年上半年上线的631部网络剧的热度指数排行来看，仙侠剧《陈情令》排在首位，刑侦剧《破冰行动》、校园青春偶像剧《全职高手》以及《庆余年》《长安十二时辰》紧随其后. 14 October 2020, https://m.weibo.cn/status/4559979988390428 (accessed 13 April 2023).
2. The series was so popular that the web novel has been translated into eleven different languages, including Vietnamese, Thai and Burmese. It also has an official English novel distributed under Seven Seas Entertainment. Significantly, while the complete series (four volumes in total) has been published in Traditional Chinese, there is only one volume published in Simplified Chinese. The incomplete publication of the Simplified Chinese version is attributed to China's 2019 crackdown on the web novel portals, affecting the publication process.
3. The show is also available on streaming platforms such as Netflix, Viki and Amazon Prime, with none of the views counted into this number. See 陈熙涵, "时隔两年,《陈情令》热度不减，播放量破95亿". 文汇, 24 June 2021, https://wenhui.whb.cn/third/jinri/202106/24/411014.html (accessed 13 April 2023).
4. Personal observation of streaming websites and their respective landing pages.
5. According to fan blogs, *wuxia* and *xianxia*s are usually grouped together. See https://www.newhanfu.com/23661.html and https://sarankita.com/blog/2872/best-wuxia-series-xianxia-chinese-dramas/
6. "Popularity and Future of Xianxia Fantasy Dramas Assessed at TV Forum", 28th Shanghai TV Festival, 9 June 2016, https://www.stvf.com/english/content?aid=import-cms-972
7. Their genders are determined through the following: Mo Xiang Tong Xiu's author interview where her voice is heard: https://www.bilibili.com/video/av28962911/?from=search&seid=6667881808626574761, Jiu Lu Fei Xiang's real name is Hong Wan Ling 洪婉玲, https://mydramalist.com/people/53337-jiu-liu-fei-xiang, Tang Qi Gong Zi was a guest actress on the drama adaptation of her novel *Ten Miles of Peach Blossoms After Story*, https://wiki.d-addicts.com/Ten_Miles_of_Peach_Blossoms_After_Story
8. Avenue X, "What's Wrong with Xianxia Dramas Today", *Youtube*, 2 November 2021, https://www.youtube.com/watch?v=0fRL8rZeT6E (accessed 14 April 2023).
9. Not to be confused with *Eternal Love* (三生三世十里桃花) (2017), the first in the *Three Lives, Three Worlds* series.
10. The full statement is: 坚定文化自信、大力弘扬中华优秀传统文化、革命文化、社会主义先进文化。树立节目正确审美导向，严格把握演员和嘉宾选用、表演风格、服饰妆容等，坚决杜绝"娘炮"等畸形审美。坚决抵制炒作炫富享乐、绯闻隐私、负面热点、低俗"网红"、无底线审丑等泛娱乐化倾向". See 国家广播电视总局, 2021. "国家广播电视总局办公厅关于进一步加强 文艺节目及其人员管理的通知", 2 September 2021, http://www.nrta.gov.cn/art/2021/9/2/art_113_57756.html (accessed 15 April 2023).
11. The Southeast Asian countries include Indonesia, Malaysia, the Philippines, Singapore, Thailand and Vietnam. See https://top10.netflix.com/united-states/tv

References

Appadurai, Arjun. 1996. *Modernity at Large: Cultural Dimensions of Globalization*. Minneapolis: University of Minnesota Press.

Blognone. 2019. "Tencent เผย "ปรมาจารย์ลัทธิมาร" ดัน WeTV โต 250%, ยอดดาวน์โหลดเฉลี่ยเดือนละล้าน [Tencent reveals "Grandmaster of Demonic Cultivation" pushes WeTV to grow 250%, monthly downloads average at millions]". 17 October 2019. https://www.blognone.com/node/112591 (accessed 14 April 2023).

Cai, Yiwen. 2023. "How China's Favourite Fantasy Realm Faded into the Background". *Sixth Tone*, 27 January 2023. https://www.sixthtone.com/news/1012137 (accessed 13 April 2023).

Chen, Jing. 2021. "China's Crackdown on Pretty Boys and Temple Temptresses: Why Are Chinese Women Feeling Targeted?". *ThinkChina*, 1 October 2021. https://www.thinkchina.sg/chinas-crackdown-pretty-boys-and-temple-temptresses-why-are-chinese-women-feeling-targeted

Deng, Iris, and Tracy Qu. 2021. "Dominance of Tencent's China Literature in Online Publishing Opens Antitrust Questions Amid China's Big Tech Crackdown". *South China Morning Post*, 10 July 2022. https://www.scmp.com/tech/big-tech/article/3140294/dominance-tencents-china-literature-online-publishing-opens-antitrust (accessed 15 April 2023).

G.H.Y Culture Media. 2022. "G.H.Y Culture & Media Announces Launch of Singapore-China Short Dramas and Entertainment IP Projects". *Cision PR Newswire*, 27 July 2022. https://en.prnasia.com/releases/apac/g-h-y-culture-media-announces-launch-of-singapore-china-short-dramas-and-entertainment-ip-projects-369770.shtml (accessed 15 April 2023).

Global Times. 2022. "Chinese Fantasy Series Seeks to Share China's Voice with the World". 30 August 2022. https://www.globaltimes.cn/page/202208/1274217.shtml (accessed 14 April 2023).

Goodfellow, Jessica. 2020. "Tencent Confirms Purchase of Southeast Asian Streamer Iflix". *Campaign Asia*, 25 June 2020. https://www.campaignasia.com/article/tencent-confirms-purchase-of-southeast-asian-streamer-iflix/461869 (accessed 14 April 2023).

Hudson, Nikki. 2020. "'The Untamed': Everything We Know About the 2020 World Tour". *Filmdaily*, 27 January 2020. https://filmdaily.co/news/the-untamed-2020-world-tour/ (accessed 13 April 2023).

Iwabuchi, Koichi. 2017. "East Asian Popular Culture and Inter-Asian Referencing". *Routledge Handbook of East Asian Popular Culture*, edited by Koichi Iwabuchi, Eva Tsai, and Chris Berry, pp. 24–33. New York: Routledge.

Jin Feng. 2009. "'Addicted to Beauty': Consuming and Producing Web-based Chinese 'Danmei' Fiction at Jinjiang". *Modern Chinese Literature and Culture* 21, no. 2: 1–41. https://www.jstor.org/stable/41491008

Kawakami, Takashi. 2019. "China Suspends Three E-Book Platforms, Citing 'Obscene' Content". *Nikkei Asia*, 19 July 2019. https://asia.nikkei.com/Business/China-tech/China-suspends-three-e-book-platforms-citing-obscene-content2 (accessed 15 April 2023).

Kishimoto, Marimi, and Jun Suzuki. 2019. "Netflix and Tencent Vie for Southeast Asia's Eyeballs". *Nikkei Asia*, 20 June 2019. https://asia.nikkei.com Chinese fantasy series seeks to share China's voice with the world/Business/Business-trends/Netflix-and-Tencent-vie-for-Southeast-Asia-s-eyeballs (accessed 14 April 2023).

Law, Julienna. 2021. "China Bans Effeminate Men and Abnormal Esthetics from TV". *Jing Daily*, 2 September 2021. https://jingdaily.com/little-fresh-meat-sissy-men-china/ (accessed 15 April 2023).

Li, Cheng Cheng. 2019. "Tencent Report Reviews the Online Video Trends of 2019". *TMTPost*, December 2019. https://medium.com/@TMTPOST/tencent-report-reviews-the-online-video-trends-of-2019-17957f5889a5 (accessed 13 April 2023).

Media Partners Asia. 2022. "Premium Online Video Category Rebounds in Southeast Asia with New Competition, Local Content and Sports Driving Expansion". 22 November 2022. https://media-partners-asia.com/AMPD/Q4_2022/SEA/PR.pdf (accessed 15 April 2023).

Naewna.com. 2019. "8นักแสดง'ปรมาจารย์ลัทธิมาร'บุกไทย เสิร์ฟความฟิน" [8 Actors of 'Grandmaster of Demonic Cultivation' Invade Thailand, Delighting Audiences]". 31 October 2019. https://www.naewna.com/entertain/450790 (accessed 13 April 2023).

Nam, S. 2023. "4 Reasons to Watch the Premiere of Breathtaking Fantasy C-Drama Snow Eagle Lord". *Soompi*, 30 June 2023. https://www.soompi.com/article/1596634wpp/4-reasons-to-watch-the-premiere-of-breathtaking-fantasy-c-drama-snow-eagle-lord (accessed 12 July 2023).

Ngo Thai Hoang Tuan. 2021. "A Glance at WeTV: Asia's No. 1 Entertainment App". *LinkedIn*, 12 April 2021. https://www.linkedin.com/pulse/glance-wetv-asias-1-entertainment-app-ngo-thai-hoang-tuan/ (accessed 14 April 2023).

Nye, Joseph. 2004. *Soft Power: The Means to Success in World Politics*. New York: Public Affairs.

Patpicha Tanakasempipat. 2019. "Tencent Launches Video Streaming in Thailand, Eyes SE Asia Expansion". *Reuters*, 14 June 2019. https://www.reuters.com/article/us-tencent-thailand-idUSKCN1TF1J8 (accessed 14 April 2023).

She, Chase. 2020. "Eternal Love of Dream Hits 5 Billion". 2 March 2020. https://dramapanda.com/2020/03/eternal-love-of-dream-hits-5-billion.html (accessed 12 July 2023).

Shim, Doobo. 2017. "Hybridity, Korean Wave, and Asian Media". *Routledge Handbook of East Asian Popular Culture*, edited by Koichi Iwabuchi, Eva Tsai, and Chris Berry, pp. 34–44. New York: Routledge.

SoHu 搜狐. 2022. "2023仙侠剧16部推荐片单！罗云熙＆白鹿《长月烬明》、肖战《玉骨遥》必看". 21 December 2022. https://www.sohu.com/a/619601860_99913067 (accessed 13 April 2023).

Telecom Review. 2022. "Tencent's WeTV to Grow New Content Partnership in Southeast Asia". 18 January 2022. https://www.telecomreviewasia.com/index.php/news/service-news/2634-tencent-s-wetv-to-grow-new-content-partnership-in-southeast-asia (accessed 15 April 2023).

Teo, Stephen. 2009. *Chinese Martial Arts Cinema: The Wuxia Tradition*. Edinburgh: Edinburgh University Press.

Tiong, Wenjie. 2023. "From Story of Yanxi Palace to Three Body, China's TV Exports Could Do What Wolf Warrior Diplomacy Hasn't". *South China Morning Post*, 26 February 2023. https://www.scmp.com/comment/opinion/article/3211185/story-yanxi-palace-three-body-chinas-tv-exports-could-do-what-wolf-warrior-diplomacy-hasnt (accessed 14 April 2023).

Wang, Shuaishuai. 2023. "How LGBTQ Content Built, Then Vanished From, China's Streamers". *Sixth Tone*, 29 March 2023. https://www.sixthtone.com/news/1012585 (accessed 15 April 2023).

Wang Yi Shou Ye 网易首页. 2021. "五大非遗艺术加盟《苍兰诀》虞书欣王鹤棣领衔演绎". 19 February 2021. https://www.163.com/ent/article/G36NIGM0000380G9.html (accessed 14 April 2023).

Yahoo. 2022. "WeTV Bets Big on Southeast Asia with New Content Partnership Opportunities". 18 January 2022. https://sg.finance.yahoo.com/news/wetv-bets-big-southeast-asia-020000591.html (accessed 14 April 2023).

Yau, Elaine. 2021. "Chinese TV Series Grow in Popularity Overseas, Movies are Another Story". 7 April 2021. https://www.scmp.com/lifestyle/entertainment/article/3128441/chinese-tv-series-grow-popularity-overseas-movies-are

13

IMPACT OF CHINESE POPULAR CULTURE ON YOUNG PEOPLE IN VIETNAM

Tran Thi Xoan

Introduction

The Qixi Festival, celebrated on the seventh day of the seventh month of the lunisolar calendar, has gained popularity among young Vietnamese. They take to social media posting pictures on their social media accounts with a variety of red bean dishes, such as steamed buns and sweet soups, and wishing for luck in their love life.[1] Various Vietnamese businesses seize this opportunity to offer special promotions, such as sale discounts.[2] Referred to as Chinese Valentine's Day, the festival is now widely recognized and practised due to literature shared on various Internet sites about this celebration. Although the Qixi Festival is known as *Lễ Thất Tịch* in Vietnam, its recent surge in popularity can be traced back to the influence of Chinese popular culture propagated through transnational media channels.

In Vietnam, exposure to foreign popular culture has seen significant growth since the country re-established contact with foreign cultures following socio-economic reforms. As Vietnam integrated itself into the global economy, this led to the flow of cultural products from East Asia countries and the West. Chinese popular culture, in particular, has long attracted the interest of generations of Vietnamese, especially since the 1990s. The recognition of the Qixi Festival reflects a renewed awareness of Chinese cultural influence.[3] In a similar vein, other Chinese cultural products, such as music, movies, and literature, are circulated widely in Vietnam's contemporary art market (Phan 2021). According to Giang (2011), the consumption of Chinese popular culture is associated with various related consumer behaviours, such as reading *wuxia* (martial arts) fiction, borrowing martial arts DVDs, and using new Han-Vietnamese vocabulary in daily conversation. These cultural exchanges have had a profound impact on Vietnamese society, influencing their preferences and language use.

Chinese President Hu Jintao's speech in October 2017 strongly emphasized the promotion of Chinese popular culture to "enhance the influence of Chinese culture worldwide" (Hu 2017). Subsequently, under President Xi Jinping's leadership, Chinese popular culture gained assiduous attention as he pledged to "modernize Chinese values and show the charm of Chinese culture to the world" (Ma and Jun 2014). The initiative was reflected in the country's five-year plan, aimed at boosting China's cultural industry by expanding its traditional and popular cultural products across various sectors, including publishing, movie, animation, television series and performance sectors (*Xinhua* 2017). The advent of Internet networks and online streaming platforms facilitated the internationalization of Chinese culture, particularly concerning the age-old cultural relations between China and Vietnam and the influence on Vietnamese cultural practices.

Despite the renewed interest in Chinese popular culture, scholars in Vietnam have shown limited attention to this development, leaving its cultural impacts largely unexplored. On the other hand, Chinese news agencies have paid more attention. For example, during President Xi Jinping's state visit to Vietnam in 2015, the Chinese press celebrated this event by highlighting ten Chinese cultural practices and products that are popular in Vietnam, which include worshipping before examinations, calligraphy, Chinese books, songs, TV dramas, and the learning of Mandarin. The Chinese media attribute the Chinese cultural influences in Vietnam to the geographical proximity between the two countries. Also, television has been considered "a cultural ambassador for China" and "a window to Chinese culture".

In this chapter, I shall discuss how Chinese popular culture occupies a place in Vietnam through the process of localization, encompassing both tangible and intangible aspects. Specifically, this article will describe the presence of Chinese popular culture and its impacts on young Vietnamese. While the primary focus of this paper is not specifically on China's soft power, the discussion on Chinese media and Chinese popular culture in Vietnam contributes to a deeper understanding of their relevance to China's soft power.

Theoretical Consideration

Cultural studies often intersect with media studies due to their natural association. Scholars often investigate the possible impact of popular culture on the audience through the lenses of cultural imperialism, asymmetric cultural development, cultural development, and cultural globalization (Willnat, Zhou, and Hao 1997). One dominant theory in cultural development, namely cultural imperialism in globalization argues that developed countries dominate the international flow of cultural products, contributing to cultural homogenization and synchronization seen in the Third World. According to this theory, media influences are often likened to the "hypodermic needle" model, where foreign values are viewed as invasive to the consumers' minds. Gerbner (1969) views television as having a small but significant influence on viewers' attitudes, beliefs, and judgements concerning the social world. Critiques challenge this approach by proposing the "active audience" argument that the audience actively decodes media content (Ang 1985; Tomlinson 1991). As such, Ang points out that the audience makes active choices in their tastes and behaviours.

Building upon the work of Willnat, Zhou, and Hao (1997) and Xiaoming and Teh's (2008) theorization of foreign media exposure and perception accessing cultivation and formation of stereotypes, this paper highlights how the consumption of Chinese cultural products can influence the perceptions of young Vietnamese to a certain degree. Moreover, this chapter argues that young Vietnamese people's cultural consumers possess the ability to recognize Chinese products' cultural territory and make informed decisions as to whether to consume them or not. By acknowledging the active agency of young Vietnamese cultural consumers, this paper contributes to a nuanced understanding of the complexities involved in the reception and interpretation of Chinese cultural influences in Vietnam.

An Overview of Chinese Popular Culture in Vietnam

The term popular culture emerged in English during the 1960s and has since become an important part of Cultural Studies. Coined to present the everyday culture of youth and working people (King 1997), "culture" itself, as described by Williams (1984), encompasses "a whole way of life" and all forms of signification (novels, films, but also advertising and television) that circulate in society. In textual usage, Hartley defined popular culture as the products and social practices of the media and entertainment industries (Hartley 2019). "The understanding of popular culture can vary depending on whether one is interested in the meanings produced 'by' or 'for' people and whether one takes these meanings as evidence of 'what the public wants' or 'what the public gets.'"

In recent years, China's cultural landscape has experienced a significant transformation, driven by the nation's international ambition and its desire to present a more open China, exemplified by the hosting of the Beijing Olympic Games in 2008. Scholars like Keane (2010) interpret this trend as a manifestation of China's soft power, prompting the country to reform its cultural, media, and creative industries to expand its cultural products. In the same spirit, the Chinese government aims to liberate its cultural products and broaden its reach beyond domestic boundaries (Otmazgin 2018). This ambition, for example, leverages the number of movies to compete in overseas markets.

Meanwhile, Vietnam's contact with foreign products flourished after the Economic Reform (Đổi Mới) of the 1980s, ushering in a new era of globalization and the rise of the Internet. Following the normalization of relations between Vietnam and China, along with their cultural similarities, Chinese popular culture, especially historical series, music, movies, and kung fu novels, has gained significant popularity. According to Hiep (2012), previous literature regarded Chinese cultural products that appeared in Vietnam were perceived as representatives of China's "soft power". However, as the market became more competitive, Vietnamese consumers shifted their preferences, leading to a decline in the consumption of Chinese cultural products in favour of offerings from Hong Kong, Taiwan, and other Southeast Asian countries (Xu 2015). As a result, local Vietnamese media started to cover a more comprehensive range of products leading to a light attention on Chinese products unlike before.

With the normalization of the Vietnam-China relationship in the late 1980s, the presence of Chinese cultural products in Vietnam become more apparent (Ge 2017). In particular, the two countries increasing volumes of bilateral trade and regular state visits have played key roles in enhancing the relationship. These strengthening social linkages between the two countries facilitated the incorporation of *wuxia* fiction, detective literature, and motion pictures into the minds of the Vietnamese. Chinese celebrities have become "closer and dear" (Phan 2021). This engagement has also enabled China to send more "outward bound" products, particularly Mandarin language content, to Vietnam (Otmazgin 2018). These products also grasp the boom of consumers who devote time and money to social media products, especially films and online literature.

Though the consumption of Chinese online literature led to a public outcry in Vietnam, especially for its toxic romantic themes, its proliferation is evident (Tranh 2016).[4] A significant number of Chinese romantic novels are readily available online, with numerous websites and fan pages dedicated to them. Various media agencies in China have also reported on the renewed popularity of Chinese products in Vietnam, as can be seen in Table 13.1.

The influence of Chinese popular culture has played a significant role in shaping the dynamic of media and cultural landscapes in Vietnam. However, such Chinese cultural products have not yet gained the attention of local and international scholars. Thus, a case study of Chinese popular culture in Vietnam is necessary to reassess its state of the art and its footprint among Vietnamese consumers. By examining this phenomenon in depth, we can gain valuable insights into how Chinese cultural elements have integrated into Vietnamese society and how they have influenced the preferences and behaviours of the local population.

2018: Initial Research on Vietnamese Students' Attitudes towards Chinese Popular Culture

This research draws on survey data collected in January 2018 for my master's thesis, which studies the perception of Vietnamese students towards Chinese popular culture. To explore this topic, I applied a quantitative method using the Likert Scale. An electronic survey was distributed to university students nationwide, and the informants needed to meet a prerequisite requirement to consume one of the Chinese products. After a fifteen-day distribution period, I analysed the collected data using descriptive statistics. Among the 424 participants, a small proportion of the students had Chinese connections, with 2.83 per cent travelling to China, 21 per cent having Chinese friends, and 9.20 per cent having Chinese-Vietnamese relatives. Furthermore, despite their different undergraduate programmes, two-fifths of the students learn the Chinese language (hereafter known as Mandarin).

Table 13.2 presents a summary of the most consumed products by the participants, indicating that exposure to Chinese media-distributed products is quite common among the respondents. Forty per cent of the students reported always or often watching Chinese films, while over one-third of them listened to Chinese music and used new Chinese-Vietnamese colloquial vocabulary.

The study proposed four hypotheses as follows:

(H1) The respondents would perceive Chinese products favourably.
(H2) The respondents with a certain level of exposure to the products would have a positive feeling towards the Chinese.

TABLE 13.1
Chinese Media Portrayal of Chinese Popular Culture in Vietnam

Time	Agencies	Titles	Contents
November 2015	China Daily	Vietnam's Cultural Ties with China	• Students worship Confucius before the Vietnamese national entrance exam with the lucky character "Deng Ke 登科—pass the exam." • Chinese-style stone lions as decorations/Lion dance • Chinese books, songs, and TV dramas popular in Vietnam, such as *Journey to the West* and *Romance of Three Kingdoms* • Chinese pop songs, especially some cover versions sung by Vietnamese stars, are quite popular in Vietnam.[a] For example, "I am not crossing her" 渡我不渡她 which was performed by different Vietnamese singers and ranked at the top of many national music lists in 2019. • The TV drama *The Legend of Wu Zetian*, starring Chinese actress Fan Bing Bing, was a hit on the Vietnamese screen. • Mandarin Fever/Calligraphy Contest/Peking Opera Masks • "Made in China" prevails in Vietnam, such as Chinese restaurants, goods imported from the Chinese mainland/China-Vietnam Joint Venture Enterprise • Toys printed with Chinese characters from *Where Are You Going*, a Chinese reality show.
June 2016	China Daily	Chinese TV Dramas and Movies Thrill Vietnamese	• Chinese TV dramas and movies attract more Vietnamese audiences resulting from their growing market share. The films have sold well with rave reviews. A science-fiction fantasy movie, *Mermaid*, swept over box offices during the Lunar New Year.[b] The movie, an environmental

			parable and a comic love story between a rich businessman and a mermaid created a "mermaid fever" in Vietnam, with audiences expressing their deep enjoyment of the film that made them both laugh and cry.
July 2017	Xinhua	Chinese TV Shows Being Lapped Up by Vietnamese Youngsters	• For many Vietnamese youngsters, Chinese TV shows have gradually become an important part of their entertainment diet. • Chinese music shows such as *Sing My Song* are also popular among Vietnamese youngsters. • Various genres of Chinese variety shows were screened online to meet the new diet of young Vietnamese audiences, such as travelling programmes (*Divas Hit the Roads* and *Flowers on Trip*), reality shows (*Awesome Challenge* and *Up Idols*), and other genres such as dating (*We Are in Love*) or family-related shows (*Dad, Where Are We Going*)
June 2017	Xinhua	Chinese TV Sparks Love of Language in Vietnam's Youth	• The popularity of Chinese TV appeals to many translators, which facilitate the flash translation of Vietnamese subtitles of original Chinese released in several movies: Chinese drama *Princess Agents* and *Ten Miles of Peach Blossoms*.
June 2018	Xinhua	Chinese TV Shows Find Fans in Vietnam	• The Internet enables many Chinese TV series, such as *The Journey of Flower* and *Once Upon a Time*, to be available in Vietnamese shortly after they are released in Chinese. The latter was streamed more than 30 million times on a video-streaming platform in Vietnam, while the former has been adapted as a local series in the Southeast Asian country.

continued on next page

TABLE 13.1 — *cont'd*

Time	Agencies	Titles	Contents
November 2021	Global Times	Chinese Female's Warrior Costume Drama to Air on Vietnamese National TV	• *The Legend of Fei,* an adaptation of a novel is set to air on VTV-2, a Vietnamese state-run broadcaster. • "Ever since 2010, Chinese TV dramas began to have an absolute advantage in both broadcast time and ratings on stations ranging from Vietnamese national TV stations to local stations", Chen Shishui, a researcher at the Institute of Chinese Studies, Vietnam Academy of Social Sciences, told the Xinhua News Agency.

Notes:
a. "Why Do Vietnamese Singers Keep Lingering on a Chinese-Made Song?", https://nld.com.vn/van-nghe/sao-cu-bam-viu-vao-ca-khuc-nhac-hoa-do-ta-khong-do-nang-20190615193211753.htm
b. "The 'Mermaid' of Stephen Chow Grossed Around $4 million in the Vietnamese Market", https://vnexpress.net/my-nhan-ngu-cua-chau-tinh-tri-thu-80-ty-dong-o-viet-nam-3359838.html

TABLE 13.2
Consumption of Popular Chinese Cultural Products in Vietnam

Order	Chinese Cultural Products	Always	Often	Seldom	Never
1	Chinese literature	5.19	16.82	47.17	27.83
2	Chinese entertainment news	5.90	20.52	58.49	15.09
3	Chinese reality shows	5.19	17.45	55.66	21.90
4	Chinese music videos	8.96	19.10	51.89	20.05
5	*Chinese films*	*8.73*	*30.66*	*53.30*	*7.31*
6	*Chinese music*[a]	*12.50*	*21.23*	*45.52*	*20.75*
7	Chinese celebrities	6.60	19.10	45.05	29.45
8	Fandom	7.08	10.98	20.05	62.50
9	New Chinese-Vietnamese colloquial vocabulary	7.78	25.24	46.93	20.05
10	Online games	2.36	5.90	19.34	72.41

Note:
a. Chinese music, or *Nhac Hoa,* is a complicated theme to study. "*Hoa*" means "Chinese". However, *Nhac Hoa* has been used to refer to music from Hong Kong and Taiwan. When I began my research, the students showed their ambiguity in determining the origin of Chinese music. They took music from film tracks as a source from mainland China.

(H3) The respondents consuming Chinese cultural products would perceive the Chinese as superior to the Vietnamese.
(H4) The respondents consuming Chinese cultural products would have a stronger desire to experience them.

Pearson Correlations revealed a positive association between consumption and the respondents' perception of Chinese cultural products. To explore this relationship further, a multiple regression test was conducted to feature their relationship, and the results supported all of my hypotheses on consumption and its impacts on perceptions, which generally predicts that students with a higher level of consumption would perceive Chinese products more favourably than Vietnamese products.

However, the study also identified some limitations, including the inability of quantitative data to fully explain why respondents supported the hypothesis that Chinese products are better than local ones. Furthermore, considering the positive Vietnamese attitude towards the Chinese revealed by this research, questions arise about the potential long-term implications. To provide probable answers to these queries, I extended the former research on Chinese product consumption and Vietnamese consumers' perceptions and feelings in the current context of 2022.

2022: Further Research on Vietnamese Students' Attitudes towards Chinese Popular Culture

To provide an up-to-date understanding of consumption and its relative impact, I conducted semi-structured interviews with six participants. All six individuals, consisting of three males and three females, replied to my email and agreed to take part in the interviews based on the past data. In this research, I adopted a phenomenological approach to discover the participants' life experiences regarding consumption and how it influences their everyday thinking (Creswell and Poth 2016). Regarding the process behind the method, I applied the following techniques: explaining the research's purpose, bringing up contextual situations and related comments from different sources, and posing open questions. I first contacted the participants and asked for their consent. Before conducting the interviews, I sought and obtained informed consent from each participant. To maintain confidentiality and anonymity, I assigned pseudonyms to the participants as P1, P2, P3, P4, P5 and P6 (see Table 13.3). The interview transcripts

TABLE 13.3
Participants in This Study

Code	Gender	Age
P1	Male	20–30
P2	Male	20–30
P3	Male	20–30
P4	Female	20–30
P5	Female	20–30
P6	Female	20–30

were shared with the participants for their approval before using them for analysis. For data interpretation, I focused on the experience of their consumption, which leads to perceptions and feelings towards the products, by using interpretive phenomenological analysis.

The current extension of research asks three main questions:

1. Are the respondents still consuming Chinese products?
2. What are the reasons for the popularity of Chinese cultural products?
3. Is Chinese popular culture a successful example of a political situation that does not affect consumption?

Key Findings: "Localization and Consumption"

After five years, the landscape of Chinese cultural artefacts has expanded to encompass a more comprehensive array of media-circulated products. During the interviews, the interviewees revealed consuming various products, with films still holding the most significant position, even in the form of short/cut videos. New products have gained popularity, especially the Vietnamese version of Weibo Viet Nam, which includes a Facebook group, pages and landing websites with millions of followers. Additionally, idyllic pastoral vlogs, memes, and domestic Chinese products have become widely consumed by the interviewees.

Among the participants, celebrity news attracts the most attention, with actors, actresses, and rising stars in new dramas being their favourite subjects. Therefore, not only Facebook fan pages but also Vietnamese news websites actively update people on trending search names.

More notably, five out of the six interviewees used to and have been learning the Chinese language. Two took elective courses during the undergraduate period, while three learned Chinese for daily communication, employment opportunities and studying abroad.

The emerging trend of new Chinese-Vietnamese colloquial languages is particularly intriguing to the young population. Common words like *soái ca* (帅哥, handsome guy), *trạch nam, trạch nữ* (宅男宅女, homebodies or stay-at-home boys/girls), *tra nam, tra nữ* (渣男渣女, philanderer) are widely accepted in daily conversations. Despite this trend, there is also resistance. While two participants acknowledged the usage of these terms, they expressed difficulties in avoiding them once they encountered them on social media:

> I can understand those words, but I cannot avoid them once I scroll through social media posts. (Interviewee P5 responded)[5]
>
> I do not, but my students do. So, these terms are ubiquitous in my social media feeds. (P1)[6]

With the growing popularity of Mandarin, more people are interested in Chinese linguistic patterns. However, one interviewee took a stance against adopting such language, preferring to preserve the purity of the Vietnamese language:

> "We do not need to use "*tra nam*—philanderer", we can use our Vietnamese metaphor figure—*Sở Khanh*,[7] with the same meaning. (P2)[8]

Overall, these insights from the interviews highlight the dynamic interplay between Chinese popular culture and young Vietnamese individuals' preferences and linguistic trends.

"We Should Not Compare Chinese and Vietnamese Products"

The interviewees mostly shared the same perspectives when comparing Chinese and Vietnamese films. For many interviewees, their taste and genre selection have experienced "the changes" in putting the reflexivity as one stated, "I do not know why I used to choose to watch these series, their topics are *cổ súy tư tưởng cổ hủ*—promote antiquated ideas." (P3)[9]

The first unexpected insight derived from the conversations was that the participants were unwilling to accept that Chinese products were superior to Vietnamese ones despite acknowledging the advancement of Chinese products. All participants expressed the sentiment that Vietnamese and Chinese cannot be compared as they are "incompatible to start with". An interviewee further elaborated on the differences, noting that the Chinese film industry tends to focus on familiar genres such as romance, historical dramas, and imperial palace dramas. Additionally, they perceived the acting leads in Chinese films as an amateur and selected them primarily for their physical attractiveness. The interviewee also described the film plots as linear and pandering to popular taste, unlike in the past when they might have been more diverse. However, the interviewee acknowledged the significant investments made in "designing costumes, transcription, and visual effects, which Vietnamese producers can barely access". This observation underscores the Vietnamese audience's close attention to the intricacies of Chinese film production.

> Vietnamese products, compared with Chinese products, are incompatible to start with. (All participants expressed so)[10]
>
> I think the Chinese film industry does not create new genres, mostly screening romantic stories, historical or imperial palace dramas. Even the acting leads are amateur and were selected based on charming looks. Film contents are linear with popular taste, unlike in the past. On another note, I can see that the industry receives huge investments in designing costumes, transcription, and visual effects, which Vietnamese producers can barely access. (P2)

"Chinese Popular Culture Is Successful in Separation with the Two Countries Disputes"

In this study, I used a quote from Lim (2020) to prompt responses from the interviewees, exploring their views on the success of Chinese popular culture in Vietnam and its potential separation from political influences.[11] The quote states, "Chinese popular cultural products appreciation can take place through separation of politics and culture. Even in regional geopolitical rival Viet Nam, Chinese films and TV dramas have attracted fandom due to their similar cultures", suggesting that appreciation for Chinese cultural products can exist independently from geopolitical tensions, even in countries like Vietnam, which have complex relations with China.

All interviewees acknowledged the success of Chinese popular culture in Vietnam from different perspectives. For instance, one admitted to enjoying the Chinese martial arts genre, expressing admiration for the heroic figures. Another interviewee (P2), however, raised concerns about the potential dangers of prioritizing foreign culture over their own, leading to a sense of cultural disconnect among Vietnamese people, identifying the irony of Vietnamese being "clueless" about their own history while being able to "talk about Chinese history and their costumes". Despite these concerns, the participants recognized the significance of understanding and appreciating foreign popular culture, with one participant (P3) suggesting the potential for cooperation and mutual learning between Vietnam and China through their shared cultural elements. P5 mentions that the proliferation signifies the possibilities for cultural exchange and understanding.

However, divergent opinions arose among the interviews when the discussion shifted to actors and actresses who shared their views on China's nine-dashed line maps. Some participants called for cancelling these persons and their products even though "we should stand in their position to know why they have to post that information". On the other hand, P5 emphasized the importance of separating content from the private lives of celebrities, adding that consuming Chinese popular culture is "merely my enjoyment and is not an endorsement of political views pushed by the celebrities".

Limitations and Implications for Further Study

For the 2022 research, due to time constraints and the delayed interview after five years, an apparent limitation is the number of participants for the interview.

This updated research tries to fill in the vacuum of the previous one on the happening attitude of young Vietnamese people towards Chinese popular culture. The results suggest that their preference is not simply a fad but more than a way of entertainment, and the consumer's choice matters.

Conclusion

This chapter provides an overview of the state-of-the-art Chinese popular culture in Vietnam from 2018 to 2022. The study shows that Chinese popular culture has shared a significant proportion of the Vietnamese market for foreign products. The localization of Chinese products in Vietnam contributes significantly to the popularity. The impacts are obvious as Vietnamese consumers have positive perceptions of China and its products. A similar result can be found in other products, especially Korean products, coming to Vietnam.

Notes
1. https://saigoneer.com/saigon-culture/19162-ghosts-and-other-myths-how-vietnam-celebrates-the-7th-lunar-month; https://tuoitrenews.vn/news/

society/20200827/saigon-vendors-rush-to-slake-craving-for-red-bean-soup-on-chinese-valentines-day/56407.html
2. A Vietnamese coffee brand occasionally posted such a promotion. For further information, see https://www.facebook.com/highlandscoffeevietnam/posts/pfbid0PxC3H2hKKGgKsXmntQSNgBbJtpfdxpmQiMEEFR7ohY5kCL9gYSFoBmHQgVV7YwWql
3. https://www.eastasiaforum.org/2012/02/01/vietnam-confronts-the-chinese-charm-offensive/
4. This is especially so with Chinese online literature in Vietnam, as reported by Tranh (2016):
   - there are around 11,000,000 results for Chinese romantic novels within 0.27 seconds;
   - various links to Chinese novel websites;
   - top websites for Chinese novels; and
   - thousands of fan pages for novels.
5. Interview with P5, in September 2022.
6. Interview with P1, in September 2022.
7. So Khanh is a character from the tale of Kieu stereotyped as a faithful lover. For further information, see https://vovworld.vn/en-US/culture/vietnam-national-drama-theatre-stages-the-tale-of-kieu-490592.vov
8. Interview with P2, in September 2022.
9. Interview with P3, in September 2022.
10. Interviews with P1, P2, P3, P4, P5, P6 in September 2022.
11. https://www.cnbc.com/2023/07/04/vietnam-bans-barbie-movie-over-south-china-sea-map.html, https://e.vnexpress.net/news/life/arts/netflix-series-depicting-china-s-nine-dash-line-opposed-in-vietnam-4152554.html

References

Ang, I. 1985. *Watching Dallas*. London: Methuen.

Creswell, John W., and Cheryl N. Poth. 2016. *Qualitative Inquiry and Research Design: Choosing among Five Approaches*. USA: Sage Publications.

Ge, S.S. 2017. "The Influence of Chinese Culture on Television to Young People in Vietnam". Master's thesis. VNU University of Social Sciences and Humanities. Cited in Phan, A.Q., 2021. "From Print Texts to Online Gaming: The Cross-Cultural History of Wuxia Fictions in Vietnam". *SAGE Open* 11. no. 2, p.21582440211021392.

Gerbner, G. 1969. "The Television World of Violence". *Mass Media and Violence* 11: 311–39.

Giang, Nguyễn Thu. 2011. "Hiện tượng người nổi tiếng và chức năng xã hội của nó". *VNU Journal of Science: Social Sciences and Humanities* 27, no. 3.

Hartley, John. 2019. *Communication, Cultural and Media Studies: The Key Concepts*. Routledge.

Hiep, Le Hong. 2012. "Vietnam Confronts the Chinese 'Charm Offensive'". *East Asia*

Forum, 1 February 2012. https://www.eastasiaforum.org/2012/02/01/vietnam-confronts-the-chinese-charm-offensive/ (accessed 14 August 2013).

Hu, Jintao. 2007. "Hu Jintao's Report at 17th Party Congress". *China.org.cn*, 15 October 2007. http://www.china.org.cn/english/congress/229611.htm#7

Keane, Michael A. 2010. "Re-imagining China's Future: Soft Power, Cultural Presence and the East Asian Media Market". In *Complicated Currents: Media Flows, Soft Power and East Asia*, edited by Daniel Black, Stephen Epstein, and Alison Tokita, pp. 1–13. Australia: Monash University Publishing.

King, Anthony D., ed. 1997. *Culture, Globalization, and the World-System: Contemporary Conditions for the Representation of Identity*. University of Minnesota Press. NED-New ed. http://www.jstor.org/stable/10.5749/j.ctttsqb3

Lim, Tai-Wei. 2020. *Evolving Social and Political-Economic Impacts of Chinese Popular Cultural Development*. Singapore: East Asian Institute.

Ma, Xiao Chun, and Liang Jun, eds. 2014. "China's Xi Points Way for Arts". *People's Daily Online*, 16 October 2014. http://en.people.cn/n/2014/1016/c90785-8795635.html

Mertens, Donna M. 2019. *Research and Evaluation in Education and Psychology: Integrating Diversity with Quantitative, Qualitative, and Mixed Methods*. USA: Sage Publications.

Otmazgin, Nissim. 2018. "A New Cultural Geography of East Asia: Imagining a 'Region' through Popular Culture". In *The Relevance of Regions in a Globalized World: Bridging the Social Sciences-Humanities Gap*, edited by Galia Press-Barnathan, Ruth Fine and Arie M. Kacowicz, pp. 79–92. Routledge.

Phan, Anh Quang. 2021. "From Print Texts to Online Gaming: The Cross-Cultural History of Wuxia Fictions in Vietnam". *SAGE Open* 11, no. 2.

Phương, Nguyễn Thu. 2010. "Trung Quốc gia tăng sức mạnh mềm văn hoá ở khu vực Đông Nam Á". *Tạp chí Nghiên cứu Trung Quốc*, số 2, no. 102.

Tomlinson, John. 1991. *Cultural Imperialism: A Critical Introduction*. Baltimore, MD: Johns Hopkins University Press.

Tranh, T.L.H. 2016. *Tiểu thuyết ngôn tình Việt Nam dưới góc nhìn văn hóa đại chúng*. Vietnam: Hue University of Sciences.

Williams, Raymond. 1984. "State Culture and Beyond". In *Culture and the State*, edited by L. Appignanesi, pp. 3–5. London: Institute of Contemporary Art.

Willnat, Lars, Zhou He, and Hao Xiaoming. 1997. "Foreign Media Exposure and Perceptions of Americans in Hong Kong, Shenzhen, and Singapore". *Journalism & Mass Communication Quarterly* 74, no. 4: 738–56.

Xiaoming, Hao, and Teh Leng Leng. 2004. "The Impact of Japanese Popular Culture on the Singaporean Youth." *Keio Communication Review* 26, no. 2004: 17–26.

Xinhua. 2017. "Xinhua. China to Develop Culture into Pillar Industry by 2020". 9 May 2017. https://www.chinadaily.com.cn/culture/2017-05/09/content_29267046.htm (accessed September 2022).

Xu, Minghua. 2015. "Chinese TV Drama in a Regional Market: Aspiring to be a Cultural Actor?". *Telematics and Informatics* 32, no. 1: 98–107.

14

PRC SOFT POWER AND CHINESE INDONESIAN ARTS
Reports from the Ends of the Spectrum

Josh Stenberg

INTRODUCTION

A standard definition of soft power is the ability to "affect others to obtain the outcomes one wants through attraction", an ability that relies on a country's "resources of culture, values, and policies" (Nye 2008). However, while economic soft power initiatives, especially infrastructure, are the subject of intense popular and academic interest, the international cultural projects of the People's Republic of China (PRC) are not subjected to the same degree of interest, especially outside China. Nonetheless, cultural diplomacy sustains important narratives about bilateral relations and can contribute to a country's geopolitical position. An important audience for cultural diplomacy is the ethnic Chinese such as the Chinese Indonesians, and the PRC's pitch for engagement draws on a narrative of cultural ties and consanguinity.

While assertions of Chinese cultural nationalism can potentially affect Chinese populations globally, it is especially critical for Southeast Asia's large and culturally mixed ethnic Chinese communities. This is nowhere truer than in Indonesia, where ethnic tensions and recurrences of persecution have marked the recent history of the ethnic Chinese. At times of tension, Indonesia, like other Southeast Asian states and populations, has tended to associate locals of Chinese descent with political China. How local Chinese communities perform (or avoid performing) ethnic identities is keyed to these geopolitical dynamics. Nowhere else is the phenomenon of Chinese soft power projects more likely to affect interethnic dynamics than in Indonesia, where China's current exercise of global soft power has the potential to reshape Sino-Southeast Asian cultural forms and social expression once again.

Multiculturalist approaches, the predominant perspective in Western liberal academia, assume an ongoing integration between ethnocultural minorities and the majority society. Many observers and members of the Chinese-Indonesian community remain optimistic that engaging with China is compatible with greater acceptance of ethnic Chinese within a pluralist Indonesian polity and that the role of "bridge-builders" will be appreciated domestically and internationally. The post-Suharto era has witnessed the removal of racist restrictions on Chinese culture, generating a revival of Sino-Indonesian cultural endeavours over the last twenty years. Patrons and practitioners emphasize the hybrid and integrated aspects of Chinese-Indonesian productions, positioning the community as one ethnicity among many in a plural Indonesia. Explicitly or implicitly, this serves as a riposte and remedy to the anti-Chinese rhetoric sentiment and legislation that marked the Suharto period. It also counters limited views of Indonesia that define it through narrow religious interpretations or definitions of autochthony.

At the same time and increasingly, the rise of the PRC as a power in Southeast Asian geopolitics can pull in a different direction from the assumptions of multiculturalism or pluralism discourses. The PRC exerts a complex influence on Chinese Indonesian perspectives while having the potential to revive historical Indonesian rhetoric and anxiety about mixed loyalties. On balance, the rise of the PRC encourages and motivates Chinese Indonesians to increase their engagement with China and adopt models of Chineseness from China—rather than drawing from the complex history of the Chinese presence in Indonesia or alternate models such as Singapore or Taiwan—and to improve their knowledge of Chinese and especially Mandarin. These aspects constitute a part of the PRC's soft power insofar as Chinese Indonesians are more engaged with China and more attracted to China now than in periods of relative weakness or hostility.

In casual discussion, the diversity of Chinese Indonesian arts is frequently reduced to a single position, even more so than is the case when the community is considered from social science approaches. The arts are either taken to represent diasporic continuity with a rising homeland or taken to represent greater minority integration into Indonesian culture. However, the cultural response to China's rise is uneven. It is much more effective among the small (yet visible and financially powerful) minority that reads and writes Chinese than in those areas of Chinese Indonesian arts that are linguistically archipelagic. To illustrate and substantiate this view, this chapter examines two practices situated at opposing ends of the linguistic spectrum: the recent developments in the performance practice of the *Hokkien*-origin puppet theatre of *wayang potehi* (linguistically most acculturated); and the Sinophone Indonesian writing of the past quarter-century (linguistically most "Chinese").[1]

In the stage practice and marketing of *wayang potehi*, the pressure to enlist indigeneity as part of Indonesian pluralism has meant the increasing representation of the genre as a form of *wayang*, a family of arts that is expansive but grouped around Java-Bali's shadow puppetry and partly for that reason one of Indonesia's central and official cultural touchstones. On the one hand, *wayang potehi* circulates in and outside Indonesia as one among a network of fraternal genres, and contact with the Fujian troupes who in some way represent the ancestral genre is limited.

On the other hand, Sinophone Indonesian writing is thematically and institutionally concerned with maintaining cultural identity among Chinese Indonesians. While such discourses can retain and incorporate integration discourse, the use of the Chinese language as a means of expression that these writers and readers are drawn from the population pool most likely to be friendly or even attached to political China and therefore, receptive to PRC soft power. Chinese Indonesian arts need to be differentiated with a close eye to socio-linguistic alignment in order to properly understand their relationship to PRC soft power. This dynamic is most apparent when considering the arts but has implications across the community.

Wayang Potehi and the Outer Boundary of Chineseness

Potehi, known in Mandarin as *budaixi* 布袋戏, is a glove puppet theatre that had developed in southern Fujian by the eighteenth century. Towards the end of that century, *potehi* was already being performed on Java. It was a widespread part of transnational Hokkien culture during the Qing and Republican periods, travelling with emigrants to Taiwan and Southeast Asia. Many of the existing puppetry lineages in Indonesia trace their arrival to the late nineteenth century or early twentieth century. Areas of Hokkien settlement across Southeast Asia have a history of *potehi*, including Indonesian sites on Sumatra and Kalimantan from which the practice has long disappeared. Records indicate that the genre's historic range stretched from Yangon in the west to Manila in the east (Fushiki and Ruizendaal 2016; Stenberg 2020). In Indonesia, it is in east and central Java that the genre has endured. In the early post-1949 era, *potehi* continued to play a part in both Beijing and Taipei's cultural exchanges with Southeast Asia, as both deployed Hokkien culture as a means of tying diaspora to their respective states.

Today, decimated by a general decline in the popularity of puppet forms as well as recent suppression or discouragement of Chinese cultural forms in polities such as Myanmar and Indonesia, *potehi*'s practice is geographically more restricted, with only Taiwan, Fujian, Penang, Singapore and Java retaining active troupes (Fushiki and Ruizendaal 2016). Taiwanese *potehi*, which has made several radical technological, aesthetic, and narrative departures, has become the most iconic branch of the puppet theatre (Chen 2019), but its Indonesian cousin, now known as *wayang potehi*, has in recent years gained in prominence as an emblem and vehicle of Sino-Indonesian identity.[2] The frequent claim that *wayang potehi* is on its last legs tends to be, in my view, more of a research or journalistic shorthand than a fact on the ground—while the number of active troupes is relatively small, patronage systems and institutional support put *potehi* in as prominent and comfortable position as it has been, perhaps since the beginning of New Order or even earlier.[3]

Its present relatively secure condition has in large part been due to the willingness of patrons and temple communities in cities and towns to embrace this genre of puppetry, performed in Indonesian since the 1970s, as a symbol of the local Chinese contribution to Indonesian culture. Given its widespread familiarity and integration into Javanese communities, *wayang potehi* is well suited to serve as a symbol of Sino-Indonesian culture. In recent years, it has served as a vehicle of patriotic sponsorship to emphasize Chinese Indonesian loyalty to Indonesia. Furthermore, there has been a diversification of venues, international collaborations and tours, and the emergence of new hybrid forms (Fushiki 2019; Gao 2021; Stenberg 2017, 2019; Tung and Mastuti 2022). Scholars, especially in Indonesia, have been at pains to emphasize its role in Javanese culture (Mastuti 2004). To understand what full acculturation can look like for performer-practitioners on the most thorough end of hybridization, we turn to a recent, specific example of *potehi* performance and representation.

The date is 31 January 2020, and the venue is the Salihara Community in South Jakarta, nationally known for providing critical and innovative voices and platforms for diverse groups through performances, art exhibits, and literary events. Woro Retno Mastuti, frangipani blossom in her grey bun, leaps up from behind the *potehi* stage in welcome—I have known her over years of performance and fieldwork. The main driving force behind this performance and other related *potehi* performances and events, she is trained as a Javanist, specializing in literature. Involved in *wayang potehi* a scholar and enthusiast since 2004, she took the initiative to found *a wayang potehi* group at Universitas Indonesia in 2015, calling it Rumah Cinwa. The name combines "*Rumah*", meaning home or house, with "*Cinwa*", officially referring to "*Cin'ta 'wa'yang* (love *wayang*), but potentially also implying "*Cin'a wayang* (Chinese *wayang*): Home of Love for [Chinese] Wayang. While Bu Woro initially acted as the *dalang* (the puppet master), she has now passed all performing responsibilities to the student members, most of them from Universitas Indonesia, drawn from a variety of departments. Her husband, a UI law academic, is involved as well, playing gongs in the musical ensemble.

In the preceding months, a significant amount of time has been dedicated to rehearsals for the long-planned Festival Potehi, an event to which I have also been invited to participate. The day-long event features performances as well as informational segments such as *Behind the Screen of Potehi* and involves Bu Woro interviewing Ki Mujiono, the well-known Surabaya-based *potehi dalang*. Although a Javanese Muslim, Ki Mujiono strictly observes the Chinese ritual requirements for potehi performance, and explains them in his conversation with Bu Woro. He later makes some corrections to the opening ritual of Rumah Cinwa's performance, which involves placing spirit paper in the corners of the *potehi* stage. My participation also takes the form of an interview, presumably as a way of showcasing international interest in *wayang potehi* and putting the Indonesian iteration in the larger international context.[4] Another section features two prominent Chinese-Indonesian public intellectuals, Didi Kwartanada and Udaya Halim, taking the stage to present the history and culture of the Peranakan Chinese and provide short talks relating to their areas of expertise. Such programming integrates *potehi* into the narratives surrounding Peranakan culture: the shared interest in Sino-Indonesian culture as an enduring part of Indonesian culture forms a community of interest that embraces all narratives of acculturation. Thus, Halim, founder of the Benteng Heritage Museum in Tangerang, is focused on a community not usually associated with *wayang potehi*, and without an extant practice. The framing of *wayang potehi* in terms of acculturation places it in conversation with established approaches to Peranakan culture and heritage.

As for the festival's *potehi* performance, the repertoire programming first follows relatively conventional patterns and draws from familiar tales such as *The Journey to the West*: the struggle of *Sun Go Kong* (i.e., Sun Wukong) against Princess Iron Fan and the Bull Demon King.[5] Ritual aspects are meticulously observed, including the incense burning in front of the stage, and the initiation of the performance by the *banxian* ritual, featuring propitious deities. The fact that both the dalang and the orchestra are non-Chinese has been the norm in East Java for a generation, and the Sino-Indonesian orchestra too follows practices of the existing troupes of that region. For these performances, the troupe relies substantially on the information gathered by Bu Woro through years of fieldwork in the region.

However, certain aspects of the Rumah Cinwa performance are rather unusual for *wayang potehi*. Firstly, the *dalang* and orchestra members are notably young, most of them being in their early twenties. The audience also appears to be a diverse mix of Jakarta's cosmopolitan middle class. Perhaps for that reason, the *dalang* mixes in English—the meowling Princess Iron Fan exclaims, "Oh my god! You *terus* steal [keep on stealing] my fan" while Sun cheekily answers her "bye-bye!". Some familiar Mandarin vocabulary and the occasional *Hokkien* phrase also make their way in. The two male students in their early twenties who share the *dalang* role employ a juxtaposition of absurd and comedic elements, drawing inspiration from Indonesian folk theatres and screen performances. The scripts they create, with the assistance of Bu Woro, are enriched and enlivened by spontaneous improvization. Percussion is used, as in Chinese puppetry or opera, to create suspense, to suggest disturbance or tumult, to accent movement, and to represent the mental processes of the characters.

The festival's evening performances represented a much more radical departure from traditional *potehi* practice. First and foremost, this is because the underlying narrative is not of Chinese origin. Instead, the story revolves around a well-known narrative about Majapahit familiar to *wayang* and folk drama audiences of Java.[6] Consequently, we are confronted with an entirely new theatrical landscape. The story, theoretically set in the fifteenth century, concerns the hero Darmawulan, a warrior who must defeat and kill the nefarious king of Blambangan to win the hand of the maiden queen Kencanawungo, and defend himself against multiple plots against him. While the stage has not changed—it is still the portable Sino-Indonesian type, modelled by Bu Woro on the stages in use in East Java—a *gamelan* orchestra furnishes the music with voice supplemented by *dalang* speaking as well as by a Chinese gong. The puppets, commissioned by carvers in Yogyakarta, depict these ethnic Javanese characters, their features resembling *topeng* masks or the white-faced varieties of *golek* puppets. Although the story, language, and music are distinctly Javanese, the physical vocabulary and the overall puppetry style scale remain derived from *potehi*.

During the post-show question and answer session, an audience member poses a question that in one formulation or another is surely on many minds: "At what point does it cease to be *potehi*?" This question asks for a definition of *potehi*'s essence and boundaries. Examining this question in depth inevitably intertwines with the broader issue of the Chinese minority's position in Indonesia. It raises inquiries about the boundaries of genres and the ethical implications involved when performance extends beyond its original ethnic affiliation. Are these considerations different in Indonesia, China, Taiwan, Europe, and the "New World" settler/migrant states? Furthermore, what responsibilities exist regarding consultation, and how are they established? What makes this kind of adaptation, which could be interpreted as appropriation in other contexts, generally embraced by the representatives and associations of Chinese Indonesians?

Undoubtedly, the Rumah Cinwa performances represent the most fully Javanized manifestation of the ongoing transformation of *wayang potehi*. Since the end of the Suharto period, this Hokkien-derived glove puppetry practice has expanded beyond its original confines of the temple circuit in Central and East Java. Increasingly, troupes travel abroad to interact with related puppetry forms, above all in Taiwan, while also engaging tourist audiences and performing in galleries, churches, and shopping centres (Stenberg 2019; Fushiki 2023). Given the contested nature of Chinese Indonesian identities, patrons use the genre as an opportunity to frame this cultural product as an ethnic contribution to Indonesia's vibrant performance arts heritage. Indeed, the genre has increasingly been identified by its sympathizers as a form of *wayang*, and Indonesian institutional actors (such as the Wayang Museum or editors of a recent *wayang* encyclopaedia) are beginning to countersign this taxonomical shift. Rumah Cinwa's performances demonstrate that even the Chinese narrative and the carving and costuming conventions can be substituted from *potehi* without severing its visible connection to the Chinese "original".

A university-based student troupe, Rumah Cinwa has little or no direct involvement from ethnic Chinese individuals or Chinese community organizations. At the same time, due to the recent intensification of Indonesia's identity politics, symbols such as *wayang potehi* constitute an important way for Chinese Indonesians and non-Chinese allies to advocate for pluralism without having to abandon the moral high ground of "tradition". In the case of Rumah Cinwa, the ideological project to naturalize the genre for the majority population has reached an unprecedented phase, both by constructing a Sino-Southeast Asian region across related puppet forms and seeking to exceed the recent regionally defined itinerary of Chinese temple performances in East and Central Java.

Rumah Cinwa's performances compel viewers to contemplate the expanding nature of traditions in terms of geography, genre, performance style, and materiality. Deployed here for the purpose of "multicultural conciliation", *potehi* can be "utilized for the identity formation of certain nationalism in a shifting social context", particularly since the Javanized form allows for the enactment of "local folktales or brand-new scripts", without Chinese origins, and Javanese musical elements can be performed through the format of *wayang potehi* (Tung and Mastuti 2022, p. 14).

These considerations operate within the complex matrix of ethnic relations in Indonesia, with China appearing as a signifier of ancestry rather than as a geopolitical power. In this context, the PRC, home of the ancestral genre, remains wholly absent from this artistic exploration of the complete hybridization of a Chinese cultural element, despite its soft power push and the impact of its geopolitical rise. *Wayang potehi*'s developments and concerns seem independent from the international geopolitical situation even as the response and support of the Chinese Indonesian (and especially the Peranakan) community remain vital. At this time of great attention to Chinese soft power, it is important to note that in certain circumstances, a signifier such as "Chinese" can remain untouched by the rise of China in Southeast Asia.

Chinese-Indonesian Literature in Indonesia

While *wayang potehi* can adapt and be embraced and adapted by non-Chinese Indonesians through strategies of indigenization, the linguistic core of Sinophone literature necessitates an extremely broad understanding of pluralism before such a group can be recognized as Indonesian. As a result, few writers outside the Chinese-speaking community have attempted to engage in such writing. As a consequence, this writing tends to occur at the other end of Sino-Indonesian identity politics: being deeply concerned with Chinese cultural identity, Chinese Indonesians also display far greater interest in and receptiveness to the soft power initiatives of the PRC.

As with *wayang potehi*, the loosening of restrictions towards the end of the New Order and in the subsequent *Reformasi* era ushered in the resumption of the cultural practice of Chinese-language writing after years of suppression. Chinese-language texts had, at the height of the New Order, been treated almost like a narcotic substance, and the publication of Chinese-language literature in Indonesia was limited to a minor element of the single, military-controlled Chinese-language newspaper.[7] There remains limited scholarship on the oeuvre. Leo Suryadinata (2004) provided a chapter-length account of the initial post-Suharto resurgence of Chinese-language writing in Indonesia, even before the *Reformasi* had fully ended. Christine Winkelmann's *Kulturelle Identitätskonstruktionen in der Post-Suharto Zeit* (2008) is an extensive and methodical examination of Chinese-language fiction and press during the early *Reformasi* period. Secondary literature in Chinese remains substantially focused on the euphoria of revival and it is mostly written by members of the community (Dongrui 2003, 2006), with the most notable exception being the more analytical work of the PRC academic Ma Feng 马峰. While many themes within this corpus are not easily distinguished from other branches of Sinophone literature, a focus on language use, Chinese-Indonesian history, and the articulation of ethnic identity can be discerned (Stenberg 2022a).

In the quarter-century since the *Reformasi* began, Chinese-language literature in Indonesia has largely been the province of a small group of enthusiasts educated in pro-Beijing schools in the Sukarno years. Most were born and all were brought up in Indonesia, with only a few of them having received any education in the Chinese-speaking world. Typically, Indonesian citizens and identifying themselves as Indonesians, these writers also openly express their admiration of the PRC in their works, with some authors even exhibiting a sense of identification with China. The long-term viability of this literature is in doubt, for there has been limited succession to this group from younger Chinese Indonesians, given the declining proficiency of Chinese and the status of literature among younger Indonesians. The group's literary output is likely to continue diminishing, although Chinese soft power initiatives—including conferences, networks, and publications—do much to sustain associations and output by offering international platforms, prestige and exposure.

The revival of writing in Chinese post-1998 was motivated not only by the desire to explore new freedoms but also by the hope of connecting with a rising China as well as re-establishing a place in the wider diasporic network. The editorial in the inaugural issue of the key periodical *Yinhua Wenyou* 印华文友 stated both that "Chinese-language Indonesian writing is an inalienable constituent of global Chinese-language writing", and that it is "'rooted in Indonesia', an inalienable and organic part of Indonesian literature as a whole" (*Yinhua wenyou* 1999). The return of Chinese-language work represented a triumph for authors who had long remained silent, a sentiment that can be perceived in these lines from a poem by Xiaobaige (小白鸽) published in 2000:

> For thirty years, with the resolution of tough grass
> We have been squeezing up through the cracks

Boring up from the rubble
Drawing on the paltry paltry nourishment
Struggling to get more and more sunlight
Ah, friends! We have finally seen a new dawn.
(Xiaobaige 2000, p. 18)

These lines by Gu Changfu (顾长福) in his 2015 ode for the anniversary of a literary society express a similar warm admiration for the enduring value of literary creation:

Poetic glory endures,
Crossing
Blue sky and emerald sea,
Soaring like gulls.
(Gu 2016, p. 83)

On a similar occasion, Yan Yan Fei (燕雁飞) penned these thoughts for the largest writing association's tenth anniversary in 2010:

The era gave you a glorious mission:
To suture Chinese culture, split open for thirty years,
To build once again Sino-Indonesian literature, long overgrown,
Do bilingual translation,
Engage with literary organizations of friendly ethnicities. (Yan 2013, p. 9)

Yan Yan Fei's collection contains poems that celebrate various themes such as the spirit of high Maoist hero Lei Feng, China's 5,000 years of glorious history, sporting successes, and even feature in its frontmatter pictures of Chinese-Indonesians at the China and Indonesia pavilions during the 2010 Expo in Shanghai.

Given these paratexts, it is unsurprising that several of the Chinese-language authors in Indonesia have been similarly explicit about the geopolitical context of their identities as Sinophone authors, expressing pride and support of PRC while also writing rhapsodies about the Indonesian scenery, ethnic relations, and occasionally expressing admiration for Indonesian politicians such as Gus Dur. Thus, Indonesian poets have written in praise of the Beijing Summer Olympics, in one case hailing it as "not a sporting event / but the century-old dream / of a strong people and a rich nation", while drawing a contrast between the Olympic and historical episodes of foreign humiliation, such as the Opium Wars and the burning of the Summer Palace. The same poem assures the reader that "historical burdens are turning to strength" through the Games, "weaving another centenary dream" (Yu 2009). Another poet wrote about "Watching the

Chinese National Day Celebrations on a Television Screen", in which he highlights the "cutting-edge weapons" and the "invincible military force" of the PRC army, and assures the reader that "the overseas children of the dragon/without exception/are excited, proud/of the ancestral nation" (Xiao 2009). Such literary works construct a narrative in which the present strength of China makes up for past humiliations.

Unsurprisingly, the West is often portrayed as the implicit antagonist in Chinese-language literature in Indonesia. For example, a Sumatran poet addresses the tension between China and the West (or perhaps the US specifically) during the 2009 Copenhagen climate conference—"big brother are you really trying to loosen our buttons/or are you just waving a big stick/forcing everyone else to cry uncle" (Xiaoxing 2012)—questioning whether the West, symbolized by "big brother", is genuinely concerned about the climate crisis or simply using its power to force others into submission. Other authors adopt a more wistful perspective on the cultural expectations associated with being Chinese. A poem by Ge Feng 戈峰 references Mao Zedong's exhortation, "One who fails to reach the Great Wall is not a hero", but concludes with, "I came I saw I climbed/as for that visible but unattainable vantage point / it's alright not to get there" (2012, p. 39). The reaffirmation of Chinese masculinity while acknowledging the political complexities suggests that full Chineseness may remain out of reach for the Chinese diaspora.

In the writings of Yuan Ni, one of the most prominent living Chinese Indonesian authors, identity issues are skilfully explored, often intersecting with cultural and political questions of Chineseness. In the story *Half a Bag of Sunflower Seeds* (半包瓜子 *Banbao guazi*), the affluent Jakarta Chinese narrator goes to Guangzhou as a tourist and visits a friend who had admired her during her youth in Jakarta, a time when Chinese schools were abruptly closed. However, the author feels alienated in Guangzhou, and as she walks, she feels that she sees "one stranger's face after another, all seemingly enveloped in a layer of indifference, making her feel the anxiety of an outsider". The unexplored path of "returning" to China, which her dying admirer has chosen, is presented as profoundly alien, even though her connection to the Chinese motherland or homeland remains inescapable. As with Ge Feng, the allure of cultural affiliation and the yearning for the homeland is complicated by the narrator's awareness of her knowledge of her own distance from China.[8]

These thematic explorations of attachment and detachment from China represent one side of the soft power reception question; another dimension of soft power in literature is literary infrastructure. Secondary literature, particularly publications from mainland China such as *Huawen wenxue* (华文文学), *Huawen wenxue pinglun* (华文文学评论) and *Bagui qiaokan* (八桂侨刊), have played an important role in sustaining minority writing. These publications, primarily based in the southern provinces that were the main source of migration to Nanyang, focus on the cultural production of the Chinese diaspora and thus provide a major opportunity for Sinophone Indonesians to publish. The largest Chinese-language newspapers in Indonesia also feature material from the PRC, including *Renmin Ribao* (人民日报) supplements in Jakarta's leading *Guoji ribao* (国际日报), and generally maintain friendly coverage of China, indicating a special relationship (Hoon 2006; Suprajitno 2020). The same papers are also among the main platforms for Chinese-Indonesian literature. Indirectly, the ties between the literary communities and the PRC provide publication opportunities, conference travel, the legitimation of scholarly interest, and much of the writing platform.

However, the group of Chinese Indonesians who write in Chinese is ageing, and the Chinese-language cultural world in Indonesia is shrinking. Certain key cultural positions—newspapers, language and music teachers—already depend on PRC educators specifically sent to Indonesia to minister to the community, though their contribution to literary production has been limited thus far. Chinese-language writers themselves are not always optimistic about the long-term survival prospects, despite the growth in Chinese-language learning. In the future, Chinese-Indonesian literary interaction may be found among the literary works of Indonesians working in China or Taiwan, as evidenced by several stories in migrant worker anthologies. The same ageing group of Chinese Indonesians, who received patriotic education before 1965, is culturally inclined to amity with China. All of them would have had many classmates who left for China, and some who returned, witness Yuan Ni's stories. Despite the complexity and sometimes the tragedy of that history, they are likely to maintain engagement with the PRC.

The initial euphoria of the language's revival in Indonesia has waned, and the prospects for an ongoing practice of Chinese-language literature seem limited. Younger authors such as Fu Huiping (符慧平, b. 1974), Lianxin (莲心, b. 1977) Huang Jingtai (黄景泰, b. 1978), are included in anthologies, but their output seems limited. Conspicuously, Fu and Huang are both Chinese language teachers, which suggests that literature is principally sustained among those who are professionally committed to the cause of preserving Mandarin. Fu's poem "Language" seems to address this phenomenon directly, lamenting that language is "no longer a bridge/

the hypocritical blows/have collapsed you to rubbish/lying in silence", for, it seems they have, "shipped you away/smelted, processed, refined you/into an elegant decoration" (Fu 2021, p. 35). While the poem can be interpreted as a critique of the general debasement of language or the vapidity of political discourse, it also reflects Fu's struggle to revitalize a minority literary language on the margins of the Chinese-language literary world. To a substantial degree, the viability of Chinese-language literature in Indonesia may depend on the sustaining force of Chinese soft power.

Conclusion

If the Rumah Cinwa performances demonstrate that a given "Chinese" cultural practice can remain untouched by the rise of PRC soft power, Chinese-language literature shows that PRC soft power is a necessary presence in other areas. It is crucial for observers, including scholars, to resist simplistic narratives that reduce Chinese Indonesians to a singular identity or a predetermined trajectory. The potential for Chineseness to be part of a pluralist vision of Indonesian or even a claim to archipelagic indigeneity is always present. Similarly, especially among the small Sinophone minority, openness to Chinese soft power is also a possibility.

Despite the suspicions surrounding the explanatory power of language use, often rejected *a priori*, due to anxieties about linguistic determinism and a lack of regard for individual preference, language choice and use are a major element in attitudes towards Chinese soft power. Different discourses on identity in Indonesian, Chinese and English have distinct boundaries of acceptable speech. These boundaries vary between popular and academic levels and differ by region. Notably, the window of acceptable speech in Chinese in Indonesia is wider than in the PRC.

The key generational difference lies in the ability to read Chinese. With the ageing of the older Chinese-educated generation, time works against PRC soft power. Compared to other diasporic communities, the challenges faced by Chinese soft power in Indonesia are particularly high. While the PRC can rely on large Chinese-speaking cohorts in the US or Australia, the Chinese-speaking cohort in Indonesia, although not absent, is small and politically all but negligible. Malaysia and Singapore have higher levels of Chinese proficiency and broader accessibility to soft power methods. In Indonesia, the vast majority of the population does not speak Chinese, and Chinese Indonesians who do not read Chinese may be only slightly more susceptible to Chinese soft power narratives than the general population. Increased exposure to study opportunities in China and a higher level of

Mandarin proficiency among Chinese Indonesians are the factors most likely to enhance Chinese soft power.

The two case studies presented serve as illustrations of separate ends of the spectrum of Chinese Indonesian activity: one in which an originally Chinese cultural product becomes absorbed into Indonesian culture, leaving only notional and folkloric traces, and another in which the bond between ethnic, cultural, linguistic and political identity is deemed valid. These tendencies vary in intensity and proportion regionally and across social classes. It is essential to keep both possibilities in mind when discussing not only Chinese soft power in the diaspora but also any aspect of contemporary Chinese Indonesian identity.

Notes

1. This research was conducted with the support of Discovery Early Career Research Award (DE210100457) of the Australian Research Council. Though aware of the important and varied contributions of Sinophone studies, I use the term here in its most denotative sense: to describe writing in Chinese rather than in archipelagic or colonial languages.
2. *Wayang*, originally a Javanese word meaning "shadow", is internationally most familiar designation of narrative genres of Java and Bali with traditional origins and ritual aspects, first and foremost *wayang kulit*. It has historically been broadly applied to entertainments in the Malay world and continues to designate "Chinese opera" in Singapore and Malaysia as well as its use of the term *wayang potehi* allows practitioners and supporters of the genre to situate *wayang potehi* in an Indonesian family of arts.
3. In general, the activities to incorporate aspects of Chinese performing arts into Indonesian concepts have been effective in Java, so that the rebirth of *wacinwa* (also known as "*wayang China Jawa kulit*") practices has actually restored a genre that had been dormant for a half-century. On the other hand, Chinese-Indonesian *xiqu*, orchestral, and puppetry practices in Sumatra and Kalimantan do not benefit from similar networks of support, and those genres are much likelier to disappear.
4. I would like to acknowledge the support of the Canadian Embassy in Jakarta, which Salihara successfully applied to for funds to support my travel.
5. *Journey to the West* has impeccable credentials as an important Chinese narrative, and it was translated into Malay in its entirety or in parts in the mid- to late nineteenth century (Oey 2013). Judging from earlier newspaper accounts and troupe materials, I think it was likely not central to *potehi* until the influence of Chinese television from the 1990s brought the immensely popular story to greater prominence among Chinese Indonesians. Specifically, the 1997 airing of the popular PRC series brought it to a wider audience, and in the last decade, it has been aired again on more than one occasion.

6. It is particularly central to the performance of the wood-puppet genre *wayang klitik* (Liaw 2013, p. 90).
7. As Ariel Heryanto notes, "printed matter in Chinese characters [fell] under the same category as pornography, arms, and narcotics in the short list of items visitors are prohibited from bringing into this, the world's fourth largest, country" (Heryanto 1997, p. 27). Some authors sent their works abroad for publication, and others had moved there permanently, and wrote about Indonesia.
8. These are of course not the only types of political thinking in Sinophone Indonesian writing. Perhaps due to resonance with Western multiculturalist projects, authors such as Wilson Tjandinegara and Soeria Disastra have received particular attention in English writing for their concerted efforts to bridge Chinese-language and Indonesian-language communities (Allen 2003; Stenberg 2017).

References

Allen, Pamela. 2003. "Literature and the Media Contemporary Literature from the Chinese 'Diaspora' in Indonesia". *Asian Ethnicity* 4, no. 3: 383–99.

Chen, Jasmine Yu-Hsing. 2019. "Transmuting Tradition: The Transformation of Taiwanese Glove Puppetry in Pili Productions ". *Journal of the Oriental Society of Australia* 51: 26–46.

Dongrui 东瑞. 2003. "Xin shiqi Yinhua wenxue gaishu (1996–2002) 新时期印华文学概述 (1996– 2002)". *Shijie huawen wenxue* 《世界华文文学》 no. 1: 3–7.

———. 2006. *Liujin jijie xubian* 流金季节续编. Huoyi chuban 获益出版.

Fu, Huiping 符慧平. 2011. "Yuyan 语言 [Language]". In *Yinhua xinshi erbaishou 印华新诗二百首*, edited by Dongrui 东瑞. Indonesia: Yinhua zuoxie 印华作协, p. 35

Fushiki, Kaori. 2019. "Embracing New Performance Spaces to Survive: The Changing Social Context of Indonesian 'Wayang Potehi'". *Journal of the Oriental Society of Australia* 51: 70–83.

———. 2023. "Wayang Potehi: Cultural Connection between Taiwan and Indonesia". In *When East Asia Meets Southeast Asia: Presence and Connectedness in Transformation Revisited*, edited by Yumi Kitamura, Alan H. Yang, and Ju Lan Thung, pp. 323–50. Singapore: World Scientific.

———, and Robin Ruizendaal. 2016. *Potehi Glove Puppet Theatre in Southeast Asia and Taiwan*. Taipei: Taiyuan Publishing.

Gao, Xiao. 2021. "Chinese Indonesian Musical Culture in Java: Identity and Meaning in a Long-term Diaspora". PhD dissertation, University of Sheffield, England.

Ge Feng 戈峰. 2012. "Deng Changcheng 登长城". *Yinhua xiaoshi senlin 印华小诗森林*, edited by Sha Ping 莎萍, p. 39. Indonesia: Yinhua zuoxie 印华作协.

Gu Changfu 顾长福. 2016. *Gu Changfu zhongbai shiji 顾长福钟摆诗集* [Gu Changfu's Pendulum Poetry]. Kowloon: Holdery Publishing.

Heryanto, Ariel. 1997. "Silence in Indonesian Literary Discourse: The Case of the Indonesian Chinese". *SOJOURN: Journal of Social Issues in Southeast Asia* 12, no. 1: 26–45.

Hoon, Chang Yau. 2006. "'A Hundred Flowers Bloom': The Re-Emergence of the Chinese Press in Post-Suharto Indonesia". *Media and the Chinese Diaspora: Community, Communications and Commerce*, edited by Sun Wanning, pp. 91–118. UK: Routledge.

Kuardhani, Hirwan. 2012. *Mengenal Wayang Potehi di Jawa*. Yensen Project Network.

Liaw, Yock Fang. 2013. *A History of Classical Malay Literature*. Translated by Razif Bahari and Harry Aveling. Singapore: ISEAS – Yusof Ishak Institute.

Mastuti, Dwi Woro R. 2004. "Wayang Cina di Jawa Sebagai Wujud Akulturasi Budaya dan Perekat Negara Kesatuan Republik Indonesia". Conference Proceedings of Seminar "Naskah Kuno Nusantara dengan Tema Naskah Kuno Sebagai Perekat Negara Kesatuan Republik Indonesia", Jakarta.

Nye Jr., Joseph S. 2008. "Public Diplomacy and Soft Power". *Annals of the American Academy of Political and Social Science* 616, no. 1: 94–109.

Oey, Eric M. 2013. "Lie Sie Bin Yoe Tee Hoe Six Malay/Indonesian Translations of a Chinese Tale". *Literary Migrations: Traditional Chinese Fiction in Asia (17th-20th Centuries)*, edited by Claudine Salmon, pp. 315–35. Singapore: ISEAS – Yusof Ishak Institute.

Setijadi, Charlotte. 2022. "'We Are People of the Islands': Translocal Belonging among the Ethnic Chinese of the Riau Islands". *Asian Ethnicity* 24, no. 1: 108–31.

Stenberg, Josh. 2017. "The Lost Keychain? Contemporary Chinese-Language Writing in Indonesia". *SOJOURN: Journal of Social Issues in Southeast Asia* 32, no. 3: 634–68.

———. 2019. *Minority Stages: Sino-Indonesian Performance and Public Display*. Honolulu: University of Hawai'i Press.

———. 2020. "Xiqu in the Philippines: From Church Suppression to MegaMall Shows". *Journal of Chinese Overseas* 16, no. 1: 58–89.

———. 2022a. "Diverse Fragility, Fragile Diversity: Sinophone Writing in the Philippines and Indonesia". *Asian Ethnicity* 24, no. 1: 59–77.

———. 2022b. "'Finding the Distant Homeland Here': Contemporary Indonesian Poetry in Chinese". *Journal of Chinese Overseas* 18, no. 2: 312–34.

Suprajitno, Setefanus. 2020. "Reconstructing Chineseness: Chinese Media and Chinese Identity in Post-Reform Indonesia". *Kemanusiaan: The Asian Journal of Humanities* 27, no. 1: 1–23.

Suryadinata, Leo. 2004. "Ethnic Chinese Literature in Indonesia: Ethnicity and Nationhood". *Chinese Indonesians: State Policy, Monoculture and Multiculture*, edited by Leo Suryadinata, pp. 82–100. Singapore: Eastern Universities Press.

Tung, Yuan-Hsin, and Dewi Woro Retno Mastuti. 2022. "Revitalizing Potehi Practice: Preservation, Innovation, and Transmission by Rumah Cinwa in Contemporary Indonesia". *International Journal of Traditional Arts* 4, no. 1.

Winkelmann, Christine. 2008. *Kulturelle Identitätskonstruktionen in der post-Suharto Zeit: chinesischstämmige Indonesier zwischen Assimilation und Besinnung auf ihre Wurzeln*. Germany: Otto Harrassowitz Verlag.

Xiaobaige 小白鸽. 2008. "Yinhua yuandi dashengfang 印华园地大盛放". *Yinhua wenyou* 印华文友, no. 5: 18.

Xiao, Zhang 肖章. 2009. "Cong dianshi yingmu shang kan Zhongguo guoqing dianli 从电视荧幕上看中国国庆典". Indonesia: Yinhua zuoxie 印华作协. http://www.yinhuazuoxie.com/xinshi/xiaozhangzhongguoguoqing.html.

Xiaoxing 晓星. 2012. "Jianpai dahui 减排大会". *Yinhua xiaoshi senlin* 印华小诗森林, edited by Sha Ping 莎萍, p. 222. Indonesia: Yinhua zuoxie 印华作协.

Yan, Yan Fei 燕雁飞. 2013. *Yi tian de rizi duo meihao* 一天的日子多美好. Hui 慧.

Yao, Xiangying 姚翔鹰. 2006. *Qiandao liuhen ji* 千岛留痕集. Indonesia: *Daoyu chubanshe* 岛屿出版社.

Yinhua Wenyou 印华文友, eds. 1999. "Fakan ci 发刊词". *Yinhua wenyou* 印华文友, no. 1: 1.

Yu, Erfan 于而凡. 2009. "*Aoyun* 奥运 [The Olympics]". Indonesia: *Yinhua Zuoxie* 印华作协, http://www.yinhuazuoxie.com/xinshi/ aoyunxinshiyuerfan.html.

Yuan, Ni 袁霓. 2000. *Yuan Ni Wenji* 袁霓文集. Xiamen, China: *Lujiang chubanshe* 鹭江出版社.

———. 2021. "Two Stories by Yuan Ni". Translated with an introduction by Josh Stenberg. *Renditions*, no. 95: 93–104.

Index

A
Abdurrahman Wahid (Gus Dur), 166, 168, 175, 261
Ada Apa Dengan China? (What's Up with China?), essays, 171
Afghanistan, and ties with China, 172
Al Azhar University of Indonesia, 19
Alchemy of Souls, 232
Alibaba group, 69
Alliance Française, 182
Ang, Ien, 206
Angeles University Foundation, 48, 183
Annual Report of Kong Zi Institute, 151
anti-China attitude, 20, 39
anti-China rhetoric, 15, 21–22, 24–25
anti-Communist sentiments, 37, 80, 82
APEC, 61
Arina Safwah, 157
Arm Tungniran, 71
ASEAN, 19, 133
ASEAN+3, 61
ASEAN Plus, 71
Asia Euro University, 131
Asia International Friendship College, 20
Asian Infrastructure Investment Bank (AIIB), 61
assimilation policy, 81–82, 180
Association of Chinese in Cambodia (ACC), 122–28, 130–31
Association of Community of Social and Education of Indonesia North Sumatra Indonesian Chinese, 20
Associations for Promotion of Peaceful Reunification of China (APPRC), 17
Associations of Graduates from Universities and Colleges in China, Malaysia (*Liu Hua*), 6, 146, 156–57
Astro Malaysia, 232
Asumsi, 175
Ateneo de Manila University, 183
AUKUS (Australia, United Kingdom and United States), security pact, 18
authoritarianism, 21

B
Badan Koordinasi Pendidikan Bahasa Mandarin, see BKPBM
Bagui qiaokan, 263
Baihuawen (modern language form), 30
Bangkok University, 69
Bank of China, 155
Banpai Vocational School, 66
BBC, 21
Bedtime Story, 232
Behind the Screen of Potehi, 256
Beijing Foreign Studies University (BFSU), 48–49, 144–45, 157
Beijing Jiaotong University, 154
Beijing Language and Culture University (BLCU), 144–45
Beijing Olympic Games, 240, 261
Belt and Road Initiative (BRI), 5, 25, 64, 99, 102, 118–19, 172–73, 200, 202

Benteng Heritage Museum, 256
big power conflict, 25
Bilibili, 230
BKPBM (Coordinating Board for Mandarin Education), 167
border wars, 25
British Council, 22
Brunei Darussalam
   Chinese education in, 9, 54, 201–8
   dwibahasa (bilingualism) education system, 203, 205
   history of Chinese schools in, 203–4
   national ideology, 202
   population of, 202
   welfare state, as, 205
Bulacan State University, 183
Burapa University, 66

C
Cambodia
   Chinese education in, 5–6
   Confucius Institute (CI) in, 128–29, 134
   domestic Mandarin education in, 131–34
   foreign Chinese education in, 128–31
   immigrant population in, 126
   international reconstruction, 121
   privatization of education, 125
   traditional ethnic Chinese education in, 122–28
Cambodia Chamber of Commerce, 126
Cambodia-China bilateral relations, 126
Cambodia-Taiwan Education Program, 130
Cambodia University of Technology and Science (Cam Tech), 127, 129
Cambodia Wenzhou Polytechnic Yalong Silk Road College, 129, 133
Cambodian People's Party (CPP), 122
Capital Normal University (CNU), 147–48

"capitalist economy", 38
caravan trade, 80
CCCC Dredging Group, 154
CCTV (China Central Television), 91
Center for Language Education and Cooperation (CLEC), 19–20, 52, 65
Central and South America Association for Promotion of Peaceful Reunification of China, 17
Central Foreign Affairs Leadership group, 182
Chaguan (teahouse), social media programme, 8, 171–75
"charm offensive", 78
Chen Shui-bian, 18, 125
Chenguang Publisher Yunnan, 107
Chiang Kai-shek, 83
Chiang Mai Chinese Language Teachers Association (CLTA), 86
Chiang Mai University, 66
China-African Union Strategic Dialogue, 25
China-Cambodia Vocational Education Alliance, 133
China Central Policy Research Office, 182
China Central Radio and Television, 103
China Communication Construction Company, 157
China Council for Promotion of Peaceful Reunification, 2, 17
China Council for the Promotion of International Trade (CCPIT), 98
China Cultural Center, 23
China Daily, 242
"China-educated Malaysians", 6–7, 140, 147, 155
China Foundation for Peace and Development (CFPD), 102, 119
China Internet Audio and Video Convention, 217

China-Lao railway, 99–100, 117–18
China National Office for Teaching
    Chinese as a Foreign Language,
    119
China Overseas Association, 20
China, People's Republic of (PRC)
    Afghanistan, and ties with, 172
    civil war in, 80, 84
    economic blockade, 16
    economic power, as, 1, 19
    establishment of, 17, 31
    foreign humiliation, 261
    foreign students in, 100–101
    international students in, 161, 162,
        165
    Malaysian students studying in,
        140–47
    mass media, and impact of, 21–22
    National Day of, 84
    santris (Muslim students) in, 7–8,
        163–73
    short-term training courses in,
        147–49
    soft power policy, 15, 22–24, 61,
        78–79, 117, 175
    survey on perception of, 69–72
    university education in, 140–47
China Public Relations Association
    (CPRA), 17
China Scholarship Council, 182, 184
China Scholarship Programme, 183
China Society, Trinidad, 17
"China threat", 79, 161
China-Vietnam Friendship Association,
    17
"China Winter Camp", 146
Chinese Chamber of Commerce, 180
"Chinese Club" programme, 71
Chinese Communist Party (CCP), 16,
    20, 35, 99, 102, 172–73, 180
"Chinese diaspora", 15–16
Chinese government scholarships
    (CGS), 108

Chinese International College, 69
Chinese International Education
    Foundation, 52
Chinese language, declining standard
    of, 31, 39
"Chinese language +" structure, 154
Chinese Language Teaching School
    Club, 91
*Chinese Martial Arts Cinema: The
    Wuxia Tradition*, 220
Chinese nationalism, 39, 63
Chinese Nationalist Party, *see*
    Kuomintang
"Chinese opera", 265
"Chinese overseas" (haiwai huaren), 15
Chinese Pop-up, 71
Chinese Proficiency Test, *see* HSK
Chinese Radio International, 71
"Chinese sojourners", 15
Chinese Students and Scholars
    Association in Thailand, 68
Chinese Teachers' Association of
    Thailand, 65
Chinese textbooks, and publishers,
    106–7
Chinese Valentine's Day, 237
Chinese-Vietnamese colloquial
    languages, 247
Chinese Wayang (*Wayang Cina*), 11
Ching Hwa Middle School (CHMS
    BSB), 203
Chongqing Industry and Trade
    Polytechnic, 133
Chulalongkorn University, 71
Chung Ching Middle School (CCMS),
    203–4
Chung Ching School in Seria, 203
Chung Hua Middle School Kuala Belait
    (CHMS KB), 203–4
Chung Hua School in Kuala Belait, 203
Chung Hwa Kiudang, 203–4
Chung Hwa Middle School Bandar Seri
    Begawan (CHMS BSB), 204, 207

Chung Hwa School, 203
Chung Hwa Tutong, 203–4
civilizational ethnicity, 24
Clayton, Thomas, 133
CNN, 21
Cold War, 38, 80
colonial rule, and policy, 30
communism, 63, 81, 163, 166
Communist Party of Thailand (CPT), 81
Comprehensive Strategic Partnership, 166
Confucian-Islamic Youth Civilization Forum, 146
Confucian Religion, 35
Confucian values, 88–89, 93
Confucian worship ceremony, 84, 89–90
Confucianism, 35, 88
Confucius Classroom (CC), 19, 52, 54, 62, 64, 79, 128, 166
Confucius Day, 105
Confucius Institute (CI)
  ASEAN, in, 19
  Cambodia, in, 128–29, 134
  countries hosting, 19, 43, 53–54, 79, 165
  culture and education, and promotion of, 3, 7, 19, 79, 182
  establishment of, 165
  global propaganda, 20, 35
  Indonesia, in, 7, 50
  language promotion, 3, 19, 42, 51, 200–1
  Laos, in, 103–5, 108
  Malaysia, in, 6, 19, 149–54
  Philippines, in, 8, 183
  scholarship, 3, 25, 36, 50, 79, 182–84
  Singapore, in, 35–36
  soft power, as, 100, 139, 149, 182
  Southeast Asia, in, 35–36, 39
  teachers from China, and demand for, 42–46
  Thailand, in, 62, 64
  United States, in, 45
Confucius Institute Headquarters, 52, 119, 183
Confucius Institute Start-Up Grant, 183
Coordinating Agency for Chinese Language Education (LKPBT), 167
Copenhagen climate conference, 262
corruption, 25
COVID-19, 18, 22, 34, 46, 79, 129, 161
Cultural Department of Yunnan Province, 89
cultural diplomacy, 252
cultural identity, 11, 200, 202, 254, 259
cultural imperialism, 239
"cultural mixing", 226, 228
cultural nationalism, 252
"Culture as National Power: Soft Power", article, 182
Culture Center of Taipei Economic and Cultural Office (TECO), 89, 91

D

Dahlan Iskan, 167, 175
Data Privacy Act, 184
deforestation, 81
Democratic Progressive Party (DPP), 86
Deng Xiaoping, 16, 83
developed countries, 29, 239
dialect group (speech group) association, 30
Didi Kwartanada, 256
Disney+, 218, 230
divide-and-rule policy, 30
Duanhua School, 124
Duli Zhongxue (independent school), 33–34
dwibahasa (bilingualism) education system, 203, 205

E

East Coast Rail Link, 154

East Java-China Association
    for Promotion of Peaceful
    Reunification of China, 18
e-commerce programme, 4, 72
Eternal Love of Dream, 227

F
Facebook, 22, 71, 246
Fan Li Hua, legend of, 11
Federation of Alumni Associations
    of Taiwan Universities, Malaysia
    (FAATUM), 157
Federation of Chinese Societies
    (Mauritius), 17
Federation of Returned Overseas
    Chinese (Qiaolian), 16
Festival Potehi, 256
Field Relief Agency of Taiwan, 130
"fifth column", 180
Filipinization of curricula, 181
"Formal School", 92
Formosa Budding Hope Association, 130
Forum on China-Africa Cooperation
    (FOCAC), 25
Free China Relief Association (FCRA),
    83
free-market economy, 83
Fu Huiping, 263–64
Fudan University, 182
Fujian Huiguan Minsheng School, 124
Fujian Normal University, 48, 183

G
gaming industry, 79
GCTN English, 21
Ge Feng, 262
Geo-Informatics and Space Technology
    Development Agency (GISDA), 66
G.H.Y Culture, 232
global citizenship, 210
Global Times, 244
globalization, 100, 117, 134, 205, 227,
    239–40

"Go Out Strategy", 98–99, 109, 118, 125
Goethe Institute, 22, 182
Grandmasters of Demonic Cultivation,
    217, 227
Greater Mekong Subregion (GMS), 118
Gu Changfu, 261
Guang Huo School, 82
Guangxi University for Nationalities,
    103
Guanxi (connections), 68
Guilin University of Electronic
    Technology, 129
Guoji ribao, 263
guoyin (Taiwan phonetics), 181
Gus Dur, *see* Abdurrahman Wahid

H
hadith, 165, 172
Half a Bag of Sunflower Seeds, 262
Hanyu (language of Han people),
    34–36
hanyu pinyin, 88, 181
hard power, 15, 61, 182
Heng Samrin, 122
Hengyi Industries, 202
High-Speed Train project, 62
hill tribe groups, 81
Hokkien (*Fujian*) association, 30
Hollywood, 22
HSK (*Hanyu Shuiping Kaoshi*), 107,
    132, 151, 157, 168
Hu Jintao, 61, 182, 238
Hua Eah School, 63
Hua Xing School, 82, 85, 87–88, 92
Huang Jingtai, 263
Huaqiao University, 108
Huawei, 155
Huawen wenxue, 263
Huawen wenxue pinglun, 263
Huayu (language of Hua people), 34–36
Hubbert, Jennifer, 20
human rights, 21, 173
Hun Sen, 121–22

I

Ien Ang, *see* Ang, Ien
iFlix, 228
I-Kuan Tao Buddhist halls, 124, 130
Immigration Department, Malaysia, 151
IMPACT Arena, Bangkok, 217
Indian Ocean-China Society for the Promotion of Peaceful Reunification, 17
Indonesia
  China, relations with, 165–66
  Chinese education in, 7, 50–51
  Chinese Indonesian arts, 253–54
  Chinese-Indonesian literature in, 259–64
  communist coup in, 163
  Confucius Institute (CI) in, 7, 50
  santris (Muslim students) in China, 7–8, 163–73
  wayang potehi, 254–59, 265
Indonesia-China Friendship Association, 17
Indonesia Tionghoa Cultural Centre (ITCC), 167–68
Indonesian Chinese-China Association for Promotion of Peaceful Reunification of China, 18
Indonesian Chinese literature (*Yinhua Wenxue*), 11, 260
Indonesian Federation of Chinese Education, 51
Indonesian Student Association in China, *see* PPI Tiongkok
Instagram, 22
Institute of Border and Coastal Defense, 106
Institute of Foreign Languages, 131
International Chinese Language Teachers Scholarship, 183–84
International Islamic University of Malaysia, 146
"International School", 92

Interpretative Phenomenological Analysis, 186
iQIYI, 218, 227, 230, 232
Islam di China: Dulu dan Kini (Islam in China: Then and Now), 171
Islam, Indonesia, dan China: Pergumulan Santri Indonesia di Tiongkok (Islam, Indonesia, and China: The Striving of Indonesian Santri in China), 170
Islam Progressive (Progressive Islam), 168
Islamic boarding school (*pesantren*), 7, 163–64, 168, 171
Islamic Caliphate, 173
Islamic identity, 173
Islamic schools, 92

J

Jakarta-Bandung Highspeed railway, 172
Japanese invasion of China, 63
Java-Bali's shadow puppetry, 254, 265
Jawa Pos, 175
Jiang Zaidong, 103–4
Jiaolian Foundation, 86
Jiaolian School, 86–88, 92–93
Jinan University, 124, 183–84
Jinan University Press, 107
Jinjiang Literature City, 217, 226
Jiujiang University, 128
JJWXC, 226
Joko Widodo (Jokowi), 166
Jom Mandarin, 157
Journey to the West, The, 256, 265

K

Kanjanita Suchao-in, 69
Ki Mujiono, 256
klenteng (Chinese temple), 11
KOMPAS, newspaper, 171
Kong Zi Institute at the University of Malaya (KZIUM), 149–52, 154

Kong Zi Institute for the Teaching of Chinese Language, 48
Kongzi Institute, 19
Kosonen, Kimmo, 133
Kulturelle Identitätskonstruktionen in der Post-Suharto Zeit, 260
Kuomintang (KMT), 39, 77, 86, 180
  Chinese education in northern Thailand, 82–84
  political history of Han Chinese, 80–82
Kurikulum Berbasis Kompetensi (Competency-Based Curriculum), 167
Kwong Chow School, 92

L

Lailatul Fitriyah, 168
Lancang-Mekong Cooperation (LMC), 64
language and identity, 206
language dualism, 33
"language-in-education policy", 203
Lao National Defense Academy, 105–6
Lao People's Revolutionary Party (LPRP), 99
Laos
  China-aided schools in, 119
  China, bilateral relations with, 100, 103, 108, 116
  Chinese education in, 5, 99–118
  Chinese investment in, 100
  Chinese language learning in, demand for, 100–101
  Chinese universities established in, 109
  Confucius Institute (CI) in, 103–5, 108
  general education in, 101–2
  independence, 101
  survey on Chinese education, 110–18
Lao Soochow University, 36, 103, 107, 109

Lao-Zhong Nongbing Village Primary School (LZNVS), 102
Lembaga Koordinasi Pendidikan Bahasa Tionghoa, see LKPBT
Leninism, 166
LGBTQ+, 223, 230, 232
Li Keqiang, 133
Li Wen Huan, General, 77, 81–82
Lianxin, 263
Liaodu Public School, 5, 103, 107–9, 119
Liaoning Mechatronics, 133
Life University, 131
Likert Scale, 241
Lim Geok Tong, 18
Lin Yifu, Justin, 146
Liu Hua organization, 6
LKPBT (Coordinating Agency for Chinese Language Education), 167
Love Between Fairy and Devil, 227–28
Luban Highspeed Train Institute, 66
Luban Workshop, 129, 156

M

Maha Chakri Sirindhorn, Princess, 65
Malaysia
  China-educated Malaysians in, 6–7, 140, 147, 155
  Chinese education system, 6, 19, 48–49
  Chinese language learners in, 49
  Chinese language trainee teachers in, 48, 54
  Chinese proficiency, 264
  Confucius Institute (CI) in, 6, 19, 149–54
  ethnic Chinese population in, 142
  students studying in China's universities, 140–47
Malaysia-China Kuantan Industrial Park, 154
Malaysia-China Public Relations Association, 17–18

Malaysia One Belt One Road Committee, 18
Malaysia One China Association for Promotion of Peaceful Reunification of China, 18
Malaysian Certificate of Education (SPM), 48
Malaysian Institute of Teacher Education (ITE), 48
"Mandarin fever", 9, 166, 200, 202, 211
Manila Forum for China-Philippines Relations (Manila Forum), 25
Mao Zedong, 172, 262
MARA Education Foundation (Yayasan Pelajaran MARA), 144
Marcos, 181
Marxism, 166
Mauritius, 24
Melayu Islam Beraja (MIB, Malay Islamic Monarchy), 202, 205, 209
Memoranda of Understanding (MOUs), 64, 69, 126, 133, 140
"Memorial Day", 84
migration, 28–31, 33–34
Ming-Ai Catholic Association, Taiwan, 88
Ministry of Civil Affairs, China, 102
Ministry of Culture, Taiwan, 125
Ministry of Education and Sports, Laos, 101, 105
Ministry of Education, Brunei, 203
Ministry of Education, China, 19–20, 100, 109, 132, 140, 182
Ministry of Education, Malaysia, 48, 142
Ministry of Education, Philippine, 48
Ministry of Education, Thailand, 65, 67, 71, 82–84, 86, 92
Ministry of Higher Education, Malaysia, 140–41
Ministry of Higher Education, Science, Research, and Innovation (MHESI), Thailand, 65, 68

Ministry of Home Affairs, Malaysia, 151
Ministry of National Education, Indonesia, 167
Ministry of Science and Technology, China, 65
Ministry of Science and Technology, Thailand, 65
Mo Xiang Tong Xiu, 217, 223
Modernity at Large, 228
Mohd Radzi Md Jidin, 49
Mojok.co, online media, 171
"mother tongue" (second language), 31, 33–34, 207
Mozachiko, 232
Muangphum, 69
Mulan Education Center, 103, 106–7
multiculturalism, 126, 253
My Love from the Stars, 227

N
Nahdlatul Ulama (NU), 168
Najib Razak, 37
Nanjing University, 69
Nanjing Vocational University of Industry Technology, 129
Nanyang Technological University, 54
Nanyang University (*Nanyang Daxue*), 6, 30
Nanyang Zhongxue (Chinese secondary school), 31
National Defense Authorization Act, 44–45
National Education Act, 64, 86
national education system, 31
National Education System for the twenty-first century (SPN21), 203
National Ethnic Affairs Commission (NEAC), 16
national identity, 34, 39
National Office for Teaching Chinese as a Foreign Language, 128
"National Plus" schools, 34

INDEX

National Primary School Curriculum (KSSR), 48
National Radio and TV Administration, China, 230
National Research Council of Thailand, 69, 71
National Strategic Master Plan on Infrastructure, Logistics and Digital, 72
National University of Battambang, 129
National University of Laos (NUOL), 103–7
National University of Singapore (NUS), 6
"nationalization" of Chinese schools, 39
Nattapong Namsirikul (Kru P'Pop), 71
Nazrin Shah, Sultan, 147
Netflix, 218, 228, 230, 232
new migrants, 29–30
New Order, 7, 255, 259
Nithivadee Chanyaswas, 68–69, 71
Nongbing Village Primary School, 102
non-government organizations (NGOs), 82, 88, 130
North Atlantic Treaty Organization (NATO), 21
Northwest University, 183
Novi Basuki, 169
Nye, Joseph S., 15, 22, 61, 78, 181, 195, 218, 231

O

OCAO (Overseas Chinese Affairs Office of the State Council), 16, 50, 76, 86, 108, 146
Office of Chinese Language Council International (Hanban), 19, 35, 39, 43–46, 48, 65, 105, 167, 181, 183
Office of the Higher Education Commission, 65, 67
Office of the Vocational Education Commission, 65
Official Development Assistance (ODA), 78
On Not Speaking Chinese, 206
One Belt and One Road (OBOR) Initiative, 125–26, 128
one-China policy, 130
Open University of Fujian, 37
opium, 81
Opium Wars, 261
Outgoing Strategy, *see* "Go Out Strategy"
"overland Chinese", 80
overland trade, 81
Overseas Chinese Affairs Council (*Qiaowu Weiyuanhui*), 16, 76
Overseas Chinese Affairs Office, 2, 16, 184
Overseas Chinese Association, Taiwan, 88–89, 93
Overseas Chinese College, 37
"overseas Chinese" communities, 4
"overseas Chinese", (*huaqiao*), 15, 101
Overseas Community Affairs Council (OCAC), 16, 84, 125
Overseas Compatriot School Associations, 84

P

Pakatan Harapan coalition, 157
Palestine, 172
Paris Peace Agreement, 122
patriotism, 21, 23, 181
"Peace and Development Forum and Friends of the Silk Road Dialogue", 102
Peidu Mama (Study Mama), 37, 40
Peking University, 71, 146–47, 183
Peking University Alumni Association of Malaysia, 146–47, 158
Pengurus Cabang Istimewa Nahdlatul Ulama (PCINU), 170–71

Peranakan Chinese, 11, 256, 259
pesantren (Islamic boarding school), 7, 163–64, 168, 171
phenomenology, 186
Philippine-China APPRC, 18
Philippine Chinese Education and Research Center (PCERC), 181, 184
Philippines
 Chinese education in, 8, 180–81
 Confucius Institute (CI) in, 8, 183
 survey on China-educated Filipino scholars, 185–97
Phnom Penh Taipei Economic and Trade Representative Office, 123
Plaek Pibulsongkram, 63
Pondok Pesantren Nurul Jadid (Ponpes NJ), 164, 166–69, 174
Potehi (puppet theatre)
 boundaries of, 258
 history of, 254–55
 performing arts, as, 9, 11, 255–59, 265
 see also wayang potehi
poverty, 103, 130
PPI Tiongkok (*Perkumpulan Pelajar Indonesia Tiongkok*), 170
Pravit Thangthaweesook, 71
pribumi, 11
Private Education Commission, 84, 92
Private Schools Act, 63, 84, 92
pro-Beijing schools, 31
Program of Sending Students to China to Learn Mandarin Among Native Speakers Towards 1Malaysia, 142
Programme of Sending Excellent Students to Leading Universities Abroad (PRC), 142
Prophet Muhammad, teaching of, 165
pro-Taipei schools, 31
Pung Kheav Se, 123, 127
Pusat Bahasa Mandarin (Mandarin Language Centre), 19, 35

Q
Qiaoban, see OCAO
Qing dynasty, 80
Qixi Festival, 237
Quran, 172

R
racial hierarchy, 30
racism, 37
Rangsit University, 69
Reformasi, 259–60
Regional Teaching Chinese Private School Organizations, 65
Renmin Ribao, 263
Republika, newspaper, 171
Rising China and Chinese New Migrants in Southeast Asia, 1
Rotary Club of Taichung, Taiwan, 88
Royal Academy of Cambodia, Confucius Institute in, (CI-RAC), 128–31
Royal Malaysian Police, 151
Royal University of Phnom Penh (RUPP), 131
Rumah Cinwa, 256–59, 264
Russia, and war with Ukraine, 21

S
Saleumxay Kommasith, 99
Salihara Community, 255
"*Sanyu Xuexiao*" ("trilingual school"), 34
School of International Culture of South China Normal University, 20
Science, Technology, Education and Mathematics (STEM) subjects, 4, 66, 72
second language ("mother tongue"), 31, 33–34, 207
Second World War, 29
SEGi University, 154
Sengdeuane Lachanthaboun, 104

INDEX

Seven Seas Entertainment, 233
Shanghai Expo, 261
"sharp power", 23
Shen Jai Foundation, 154
Siam, *see* Thailand
Sie Jin Kui, legend of, 11
Silk Road, 99
Silk Road: Jasmine Flower, 103
Sin Chew Daily, 20
Singapore
  Chinese education in, 88, 204
  Chinese-medium university in, 30
  Chinese proficiency, 264
  Chinese students in, 37–38
  Confucius Institute (CI) in, 35–36
  drama series production, 232
  national schools, 6, 31–32, 34
  population, 34
Singapore Chinese Cultural Centre, 23
Singapore University, 6
Sino-Indonesian identity, 255–56, 259
Sino-Thai cooperation, 4, 62, 64–67, 72
Sino-Thai Vocational Collaboration, 64
Sinophone Indonesian writing, 254, 259, 261, 263, 266
Sirindhorn Center for Geo-Informatics (SCGI), 66
Snow Eagle Lord, 223
socialism, 99
"Socialism with Chinese characteristics", 38
Soeria Disastra, 266
soft power
  concept of, 15, 61–62, 78, 139, 181–82, 218, 252
  education, as tool of, 62, 67, 72, 77
  framework of, 186
  sources of, 62
Somsy Gnophanxay, 104
Soochow Industrial Park, 109
Soochow University in China, 109

Soochow University in Laos, 36, 109
Souphanouvong University, 104–5, 107
Southeast Asia
  Chinese education in, 28–40
  Chinese High Schools in, 32
  Chinese migration to, 28–29
  Chinese schools in, types of, 33–34, 39
  colonial powers, under, 28–29
  Confucius Institute (CI) in, 35–36, 39
  nationalism in, 31
  teachers from China, and demand for, 46–52
  xianxia drama, and popularity of, 9–10, 226–30
South Korea, 2, 43, 165, 218
Space Technology Applications, 65
Special Commemorative Volume of Ten Years of Associations of Graduates from Universities and Colleges in China, Malaysia, 2005-2015, A, 146
Special Economic Zone (SEZ), 109
Statistik Pendidikan Tinggi (Higher Education Statistics), 141
STEM (Science, Technology, Education and Mathematics) subjects, 4, 66, 72
Strategic Partnership, 166
Study Mama (*Peidu Mama*), 37, 40
Su Zhou University, 5
subversive soft power, 23
Suharto, 7, 11, 162–64, 166–69, 253, 258, 260
Sukarno, 7, 260
Summer Palace, burning of, 261
Sun Yat Sen, 63, 83–85, 180
Sun Yat-sen University, 26, 183
Susilo Bambang Yudhoyono, 166

T

Tahiti, 24, 26

Tai Kam Jeen Kam (Thai-Chinese Talk), 71
Taipei Economic and Cultural Office in Thailand, 88
Taiwan
  economic advantage, losing, 125
  KMT Chinese education, 82–84, 86
  KMT Han Chinese, 80–82
  national unification, 16
  Thailand, diplomatic ties with, 4
Taiwan Normal University, 124
Taiwanese Business Association (TBA), 89
Talented Young Scientist Visiting Program, 65
Tan Kah Kee, 30
Tan Lark Sye, 30
Tan Loke, 71
Tang Dynasty 11
Teaching Chinese to Speakers of Other Languages (TCSOL), 144, 151, 157, 183, 189
Teaching of English as a Foreign Language (TOEFL), 157
technology transfer, 172
Tencent, 226, 228
Tencent Video, 217, 231
Teo, Stephen, 220
TEP Culture and Education Association, 130
Thai Alumni Association of Chinese Universities (TACU), 68–69, 71
Thai-China Vocational College, 64
Thai-Chinese International School (TCIS), 92
Thai-Chinese Relationship Association, 17
Thai-Chinese Student Association (TCSA), 68
Thai PBS, 71
Thai-Singapore International School (TSIS), 92
Thai-Taiwan Business Association (TTBA), 82

Thailand
  Chinese influence on Thai education, 63–65
  Chinese schools in, 4
  citizenship, 81–82
  Confucius Classroom (CC) in, 62, 64
  Confucius Institute (CI) in, 62, 64
  ethnic Chinese tension in, 63
  KMT Chinese education in, 82–84
  KMT Han Chinese, 80–82
  Taiwan, diplomatic ties with, 4
Thailand 4.0 programme, 72–73
Thailand-China Association for Promotion of Peaceful Reunification of China, 17
Thailand-China Joint Research Center on Rail Systems, 65
Thailand-China Technology Transfer Center, 65
Theravada Buddhism, 82, 131
Thinking Radio, 71
Third World, 239
Three People's Principles, 180
TikTok, 22
TNN news, 71
Tong Xiaoling, 54
trade war, 68
Treaty of Amity, 180
"Triangular Threat", 163
trilingualism, 126
Trinidad and Tobago, 24
Trinidad and Tobago Association for Promotion of Peaceful Reunification of China, 17
Tsinghua University, 156, 183
Tuan Shi Wen, General, 81
"tuition schools", 33–34
"Tutoring School", 84, 86, 92
Tzu Chi School, 92

U
Udaya Halim, 256
"Un-Filipino Activities", report, 180
Ukraine, and war with Russia, 21

United Chinese Schools Committees'
  Association of Malaysia (Dong
  Zong), 49
United Front Work Department
  (UFWD), 16, 76
United Malays National Organization
  (UMNO), 37
United Nations Economic and Social
  Council, 102
United States (US), 2–3, 12, 22, 40,
  44–45, 139
United States Innovation and
  Competition Act, 45
Universitas Gajah Mada (UGM), 35
Universitas Indonesia (UI), 35, 156
Universitas Sebelas Maret, 55
Universiti Malaysia Pahang, 154
Universiti Malaysia Sabah, 154
Universiti Teknologi Mara, 144
University of French Polynesia, 26
University of Malaya, 19, 48
Untamed, The, drama, 217–22, 227–28
US-China rivalry, 3, 12, 40

V
Vientiane Police College, 105–6
Vietnam
  Chinese online literature in, 250
  Chinese popular culture in, 10,
    237–49
  Chinese-Vietnamese colloquial
    languages, 247
  Economic Reform (Đổi Mới) in, 240
Vietnam-China relationship, 240
Vit Mitri Thai-Jeen (Thai-China
  Friendship in Science), journal, 68

W
wacinwa ("wayang China Jawa kulit"),
  265
Walailak University, 37
Wang Huning, 182
Wang Ruifang, 155
Wang Wentian, 132

Wang Yi, 99
Wayang Cina (Chinese Wayang), 11
wayang klitik, 266
wayang kulit, 265
Wayang Museum, 258
wayang performance, 11, 265
wayang potehi, 254–59, 265
  see also Potehi
WeChat, 22
Weibo Viet Nam, 246
Wenyanwen (classical language form),
  30
Wenzhou Polytechnic College, 129, 133
West Philippine Sea dispute, 197
WeTV, 218, 228, 230–32
WhatsApp, 22, 145
Wife, The, 232
Willy Berlian, 51
Wilson Tjandinegara, 266
Winkelmann, Christine, 260
Wo Chi Xi Hong Shi, 223
World Trade Organization, 61, 98
World Vietnam Kampuchea and Laos
  Chinese-China Association
  for Promotion of Peaceful
  Reunification of China, 18
Woro Retno Mastuti (Bu Woro),
  255–57
Wuhan Railway Vocational College of
  Technology, 66
Wuhan University, 66
wuxia drama, 9, 10, 220–23, 226–27,
  240

X
Xi Jinping, 21, 99, 162, 238
Xia Men (Amoy) University, 30
Xiamen University, 183
Xiamen University in Malaysia, 7, 36,
  37, 140, 154–56
xianxia drama
  aestheticism in, 222, 227
  concept of, 218, 220
  demand for, 217–18

domestic restrictions, 230–31
love and romance in, 222–23
magic and fantasy action in, 221
noble and deity descent characters in, 221–22
releases, 218–19
Southeast Asia, and popularity in, 9–10, 226–30
women authors, 223, 226
Xiaobaige, 260
xin yi min (new Chinese immigrants), 122
Xinhai Revolution, 63
Xinhua, 243
Xinjiang, 172–73
Xu Lin, 105

Y

Yalong Intelligent Equipment Group, 133
Yan Yan Fei, 261
Yan'an Overseas Chinese Office, 16
Yang Qi-qiu, 122–23
Yayasan Pelajaran MARA (MARA Education Foundation), 144
Yik Chye School, 203
Yinhua Wenxue (Indonesian Chinese literature), 11, 260
YouTube, 171
Yuan Ni, 262–63

Yuhe Zhongxin, 43–44, 47, 52
Yunnanese Chinese Association (YCA), 77, 82–83, 89, 91
Yunnanese Chinese community
background of, 80
Chinese education in northern Thailand, 82–84
Chinese schools in, 4, 77–78, 86–88, 91–92
ethnicity, 80
KMT Han Chinese, 80–82
pro-Beijing perspectives among, 87, 91–94
pro-Taipei perspectives among, 87–89, 91–94
villages in, 84
Yunnanese Chinese School Network, 89

Z

Zafrul Aziz, Tengku, 156
Zhejiang People's Fine Arts Publishing House, 107
Zhigong Party, 146
Zhong Tai Education (ZTED), 68, 71
Zhongguo Guoji (China International), 21
Zhou Daguan, 122
Zongxiang Huiguan (clan associations), 29–30, 122–23
Zoom, 144

www.ingramcontent.com/pod-product-compliance
Lightning Source LLC
Chambersburg PA
CBHW040213020526
44111CB00050B/2944